INTERNATIONAL PERSPECTIVES ON THE TEACHING OF LITERATURE IN SCHOOLS

Literature teaching remains central to the teaching of English around the world. This edited text brings together expert global figures under the banner of the *International Federation for the Teaching of English* (IFTE). The book captures a state-of-the-art snapshot of leading trends in current literature teaching, as well as detailing predicted trends for the future.

The expert scholar and leading teacher contributors, coming from a wide range of countries with fascinatingly diverse approaches to literature teaching, cover a range of central and fundamental topics:

- literature and diversity;
- digital literatures;
- pedagogy and reader response;
- mother tongues;
- the business of reading;
- publishers, adolescent fiction and censorship;
- assessing responses to literature;
- the changing definitions of literature and multimodal texts.

The collection reviews the consistently important place of literature in the education of young people and provides international evidence of its enduring value and contribution to education, resisting the functionalist and narrowly nationalist perspectives of misguided government authorities.

International Perspectives on the Teaching of Literature in Schools will be of value to researchers, PhD students, literature scholars, practitioners, teacher educators, teachers and all those in the extensive academic community interested in English and literacy around the world.

NATE

The National Association for the Teaching of English (NATE), founded in 1963, is the professional body for all teachers of English from primary to post-16. Through its regions, committees and conferences, the association draws on the work of classroom practitioners, advisers, consultants, teacher trainers, academics and researchers to promote dynamic and progressive approaches to the subject by means of debate, training and publications. NATE is a charity reliant on membership subscriptions. If you teach English in any capacity, please visit **www.nate.org.uk** and consider joining NATE, so the association can continue its work and give teachers of English and the subject a strong voice nationally.

This series of books co-published with NATE reflects the organisation's dedication to promoting standards of excellence in the teaching of English, from early years through to university level. Titles in this series promote innovative and original ideas that have practical classroom outcomes and support teachers' own professional development.

Books in the NATE series include both pupil and classroom resources and academic research aimed at English teachers, students on PGCE/ITT courses and NQTs.

For a full list of titles in this series, please visit: www.routledge.com/National-Association-for-the-Teaching-of-English-NATE/book-series/NATE.

Titles in this series include:

INTERNATIONAL PERSPECTIVES ON THE TEACHING OF LITERATURE IN SCHOOLS

Global Principles and Practices

Edited by Andrew Goodwyn, Cal Durrant, Louann Reid and Lisa Scherff

Routledge
Taylor & Francis Group

LONDON AND NEW YORK

First published 2018
by Routledge
2 Park Square, Milton Park, Abingdon, Oxon OX14 4RN

and by Routledge
711 Third Avenue, New York, NY 10017

Routledge is an imprint of the Taylor & Francis Group, an informa business

British Library Cataloguing-in-Publication Data
A catalogue record for this book is available from the British Library.

Library of Congress Cataloging-in-Publication Data
Names: Goodwyn, Andrew, 1954– editor.
Title: International perspectives on the teaching of literature in schools: global principles and practices / edited by Andrew Goodwyn, Cal Durrant, Louann Reid and Lisa Scherff.
Description: Abingdon, Oxon; New York, NY: Routledge, 2018. | Includes bibliographical references.
Identifiers: LCCN 2017007946 | ISBN 9781138227194 (hardback) | ISBN 9781138227217 (pbk.) | ISBN 9781315396460 (ebook)
Subjects: LCSH: English literature—Study and teaching. | Comparative education.
Classification: LCC PR33 .I67 2018 | DDC 820.71—dc23
LC record available at https://lccn.loc.gov/2017007946

ISBN: 978-1-138-22719-4 (hbk)
ISBN: 978-1-138-22721-7 (pbk)
ISBN: 978-1-315-39646-0 (ebk)

Typeset in Bembo
by codeMantra

CONTENTS

PART III
Rationales for teaching literature   **175**

BIOGRAPHIES

David Baxter was a secondary school English teacher, head of department and regional consultant for the New South Wales (NSW) Department of Education from 1975 to 1995. He then became a lecturer in English and literacy education for the University of New England before moving to the Australian College of Physical Education (ACPE) in 2007 as Associate Dean, with responsibility for quality assurance and compliance. Since retiring from ACPE in 2013, David has done consultancy work with a range of private and public higher education providers. He was Vice-President of the NSW English Teachers Association (ETA) from 1996 to 2003 with responsibility for enhancing the involvement of rural English teachers in the work of the association and a NSW delegate to the Australian Association for the Teaching of English from 2002 to 2003. He was a participant in a number of research projects and publications, including a validation study of the first version of standards for teachers in NSW (2003–2005), a study of the characteristics of subject faculties with track records of enhancing student outcomes (AESOP, 2002–2004) and an evaluation of the efficacy of the Structure of the Observed Learning Outcome (SOLO taxonomy) in assessing the work of students in English (2004–2009). Most recently, with Dr. Dean Dudley (Macquarie University), he has been involved in research and publications concerning the use of SOLO in physical education.

Don Carter is Senior Lecturer in English Education at the University of Technology Sydney. He has a Bachelor of Arts, a Diploma of Education, Master of Education (Curriculum), Master of Education (Honours) and a PhD in curriculum from the University of Sydney (2013). Don is a former Inspector of English at the NSW Board of Studies, Teaching & Educational Standards and was responsible for a range of projects including the *English K-10 Syllabus*. He has worked as a head teacher of English in both government and non-government schools and was also an ESL consultant for the NSW Department of Education. Don is the secondary schools representative in the *Romantic Studies Association of Australasia* and has published extensively on a range of issues in English education, including *The English Teacher's Handbook A-Z* (Manuel & Carter) and *Innovation, Imagination & Creativity: Re-Visioning English in Education* (Manuel, Brock, Carter & Sawyer).

Suzanne Choo is Assistant Professor in the English Language and Literature Academic Group at the National Institute of Education, Nanyang Technological University, Singapore. Her research has been published in various peer-reviewed journals such as *Research in the Teaching of English, Curriculum Inquiry, Discourse: Studies in the Cultural Politics of Education, English Journal, Journal of Aesthetic Education, Journal of Curriculum Studies* among others. Her book, *Reading the World, the Globe, and the Cosmos: Approaches to Teaching Literature for the Twenty-first Century* (Peter Lang, 2013), was awarded the 2014 Critics Choice Book Award by the American Educational Studies Association. In 2011, she was awarded the International Award for Excellence by *The International Journal of the Humanities* for the best published article in the journal. She is interested in issues related to education for global and cosmopolitan citizenship particularly in relation to literature education. Other interests include the disciplinary history of literature in English; theorizations of literature pedagogy; world, global and cosmopolitan approaches to teaching literature; and new literacies for the twenty-first century.

Gabrielle Cliff Hodges is Senior Lecturer in Education at the University of Cambridge Faculty of Education where she co-ordinates and teaches on the secondary English PGCE course, and also supervises Masters and PhD students. Previously, she taught in three 11–18 comprehensive schools in Cambridgeshire, in the last as Head of the English department, before moving into teacher education in 1993. She is an active member of the National Association for the Teaching of English (NATE) and the United Kingdom Literacy Association (UKLA). She is also a Fellow of the English Association. Her main area of research is reading, especially young people's development as readers within and beyond the classroom. She has published many chapters and articles on reading, writing and language in secondary English teaching. Her most recent book is *Researching and Teaching Reading: Developing Pedagogy through Critical Enquiry* (Routledge, 2016).

Thomas Day is Teacher of English at Eton College, a Research Fellow in English Literature at the University of Hertfordshire and the editor of the longstanding English Association journal for secondary teachers of English, *The Use of English*. Formerly an academic, he has published widely on a number of authors, including Keats, Katherine Mansfield, T. S. Eliot and Geoffrey Hill. In 2015 he gave a TEDx talk entitled 'In Praise of Slow Learning' which is available on YouTube.

Cal Durrant retired as Associate Professor in English Curriculum and Director of the Literacy Research Hub at ACU in Sydney in 2013, but continues to work as part-time Research Officer of the innovative Pilbara Cities Internship Program in the School of Education at Murdoch University in Perth, Western Australia. He is currently the Secretary of IFTE (International Federation for the Teaching of English); he also spent sixteen years on the AATE (Australian Association for the Teaching of English) Council as Research and Initiatives Officer and then Commissioning Editor of the highly acclaimed *Interface* series. Cal's research covers the areas of English literacy and technology and media education. He was a key member of the successful Deakin/Murdoch team that delivered the $2.4 million Australian Government's Summer School for Teachers of English initiative in January 2008, and over the past two decades has been involved in projects that have applied ICTs to a range of teaching and learning contexts. Cal was ACU leader in the 2012 UNE/ACU/UWS research consortium that evaluated the impact of selected reforms of the Improving Teacher Quality National Partnership as part of the Smarter Schools National Partnerships programme that reported back to the Commonwealth in 2015.

Marshall A. George holds an endowed chair, the Olshan Professor of Clinical Practice, at Hunter College—City University of New York, where he teaches courses in the doctoral program in Teacher Leadership and the graduate and undergraduate programs in English Education. Previously, he was a professor of English Education and served as department chair of Curriculum & Teaching at Fordham University. He taught English language arts in grades 7 through 12 for ten years in North Carolina, New York and in Brazil. Marshall is a former chair of the Conference on English Education and also served on the Executive Committee of the National Council of Teachers of English. His scholarship focuses on literature for adolescents, pre-service education and teacher professional development and has appeared in journals such as *English Education, English Journal, American Secondary Education, English Leadership Quarterly, Theory into Practice, Voices from the Middle* and *The ALAN Review*. He serves as a journal editor for *Contemporary Issues in Technology and Teacher Education*.

Andy Goodwyn, after a long association with The University of Reading, is currently Professor of Education and Head of the School of Education and English Language at the University of Bedfordshire. He is President of IFTE and a former Chair of NATE. He has researched and published widely about English in education in books and journals and co-edited the previous IFTE edited collection *International Perspectives on the Teaching of English in a Globalised World* (Routledge, 2013). He has also researched and published extensively about expertise; examples include *The Expert Teacher of English* (Routledge, 2010) and *Expert Teachers: An International Perspective* (Routledge, 2016).

Andrew Green taught English in a range of 11–18 schools. He is now BA Education programme leader at Brunel University London. He has published widely on the teaching of literature and is particularly interested in post-16 English teaching. His publications cover Gothic Literature, the poetry of William Blake and Philip Larkin. Alongside books on *Frankenstein, Wuthering Heights, High Windows, The Whitsun Weddings* and *Songs of Innocence and of Experience,* he is author of *Four Perspectives on Transition: English Literature from Sixth Form to University, Teaching the Teachers: Higher Education and Teachers' Continuing Professional Development* and *Working with Secondary Schools: A Guide for Higher Education.* His latest books are *Starting and English Literature Degree* (Palgrave Macmillan 2009), *Transition and Acculturation* (Lambert, 2010), *Becoming a Reflective English Teacher* (Open University Press 2011), *A Practical Guide to Teaching English in the Secondary School* (Routledge 2012) and *Teaching English Literature 16–19* (Routledge, 2013).

Amanda Haertling Thein is Associate Dean for Academic Affairs and Graduate Programs, and Associate Professor of Language, Literacy, and Culture in the University of Iowa's College of Education. Her research focuses on socio-cultural and socio-emotional aspects of literary response; critical approaches to multicultural literature instruction; and the intersection of critical youth studies and young adult literature. Amanda's research has been published in journals such as *Research in the Teaching of English, Journal of Literacy Research* and *Journal of Adolescent & Adult Literacy.* She is co-author of four books, including *Teaching to Exceed the English Language Arts Common Core State Standards* (Routledge, 2016). Amanda is co-editor of *English Teaching: Practice & Critique,* and a member of the Conference of English Education's Executive Committee.

Jacqueline Manuel is Associate Professor of English Education in the Faculty of Education and Social Work at the University of Sydney. She holds a BA (Hons 1) in English, a DipEd and a PhD in English Literature from the University of New England. She is Program Director of the Master of Teaching (Secondary) in the Faculty and coordinator of secondary English curriculum. Jackie's teaching and research interests include teenagers' reading; creative pedagogies in secondary English; developing students' writing capacities and accomplishments; pre-service English teacher motivation; and English curriculum history. She has published widely in the field of English education. Her most recent books include *Teenagers and Reading: Literary Heritages, Cultural Contexts and Contemporary Reading Practices* (edited with Sue Brindley, AATE/Wakefield Press) and *Imagination, Innovation, Creativity: Re-visioning English in Education* (edited with Paul Brock, Don Carter and Wayne Sawyer, Phoenix Press). Jackie is a team member of *Shakespeare Reloaded.* She is a former Member of the NSW Board of Studies and has been Chief Examiner of NSW HSC English (Standard & Advanced, 2006–2011).

Debra Myhill is Professor of Education at the University of Exeter, UK. Her research has focused particularly on young people's composing processes and their metacognitive awareness of them; the inter-relationship between metalinguistic understanding and writing; the talk-writing interface; and the teaching of writing. She is Director of the Centre for Research in Writing, which promotes inter-disciplinary research, drawing on psychological, socio-cultural and linguistic perspectives on writing. Over the past fifteen years, she has led a series of research projects in these areas, in both primary and secondary schools, and has conducted several commissioned research studies for the government, including the national evaluation of the *Every Child a Writer* intervention. She is regularly invited to undertake commissioned research or advisory roles for professional bodies, policy-makers and examination boards. Debra runs numerous professional education courses for teachers, examining the practical classroom implications of her research on the teaching of writing, and in 2014, her research team was awarded the Economic and Social Research Council award for Outstanding Impact in Society.

Mary Purcell has taught Literature and Philosophy in Melbourne secondary schools for many years and is a PhD candidate at Melbourne University investigating the pedagogic possibilities of diasporic texts in a contemporary Literature classroom. Mary has presented numerous seminars and workshops for Literature teachers over many years and has contributed to the writing of literature curriculum in Victoria.

Louann Reid is Professor and Chair of the Department of English at Colorado State University, where she teaches English Education courses at the undergraduate and graduate levels. Research interests include the teaching of graphic narratives in secondary schools, censorship, the teaching of literature and English literacy teacher education. She has authored or co-authored numerous articles and eight textbooks for secondary school students, including the Houghton Mifflin *Daybook* series of textbooks for students in grades 6 through 12. Dr. Reid has edited two journals for English Language Arts teachers, including *English Journal*, the flagship journal of the National Council of Teachers of English (NCTE), and is co-editor of three books, including *Rationales for Teaching Young Adult Literature* and *International Perspectives on Teaching English in a Globalised World*. A past chair of the Conference on English Education, she has been involved in state and national initiatives regarding standards, assessments and programme accreditation. She is the recipient of the Rewey Belle Inglis Award and the Conference on English Leadership's Exemplary Leader Award, both from groups within NCTE.

Rodrigo Joseph Rodríguez is Assistant Professor of Literacy and English Education at The University of Texas at El Paso, which is located in the U.S.–México borderlands and across from Ciudad Juárez, Chihuahua, México. His research interests include academic writing, children's and young adult literatures, culturally sustaining pedagogies and socially responsible biliteracies. He is the author of *Enacting Adolescent Literacies across Communities: Latino/a Scribes and Their Rites* (2016). In addition, he is an advocate of *El día de los niños/El día de los libros* (Children's Day/Book Day), which is an initiative and daily commitment to link all children, adolescents and families to books, languages and cultures.

Lisa Scherff is currently a teacher at Cypress Lake High School (Florida). She previously taught English education at the University of Tennessee, the University of Alabama and Florida State University. Her research interests include opportunity to learn in the English/language arts, teacher preparation and development and student–teacher discussions of young adult literature. Her work has appeared in journals such as the *Journal of Teacher Education, Journal of Adolescent & Adult Literacy, Journal of Literacy Research, Research in the Teaching of English* and *Teaching and Teacher Education*. Lisa is Chair of the 2016–2017 Amelia Elizabeth Walden Award.

Melanie Shoffner is Associate Professor of English Education at Purdue University in West Lafayette, Indiana, where she holds a joint appointment in the Departments of English and Curriculum & Instruction. In 2016–2017, she was a Fulbright Scholar in the Faculty of Letters at Babeş-Bolyai University in Cluj-Napoca, Romania, teaching courses in adolescent literature and pedagogy. Her research examines issues arising from, related to and influential for secondary English teacher preparation, including the development and use of meaningful reflective practice and the role of affective and relational elements in teacher preparation. Her recent work includes the edited book *Exploring Teachers in Fiction and Film: Saviors, Scapegoats and Schoolmarms* (Routledge, 2016) and co-edited book *Teaching English Language Arts to English Language Learners: Preparing Pre-Service and In-Service Teachers* (Palgrave Macmillan, 2016), as well as articles in *The Teacher Educator, Reflective Practice* and *English Education*. Professor Shoffner is the current Past-Chair of the Conference on English Education (CEE) and Co-Editor of *Contemporary Issues in Technology and Teacher Education (CITE): English*.

Gary Snapper is a Research Associate at Brunel University, the Editor of NATE's Professional Journal *Teaching English* and a teacher of A Level and IB English. His doctoral research at the Institute of Education, London, explored the relationship between English as a school and as a university subject, and he continues to focus on issues in post-16 English. He is co-author, with Carol Atherton and Andrew Green, of *Teaching English Literature 16–19* (Routledge/NATE 2013), and has contributed chapters on post-16 English to several recent books. He is a member of the NATE Post-16 Committee and provides workshops on post-16 literature teaching for trainee teachers, practising teachers and university lecturers. He taught English in 11–18 comprehensive schools in Cambridge for fourteen years, including six years as Head of English at Impington Village College, Cambridge, and currently teaches at the Cheney School, Oxford (A Level) and for Oxford Study Courses (I.B.).

Blaine E. Smith is Assistant Professor of New Literacies and Bi/multilingual Immigrant Youth at the University of Arizona. Her research primarily centers on the digital literacy practices of culturally and linguistically diverse adolescents, with special attention to their multimodal composing processes and products. She is a 2016 National Academy of Education/Spencer Postdoctoral Fellow and is currently working on the study, 'Multimodal Composing-to-Learn: Understanding how Adolescents Analyze Literature through Multiple Modes in Digital Environments.' She is also a recipient of the Literacy Research Association's Outstanding Student Research Award and the Emerging Scholars Fellowship by the Reading Hall of Fame. Her work has appeared in *Computers & Education, Bilingual Research Journal, Elementary School Journal, British Journal of Educational Technology, Journal of Adolescent & Adult Literacy* and *Learning, Media, and Technology,* among others. Blaine received her PhD in Language, Literacy, and Culture from Peabody College at Vanderbilt University.

David Stevens is Course Director and English tutor for the PGCE Secondary course at Durham University, having previously taught English in four schools, in two as Head of English. David's research and teaching interests centre on English pedagogy, working towards a synthesis of different—sometimes apparently opposing—views of English, focusing on its radical Romantic roots and the implications of such a conception for the contemporary world. He counts as major influences the poetry of Blake, Coleridge and other Romantics, and libertarian thinkers such as William Morris, John Dewey, Herbert Read and Paulo Freire. Above all, David is concerned to promote a broad vision of English as an arts subject in a critically intercultural context, and has published widely in this field. David is a long-standing member of the National Association for the Teaching of English, and chairs its Committee for Initial Teacher Education.

David Taylor is a teacher of English at Northcote College where he is the Assistant Head of English. He is a representative on the New Zealand Association for Teachers of English council. He was a 2011 Woolf Fisher Fellow and 2015 Fulbright Distinguished Teacher.

Shirin Teifouri taught undergraduate courses in English literature in Iran before coming to the UK to complete her PhD in English literature at the University of Sheffield. Following the completion of her PhD, she was awarded two honorary research fellowships, at the University of Sheffield and Birkbeck University of London to explore pedagogical engagement with the transformative function of literature and critical theories in dialogical encounters with displaced 'communities' in non-academic settings.

Ruth Vinz is Endowed Morse Professor of Teacher Education and Professor of English Education at Teachers College, Columbia University. Her teaching experience includes twenty-three years of high school teaching before coming to Teachers College in 1992 to teach in the MA and doctoral programs. It is this extensive teaching experience that continues to inform her research and practices in the field of literacy education. Vinz's research focuses on how English teachers' curricula, instructional and assessment practices impact students' literacy learning—specifically pertaining to literature education and writing processes. She is author of *Composing A Teaching Life*, which received the Richard Meade award for outstanding research published in English education. She co-authored several books: 2nd edition of *Inside Out, Recasting the Text, Learning the Landscape, Living By Words: Writing Qualitative Research, Becoming (Other)wise: Enhancing Critical Reading Perspectives, Narrative Inquiry: Research in Literacy and Language* and the Houghton Mifflin *Daybook* series of reading literature/writing textbooks for 6th to 12th graders. Most recently, she co-edited *Educating for the 21st Century*. In 2002 Vinz founded *The Center for the Professional Education of Teachers* (CPET), an incubator for rethinking professional education, a hub of active schools-based research and an organization that provides direct services to teachers and students in sites nationally and internationally.

Monika Wagner has taught English, Literature and Linguistics across a range of year levels in secondary schools in country Victoria and Melbourne since 1999. Along with English Method, literacy and linguistics units, she has also taught inclusivity and diversity units to pre-service teachers across a number of Melbourne universities over the last few years. Although she teaches the range of Englishes, her passion remains with Literature, having completed a Master of Arts focusing on post-Modernist text and theory at the conclusion of her first degree. She has marked state-based Literature examinations for over a decade, as well as other state and national literacy examinations. Monika has presented numerous workshops and lectures over the last fifteen years, both to teachers and students. She completed her Masters of Education in 2011 at the University of Melbourne, and is currently undertaking her PhD with a focus on policy and the implementation of approaches to intercultural understanding in secondary schools. She joined the Victorian Association for the Teaching of English Council and served as President from 2012 to 2015. She was the Victorian delegate on Australian Association for the Teaching of English Council from 2012 to 2014, and held the position of AATE President/Elect in 2015 to 2016.

Annabel Watson is Senior Lecturer in Language Education at the University of Exeter, UK. She is a member of the Exeter *Centre for Research in Writing*, with research interests focusing on children's writing development and metalinguistic understanding (particularly in secondary schools), writing with technology and teacher attitudes to student writing. She leads the Secondary English PGCE and teaches on several other ITE and Masters/Doctoral programmes.

Aaron Wilson is a lecturer in the School of Curriculum and Pedagogy and an Associate Director of the Woolf Fisher Research Centre at the University of Auckland, New Zealand. His research interests are in interventions to address disparities in education, disciplinary literacy teaching in secondary schools,

English and teacher professional development. Before joining The University of Auckland, Aaron was Head of English at Aorere College.

Daniel Xerri is a lecturer at the University of Malta, the Joint Coordinator of the IATEFL Research SIG and the chairperson of the ELT Council within the Ministry for Education and Employment in Malta. He holds postgraduate degrees in English and Applied Linguistics, as well as a PhD in Education from the University of York. He has been awarded a number of international grants in order to conduct research in the United Kingdom, Australia and the United States. He is the author of many publications on different areas of English education, including articles published in *ELT Journal*, *English in Education* and *International Journal of Research and Method in Education*. His main research interests are creativity and teacher education. Further details about his talks and publications can be found at: www.danielxerri.com.

John Yandell taught in inner London secondary schools for twenty years before moving to the Institute of Education, University College London, where he has worked since 2003. As a teacher and a teacher educator, he has written extensively on policy and pedagogy, curriculum and assessment. He has a longstanding interest in school students as active and collaborative makers of meaning, and a commitment to investigating and representing classrooms as complex sites of cultural production. He is the editor of the journal, *Changing English: Studies in Culture and Education* and the author of *The Social Construction of Meaning: Reading Literature in Urban English Classrooms* (Routledge, 2013). Other recent publications include *Rethinking Education: Whose Knowledge is it Anyway?* (with Adam Unwin, New Internationalist, 2016), and *Critical Practice in Teacher Education: A Study of Professional Learning*, which he co-edited with Ruth Heilbronn.

INTRODUCTION

Louann Reid

When the editors conceived of this volume in the IFTE 'perspectives' series, we had two aims. The first was to provide a space for teachers and researchers to focus on the teaching of literature, which is a central component of English/literacy curricula. Second, we hoped to foster discussion of commonalities and differences in literature pedagogy in nations across the world where English is the mother tongue or the medium of instruction. The essays and research studies in this collection reveal that similar interests and issues transcend borders. Worldwide, educators face questions and tensions regarding the place and importance of teaching literature in schools, including topics such as text selection, theoretical and pedagogical approaches, rationales for teaching literature, and the challenges of teaching literature in countries that are seemingly obsessed with standards, accountability, and assessment.

Throughout the collection, one overarching theme is the power of story. Whether spoken or written, stories introduce us to a wider world and help us make sense of it. They can bring people together. In *The Call of Stories*, American psychiatrist Robert Coles stresses the importance of understanding the stories of others. An English major in college, he changed his life's direction when he visited William Carlos Williams, who had read Coles's thesis on Williams's poem 'Paterson'. They talked about how doctors should listen to their patients. Williams told him, 'Their story, yours, mine—it's what we all carry with us on this trip we take, and we owe it to each other to respect our stories and learn from them' (p. 62).[1] Stories also have the power to pull people apart, to engender strong emotions and impel actions, sometimes with negative results as in censorship, imprisonment, or exile to poets and the tellers of tales (e.g., Mark Twain, Anna Akhmatova, Salman Rushdie, Pablo Neruda).

The chapters in this volume underscore the passion that readers have for books and reading. Alberto Manguel, in *A History of Reading*, offers an example from about 1000 CE: 'To avoid parting with his collection of 117,000 books while traveling, the avid reader and Grand Vizier of Persia, Abdul Kassem Ismael, [had] them carried by a caravan of four hundred camels trained to walk in alphabetical order' (p. 193). Although e-books and other technological devices and tools have replaced well-trained camels for storage and constant availability, the love of reading endures.

At least, for some.

Many teachers cite their love of literature as a major reason for choosing to teach English, but students do not necessarily share that love, particularly for school reading (Carter and Manuel). Literature may no longer be widely perceived as 'Queen of the Curriculum' (Christenbury 1994),[2] yet it figures prominently as a motivation for pursuing a career as an English language arts teacher (Goodwyn 2003, Manuel and Brindley 2005, Reid and Cline 1997). Increasing the number of readers who find pleasure in reading is one common goal of teaching it.

The several tensions in teaching literature, such as that between reading for pleasure and reading for assignments and tests or between national heritage and transnational understanding, are not new but continue to influence our approaches to texts, contexts, readers, and teachers. In the last century, the inclusion of literature as a school subject has cyclically and repeatedly met challenges posed by economic downturns, initiatives for increased vocational instruction, literary and cultural theories, demands for the curricular primacy of science and mathematics, changes in demographics, and various governmental programs that aim to establish accountability through standardized curricula and high-stakes assessment schemes.

We strive in this collection to address key questions for today's teachers and students, not with the intention of resolving tensions or providing definitive answers but instead to place multiple perspectives in conversation on a subject of broad interest: teaching literature in schools. Previous cross-national collections (many from editors associated with IFTE) also have addressed teaching literature as well as the broader work of English teachers. These collections demonstrate the persistence of the tensions and the significance of literature as a school subject.[3]

What is literature and why does it matter?

Authors of the chapters in this volume demonstrate the multiplicity and complexity of what we mean when we speak of literature in the 21st century. Teaching and learning have always been influenced by the contexts in which they occur. Now we tend to speak of 'texts,' a reflection in part of the influence of available technologies that have broadened the kinds of writing worthy of study and inclusion. We are likely to refer to literature rather than Literature in a desire to eliminate the elitism associated with the capital *L*. The term of choice inflects perspectives on questions of canon formation, culture or multiculturalism, and language. Regarding literary texts in schools, authors in this volume argue that literature should not be limited to national heritage selections but also include culturally unfamiliar texts (Wagner and Purcell) and forms that have not been sufficiently valued such as literature written for adolescents (Shoffner and George), and literature from the oral tradition (Rodríguez). Authors do discuss teaching canonical texts (Teifouri, Scherff, Yandell) and poetry as well (Stevens, Xerri).

Literature matters because human expression matters. It matters as a way to think about our relationship to real and imagined worlds (Cliff Hodges) and to other human beings. Reading literature also has social, cognitive, and emotional benefits (Taylor and Wilson). Literature matters in ways that resist capture by high-stakes assessments.

Organization of this book

A reader could follow several pathways through a collection such as this one, selecting an order by title, author, country, or just reading straight through from the first page to the last. We chose to divide the book into three sections on topics of persistent significance. We selected the chapters within each section to 'speak' to the topic as well as to each other. We hope that readers will make multiple connections within and across sections, knowing that any categories are somewhat arbitrary and fully provisional.

Ways of seeing, ways of teaching

Literature invites us to enter multiple worlds and position ourselves among other people. Through literary texts, we see and know differently; sometimes we are even moved to act more ethically or empathetically. Educators and theorists claim that individuals expand perspectives of themselves and the world through their interactions with texts and other readers. They employ strategies for reading, discussing, and even assessing response to literature that reflect their beliefs and values about what literature is and the purposes of reading and teaching it. Likewise, authors in this volume offer a variety of theoretical frames and approaches to making meaning with and of texts in school settings, including cosmopolitanism (Choo and Vinz), linguistic analysis (Myhill and Watson), multimodal composing (Smith), space and place (Green), critical emotion studies (Thein), and an assessment taxonomy (Durrant and Baxter).

Readers, texts and contexts

What we believe about the nature and value of literature and what we understand about readers shapes our teaching. As a school subject, literature is influenced by governmental factors as well as the knowledge of professional educators. High-stakes testing and national curriculum initiatives prioritize certain kinds of knowledge (thus, of teaching) and types of texts. As a result, persistent tensions exist. Educators and researchers in this section provide insights into transforming or reconceptualizing classroom spaces (Wagner and Purcell, Carter and Manuel, Scherff). They argue for text selection and pedagogy that advance a literate, knowledgeable citizenry through rethinking canons (Rodríguez) and questioning pedagogy (Day). Several authors provide cases that demonstrate relationships between beliefs about literature and approaches to teaching it: teachers as gatekeepers (Xerri), the place of a class novel (Yandell), the pedagogical possibilities of a single poem (Stevens). An investigation of changes in studying English literature at the university level in Iran after the Islamic Revolution (Teifouri) highlights the impact of cultural context and serves as a case to interrogate the relationships among many of the topics addressed by other authors in this volume.

Rationales for teaching literature

This section begins with an extensive discussion of why literature matters (Cliff Hodges) and ends with a call for a radical alternative to the usual rationales for reading literature (Goodwyn). In between, authors make a case for a broader view of what counts as literature in schools (Shoffner and George), the value of non-standard approaches to curriculum (Snapper), and the contribution of re-creational reading to literary study (Taylor and Wilson).

In this volume, twenty-seven authors from seven countries tell stories that matter about teaching literature in the world. We hope that their perspectives on teaching literature and their passion for students and texts engender further conversation and informed action.

Notes

1 Story previously appeared in Louann Reid, *English Journal*, 93(4), p. 11.
2 Parenthetical references with name and no date are to chapters in this volume.
3 *English Teachers at Work*, Tchudi, 1986; *Readers, Texts, Teachers*, Corcoran and Evans, 1987; *Knowledge in the Making*, Corcoran et al., 1994; *Questions of English*, Peel et al., 2000; *English Teachers at Work*, Doecke et al., 2003; *International Perspectives on Teaching English in a Globalised World*, Goodwyn et al., 2014.

References

Christenbury, Leila. *English Journal* 83.8 (December 1994): 11.

Corcoran, Bill and Emrys Evans, eds. *Readers, Texts, Teachers*. Upper Montclair, NJ: Boynton/Cook. 1987.

Corcoran, Bill, Mike Hayhoe, and Gordon Pradl, eds. *Knowledge in the Making*. Portsmouth: Boynton/Cook. 1994.

Doecke, Brenton, David Homer, and Helen Nixon, eds. *English Teachers at Work: Narratives, Counternarratives, and Arguments*. Kent Town: Wakefield Press. 2003.

Goodwyn, Andrew, Louann Reid, and Cal Durrant, eds. *International Perspectives on Teaching English in a Globalised World*. London: Routledge. 2014.

Manguel, Alberto. *A History of Reading*. New York: Penguin Books. 2014.

Peel, Robin, Annette Patterson, and Jeanne Gerlach. *Questions of English*. London: Routledge. 2000.

Reid, Louann and Ruth K. J. Cline. 'Our Repressed Reading Addictions: Teachers and Young Adult Series Books.' *English Journal* 86.3 (March 1997): 68–72.

Tchudi, Stephen. *English Teachers at Work: Ideas and Strategies from Five Countries*. Upper Montclair, NJ: Boynton/Cook. 1986.

PART I

Ways of seeing, ways of teaching

1

THE LITERATURE TEACHER AS RESTLESS CARTOGRAPHER

Pedagogies for cosmopolitan ethical explorations

Suzanne Choo and Ruth Vinz

The cosmopolitan impulse to migrate, and explore foreign lands, occurred as early as 60,000 years ago when humans ventured out of Africa leading to the emergence of new civilizations. Sometime around the fourth century, the term 'cosmopolitanism,' which, translated from the Greek, means citizen of the cosmos, came into popular use by Cynic philosophers in Ancient Greece during a period when citizenship was a symbol of status and guaranteed one the right to vote, hold public office, and own property. Yet, when Diogenes the Cynic philosopher was asked where he came from and replied, 'I am a *kosmopolites*,' he deliberately employed the term to critique the exclusivity of citizenship offered to a privileged few. In practice, Diogenes and his band of cynic cosmopolitans rejected material comfort and were skeptical about the way identity had become defined by the rules of the state rather than tied to a broader affiliation with humanity itself. More importantly, their skepticism served to politicize social inequality by highlighting forms of discrimination arising from the parochialism of state citizenship.

Today, renewed interest in cosmopolitanism, as observed in the growing body of scholarship in fields ranging from philosophy to anthropology, international relations, and literary studies, carries some of the spirit of ancient cynic cosmopolitanism. This involves first, the understanding that the call to a cosmopolitan mindset is essentially an ethical call to recognize one's affiliation with one's familiar community *as well as* multiple communities that make up our world. Antithetical terms such as 'rooted cosmopolitanism' (Beck, 2006), 'cosmopolitan patriot' (Appiah, 1997), and 'vernacular cosmopolitanism' (Bhabha, 1996) capture how global interconnections have resulted in the contemporary paradox of living at home and in the world. Such hybrid terms ultimately aim to disrupt notions of cultural purity and convey the myriad ways that identity can be conceived of as re-attachment, multiple attachments, or attachment at a distance (Robbins, 1998). It is in this space of multiplicity that a consciousness of 'planetarity' (Spivak, 2003) becomes possible as we become aware of our allegiances to communities worldwide. Second, contemporary proponents of cosmopolitanism share cynic cosmopolitanism's strong commitment toward resisting injustice. As Peng Cheah (2006) observes, what is distinctive about the revival of cosmopolitan research in the 1990s is a shift away from articulating universal visions of a one-world utopia toward highlighting actually existing, on-the-ground cosmopolitan practices that seek to counter global injustices arising from corporate capitalism. In relation to literature education, various scholars have discussed contemporary cosmopolitanism's applications to teaching which essentially entail the ways literature provokes critical engagement with an ethics of living in an interconnected, globalized age (see Choo, 2013; Donald, 2007; Jollimore & Barrios, 2006; Nussbaum, 1997).

In this chapter, we start from the premise that cosmopolitan pedagogies are determined first by an orientation that then directs praxis. This aligns with current scholarship that conceptualizes cosmopolitanism as a transnational orientation involving global seeing (Gaudelli, 2011) or 'globality' which is 'an orientation to the world as a whole' (O'Byrne, 2003, p. 86). Its starting point is an attitude characterized by a willingness to engage the other (Mehta, 2000), a disposition that opens oneself to learn from rather than merely tolerate the other (Hansen, 2011), and a sensitivity toward empathizing with others (Nussbaum, 1997). The terms 'seeing,' 'attitude,' 'disposition,' and 'sensitivity' capture the sense of a cosmopolitan orientation in which one is attuned toward a broader human fraternity transcending territorial boundaries (Lu, 2000). Thus, we argue for the importance of cosmopolitan literature pedagogies that involve a reorientation in three areas: approaching literature, not as a platform for enclosed readings, but as an invitational space for ethical encounters; nurturing the literature student, not as a reader with a tourist mindset, but one with an exilic imagination; and reorienting the literature teacher, not as cultural guardian, but as restless cartographer.

Approaching literature: from enclosed readings to ethical encounters

For many teachers of literature, a hybrid of textual practices grounded on reader response criticism, new criticism, and poststructuralist criticism are commonly employed that encourage students to actively respond to texts, perform critical close reading of the formal features of texts, and critique the politics of texts and textual production. The predominant strand in this tapestry is a panoply of Reception Theory approaches focusing on the reader's interactions and transactions in co-'creating' the text. Popularized as Reader Response, classroom practices support readers' transaction with the text (Rosenblatt, 1994), readers' unconscious filling of gaps in the text based on prior experiences (Iser, 1972), and readers' dialogic engagement with interpretive communities (Fish, 1980).

Practices associated with reader response approaches have been widely disseminated, creating the proverbial double-edged sword in literature pedagogies.

On the one hand, these practices have liberated the classroom by encouraging multiple responses to texts, by developing students' self-reflexivity as they become sensitized to their own assumptions within a community of learners, and by connecting texts to students' experiences resulting in more student-centered teaching. On the other hand, the continued emphasis on aesthetic reading, in which the reader's attention is centered directly on what he or she is living through, implies that the production of meaning typically occurs through the reader's interactions with the lifeworld of text—its plot, character, setting, and style. In this sense, reader response approaches may overlook the cosmopolitan potential of literature to serve as invitational spaces for ethical explorations about values, beliefs, and systems within their own society and the world.

We argue that the centricity of the reader in a text-reader transaction should be disrupted to accommodate the perspective of the other, particularly the other who is marginalized, silenced, and discriminated against. A conscious desire to engage diverse others might serve as a starting point for literature discourse. By considering literature as an invitation to ethical exploration, an invitation to engage with another reality, including belief systems and values that are embedded in it, teachers can become sensitized to the kinds of issues, moral dilemmas, and tensions that can be part of classroom discussions. In selecting texts, teachers may ask questions such as: how can texts introduced in the classroom provide a hospitable space for alternative worldviews, realities, and beliefs? Which groups are currently stereotyped in students' communities and how can their perspectives be included?

Literature, in providing insights into the lived experiences of others, inherently invites ethical contemplation. Take for example, the opening sentences of Ursula Le Guin's short story, 'The Ones Who Walk Away from Omelas': 'With a clamor of bells that set the swallows soaring, the Festival of Summer came to the city Omelas, bright-towered by the sea. The rigging of the boats in harbor sparkled with flags' (p. 255). A question worthy of examination after only these opening sentences might be: what would cause anyone to walk away from Omelas as the title suggests? With such a question, we have put the reader on alert to what might be conflictual and ethical contexts within the landscapes of the fictional city Omelas. As we might anticipate, this idyllic world is shattered when the story's narrator speaks directly to the reader: 'Do you believe? Do you accept the festival, the city, the joy? No? Then let me describe one more thing' (p. 259). Then, the narrator reveals that under one of the beautiful public buildings, in a small room the size of a broom closet, a young child has been locked up for several years. The child is malnourished, naked, full of sores, and is isolated from everyone else. When the citizens of Omelas visit the child, they are told not to speak a word. In the end, they

> all understand that their happiness, the beauty of their city, the tenderness of their friendships, the health of their children, the wisdom of their scholars, the skill of their makers, even the abundance of their harvest and the kindly weathers of their skies, depend wholly on this child's abominable misery.
>
> (p. 260)

The story presents two responses—complacent people who turn away from the child to enjoy the grace of life in Omelas and those who choose to leave the city as an overt rejection of Omelas' values. Does the latter response sufficiently do justice to the oppressed other? At this point, the title takes on new meaning: to act or to walk away? Such a question invites the reader to consider what it means to act justly as well as to consider the practical limits of justice.

Marshall Gregory (2010) highlights three ethical invitations literature extends to readers that, in relation to Le Guin's story, may generate the following kinds of questions:

1 Invitations to shared feeling with others—Who is othered in this text and how is he or she othered? How does this process of othering compare with forms of othering in your own country and in the world?
2 Invitations to shared beliefs—In what ways does the story depend on our recognition of injustice? How does the implied author's conception of social injustice compare or contrast with your society or community's?
3 Invitations to ethical judgment—What ethical theories can we use to judge Omelas? How can these same theories to judging systems of governance be applied to your country as well as other countries?

Such questions push students to connect with real-world injustices in their world. The text is then no longer perceived as an enclosed artifact but an entry point to understanding ethical realities. Further, the invitation to make ethical judgments on characters and value systems in texts means that students should not only be equipped with the skills of aesthetic analysis but should also have some understanding of ethical philosophy. As George Hillocks Jr. (2014) observes, high school literature teachers focus on empowering students to appreciate the formal properties of the text but do not explicitly equip them to handle its ethical, philosophical concepts with the result that students cannot convincingly substantiate their judgments of characters or issues.

Like Shirley Jackson's 'The Lottery' and Suzanne Collins' popular *Hunger Games* trilogy, the characters in Le Guin's story cannot be sufficiently judged without serious discussions about ethical philosophy such as utilitarianism and its consequences. Starting from Jeremy Bentham's greatest good for the greatest number maxim, students can consider how individual rights are compromised for the good of the majority in the story and how, in present-day contexts, such logic has been used to justify the use of torture on suspected terrorists (Sandel, 2009). Going further, students can discuss John Stuart Mill's expansion of Bentham's utilitarianism that draws attention to the quality of pleasures arising from the consequences of action. From this perspective, the quality of life citizens enjoy at the expense of one child validates their inaction which, whether they ignore or walk away, has the same consequence. A contemporary application of this logic is the justification of modern-day slavery in which the quality of life in economically advanced nations is dependent on sweatshop laborers. In short, when literature is recognized as an important space that invites ethical encounters with individuals whose capacity to live fully has been suppressed, literature discussions may expand beyond aesthetic features of the text or readers' responses to it so that questions about living ethically in the world and our obligations of justice to others become central to literature discourse.

Nurturing the literature student: from reader with a tourist mindset to one with an exilic imagination

If our approach to literature begins from an ethical orientation, it raises the question about how teachers should envision the kind of literature student they wish to nurture. The ethical invitations we suggested previously are aimed at pushing students to see, think, and feel from the perspective of the other. Vijaydan Detha, a fiction writer from Rajasthan, India, challenges us to think of a story as more than an exploration of another person's dilemmas and circumstances. In his story 'A True Calling,' the opening paragraph provides the reader with this provocation:

> Nothing happens to a story if all you do is listen. Nothing happens if all you do is read, or memorize word for word. What matters is if you make the heart of the story part of your very life. This story is one of those.
>
> *(para. 1)*

The story is an invitation to the reader *to inhabit* the story, to travel within and in the landscapes of the story. In Detha's provocation, we see a call to blur or collapse the boundaries of many often-conceived binaries—between self and other, listener and teller, insider and outsider—and not only experience 'the heart of the story' temporarily but also to close the physical and ethical distances between self and others represented in the text and carry these into one's own life.

Literature's potential in cultivating ethical ways of inhabiting and seeing leads some to fear that it can become a tool for moral education and indoctrination. For example, see Posner's (1997) essay 'Against ethical criticism.' Here, we parse a clear distinction between moral education and ethical education so as not to conflate them. The distinction between morality and ethics can be observed in the difference between the Latin term 'moral' which stresses expected social conduct that may be expressed in terms of rules, dos and don'ts, right and wrongs (Haydon, 2006) and the Greek term 'ethics' that focuses on *reasoning* about how to cultivate oneself fully and how to live *in relation* to others (Noddings, 2003; Williams, 1985). Literature's essential power is not so much that it offers moral lessons, but that it invites ethical reflection that pushes us to move beyond the self, including the self's desire for preservation, to enact power over others, and the self's instinctive drive to read others from his or her own prior knowledge, experiences, and worldview. The kinds of other-centered, ethical questions that literature invites essentially revolve around what it means to live out the Socratic idea of the 'good life' which does not refer to a kind of self-centered, comfortable living but a life in responsible and just engagement with others as he states, 'the good life, the beautiful life, and the just life are the same' (Plato, 360 B.C.E./2002, p. 51). Given that identity is not constructed in a vacuum but develops through on-going dialogues with other real or fictional selves, literature can potentially provide a crucial site for what Kwame Anthony Appiah (2005) terms 'soul-making' which is 'the project of intervening in the process of interpretation through which each citizen develops an identity' (p. 164).

In this sense, the literature classroom can be conceived as that intervening space for cosmopolitan soul-making in which students' fashioning of identity expands beyond their familiar community or nation as they engage in conversations with diverse others in the world. One obvious pedagogical strategy would involve the inclusion of transnational literature that inquires into various crosscultural, crossborder crossings in our global age. The trope of exile constitutes a prevalent theme in transnational literatures; we have only to remember V. S. Naipaul's exilic explorations in his fiction that examines displacement in a Caribbean context or Jhumpa Lahiri's short stories that probe into the challenges of holding on to cultural traditions while seeking to assimilate into foreign lands. Such transnational literature resists fossilizations of identity by showing how individuals learn to reorient their understanding of themselves and others as they navigate the ambiguities of cultural flux, hybridity, and mixing.

Transnational literature provides rich opportunities for students to make sense of their globalized experiences as they negotiate multiple cultures they are connected to in virtual or physical affinity spaces. It is these imaginative excursions into other worlds that enable the literature student to sharpen his or her sense of critical cosmopolitanism that resists thinking about the self within the realm of the familiar (Walkowitz, 2006). Instead, such excursions aim at continual 'self-reflexive repositioning of the self in the global sphere' (Cuddy-Keane, 2003, p. 546). In this temporal space of displacement and dislocation, students cultivate an exilic imagination rather than a tourist mindset. Unlike tourists who, when visiting a foreign land, tend to interpret the other from their dominant culture's point of view, exiles are displaced and, as Edward Said (2002) has argued, it is their capacity to see the entire world as a foreign land that makes possible originality of vision: 'Most people are principally aware of one culture, one setting, one home; exiles are aware of at least two and this plurality of vision gives rise to an awareness of simultaneous dimensions' (p. 148).

With such an exilic imagination, students may find themselves located and dislocated simultaneously, feeling the familiar and the strange in the same moment, and being insider and outsider synchronously. In the process, the individual is always becoming, in transit as he or she negotiates the anxieties of non-belonging while belonging and oscillating in the in-between spaces of such binaries in a variety of global, local, and personal contexts. Further, the capacity to imagine from a position of exile enables one to see the marginalized other differently beyond institutional, national, and other ideological lenses, and this facilitates the possibility of empathy in the first place. As Martha Nussbaum (1997) argues, literature can cultivate a narrative imagination that pushes one into 'a kind of exile—from the comfort of local truths, from the warm nestling feeling of loyalties' (Nussbaum, 1997, p. 11). It is the imagination's nomadic potential that can rupture the reader's singular perspective of reality, breaking the inertia of habit and provoking a 'wide-awakeness' allowing him or her to perceive and appreciate multiple, complex realities (Greene, 1995).

Reorienting the literature teacher: from cultural guardian to restless cartographer

Cosmopolitan literature pedagogies attend not only to the kinds of ethical conversations that can be elicited from the text or the transcultural sensitivities that can be nurtured in students but also draw attention to the important role teachers play in resisting tendencies toward exclusivity and insularity as a result of contemporary anxieties of global interconnectedness. As Wendy Brown (2010) observes, today's postnational political climate has given rise to a paranoia of *walling* all over the world. The examples are numerous and include the construction of a U.S.-Mexico border to curb the flow of drugs and immigrants; the security fence in Israel constructed along the West Bank to keep Palestinians away; electric fences constructed in Botswana along its border with Zimbabwe; and walls between Egypt and Gaza, Saudi Arabia and Yemen, Brazil and Paraguay, among others. This late modern phenomenon of walling, she argues, marks an instinctive desire to maintain a boundary between 'us' and 'them' and yet, one cannot block others without remaining shut in.

Similarly in the context of teaching, fears of new and emerging canons, voices, and genres may lead teachers to become guardians of cultural texts and traditions. Proponents of a cultural heritage approach to literature education typically emphasize an appreciation of canonical or representative works perceived as products of a nation resulting in literature education becoming what Harold Bloom (1994) describes as a necessarily elitist enterprise grounded on principles of selectivity.

Increasingly, influences from progressive, constructivist, and poststructuralist education movements have reoriented the role of the teacher and ways of organizing the curriculum. In describing the transnational turn in literary studies, Paul Jay (2010) highlights how the globalizing of literary studies toward the late twentieth century has led to a radical dislocation of traditional geographical spaces teachers have used to organize the curriculum. For example, early world literature curricula were typically organized around 'Great Books' representative of civilizations, particularly the West, and premised on the notion of bounded territoriality which assumes that identities of individuals, cultures, and nation-states are fixed, determinable, and discrete. With increasing awareness of the fluidity and 'liquid' nature of culture (Bauman, 2000) coupled with growing attention to transnational studies and border criticism, the literature curriculum must now attend to extraterritorial spaces concerning issues that transgress national borders. These are the in-between, hybrid, contact zones (Pratt, 1991) where cultures clash and mix with one another, and where cultural histories intersect.

As we re-envision the literature curriculum as a site attuned to transnational flows characteristic of our age, a corresponding reorientation of the literature teacher's role as a cosmopolitan explorer, navigator, and restless cartographer occurs. Such a role is characterized by a cosmopolitan curiosity to venture beyond national and disciplinary borders as well as a restlessness that expresses itself in the constant orienting and reorienting of what it means to read, experience, and teach literature. Teaching is constant navigation, continuous charting of pathways for learning *for and with* our students. We are on a journey, attentive to markers and signposts, observant of changing contexts and circumstances, watching for pathways and byways, and always imagining the unknown, the next places to explore. As we approach literature through this changing global context, we find ourselves focusing on different questions, exploring different territories for study, discovering ways to make sense of cultural and physical landscapes that we do not fully understand and that are in constant flux and change.

Thus, we conceive the metaphor of teacher as restless cartographer, performing the cartographic act of mapping texts as sites for exploring and further understanding social and global spaces. How might we map the complexities and nuances of global landscapes onto the daily landscapes in which we walk, work, live in relation to and take action with and for others? Mapping texts into the curriculum that consciously underscore cosmopolitan ideals as plural, nuanced, and 'in process' enhances the possibility of reaching our goal of furthering intercultural and transcultural communication, understanding, and action. One pedagogical approach is to *cluster* texts, that is, map several texts, one with others, onto the landscape of a particular subject, situation, location, event, or historic circumstance as a way to interrupt singular representations. This avoids the tendency to stereotype through a single story or to simplify the complex nuances and approaches that only one perspective offers. Vinz (2000) argues that clustering texts, conceived as spiderwebs and attentive to the fragile threads of connection and complication, places these texts in configurations that are ripe for dialogue, offering multi-perspectives and dimensionality not so easily met with organizational methods that set up discrete categories (such as African or Caribbean or thematic identification). Clustering or webbing is similar in purpose and kind to the cartographic activity Fredric Jameson (1991) has called 'cognitive mapping,' a relational framework that enables 'a situational representation on the part of the individual subject to that vaster and properly unrepresentable totality which is the ensemble of society's structures as a whole' (pp. 51–54).

We find historical fiction a particularly fertile site for clustering. Historic and fictional accounts in combination with poems, films, photographs, autobiographies, biographies, or oral histories of either the same or related situations create a multi-dimensional web on the landscape, much like isopleth mapping techniques, where each perspective and nuanced or disparate piece of information adds dimensionality and relationality with the others, each text dependent on the others adds up to more than the sum of their parts. Mapping historic and reinventions of the historic onto the same point in the landscape establishes *prisms* of reference for thinking about oneself and one's place in broader social spaces. As such, literature serves a cartographic function by offering re-representations of social space, broadly understood.

For example, Edna O'Brien's (2016) recent novel *The Little Red Chairs* alludes to the siege of Sarajevo where, at the twentieth anniversary, 11,541 red chairs were placed in rows—one empty chair for every Sarajevan killed during the 1,425 days. The novel begins with a stranger-comes-to-town trope, and we soon learn that the fictional Dr. Vlad Draganand shares key similarities with those of Radovan Karadzic, the historical 'Butcher of Bosnia' who was arrested after 12 years in hiding and found guilty of genocide on March 24, 2016 by the International Criminal Tribunal at the Hague just two days before O'Brien's novel was published. In this novel, the two landscapes of historic and fictional fuse as embodiment of the forces of war and misery that extend out into the world, not only leaving us to ponder the symbolic empty chairs as part of a topography of lives touched by such outrageous acts but also *to feel, to experience,* and *to imagine* along with others, real and/or fictional, *theirs/our* experiences. The dialogic spaces opened by the combined gestures of historical/fictional in this novel offer a network of pathways for the types of cosmopolitan explorations that we envision possible when clustering texts onto the landscapes. From this original pairing, we become restless cartographers. Add a small book of drawings and poems by children of Sarajevo, *I Dream of Peace,* the title inspired by UNICEF interviews and discussions with child victims. That might lead the inquiry to *Zlata's Diary,* another version of a child's perspective of wartime in Sarajevo. Or, we might read some of the poems by Karadzic, the Butcher, himself. It is worthwhile to pause and consider how such a poet becomes leader of a war toward ethnic cleansing. A photo essay in *The Atlantic,* April 13, 2012, documents multiple images of Sarajevo from citizens and soldiers to war-torn landscapes. The film documentary *Perfect Circle* is rich with questions about the loss of culture in the aftermath of war. Another possible pathway is to move into the texts written and recorded by Muslims in Sarajevo but map outward to literature about Muslims in other cultural and political contexts. The possibilities for clusters are rich and varied. It takes restlessness and curiosity to develop the cartographic capacities we hope to nurture in ourselves as teachers and in our students causing us to reorient our own perspectives as we reconsider the complex and nuanced landscapes of our globe.

Re-imagining possibilities

In conceiving cosmopolitan literature pedagogies, we have been exploring ways to nurture ours and our students' abilities to feel *for and with* distant others and to imagine other people's lives, experiences, victories, injustices, and values even those very unlike our own. It might be said that both imaginative and emotional attachment to others, as fellow travelers on our shared although distinctly diverse global landscapes, can be experienced through fictional characters and landscapes, and this, in turn, might be one of many fertile spaces to cultivate not only our cosmopolitan ethical imagination but also to consider the 'what ifs' of how we might respond to these differences and injustices through various forms of ethical action. We are not suggesting that every student and teacher will find fertile spaces for ethical explorations in every text they read, but we do advocate for reorienting the relationships between fictional worlds and the worlds of difference we confront in our lives and particularly in our increasingly global landscapes of the present and future.

References

Appiah, K. A. (1997). Cosmopolitan patriots. *Critical Inquiry, 23*, 617–639.

Bauman, Z. (2000). *Liquid modernity.* Cambridge: Polity Press.

Beck, U. (2006). *The cosmopolitan vision.* Cambridge: Polity Press.

Bhabha, H. (1996). Unsatisfied: Notes on vernacular cosmopolitanism. In L. Garcia-Morena & P. C. Pfeifer (Eds.), *Text and nation* (pp. 191–207). London: Camden House.

Bloom, H. (1994). *The Western canon: The books and school of the ages.* New York: Penguin.

Brown, W. (2010). *Walled states, waning sovereignty.* New York: Zone.

Cheah, P. (2006). *Inhuman conditions: On cosmopolitanism and human rights.* Cambridge, MA: Harvard University Press.

Choo, S. S. (2013). *Reading the world, the globe, and the cosmos: Approaches to teaching literature for the twenty-first century.* New York: Peter Lang.

Cuddy-Keane, M. (2003). Modernism, geopolitics, globalization. *Modernism/Modernity, 10*(3), 539–558.

Detha, V. (2004). A true calling. Retrieved on May 19, 2016 from www.wordswithout borders.org/article/a-true-calling.

Donald, J. (2007). Internationalisation, diversity and the humanities curriculum: Cosmopolitanism and multiculturalism revisited. *Journal of Philosophy of Education, 41*(3), 289–308.

Fish, S. (1980). *Is there a text in this class? The authority of interpretive communities.* Cambridge, MA: Harvard University Press.

Gaudelli, W. (2011). Global seeing. *Teachers College Record, 113*(6), 1237–1254.

Greene, M. (1995). *Releasing the imagination: Essays on education, the arts, and social change.* San Francisco, CA: Jossey-Bass.

Gregory, M. W. (2010). Redefining ethical criticism: The old vs. the new. *Journal of Literary Theory, 4*(2), 273–301. www.jltonline.de/index.php/articles/article/view/287/879.

Hansen, D. T. (2011). *The teacher and the world: A study of cosmopolitanism as education.* New York: Routledge.

Haydon, G. (2006). *Education, philosophy and the ethical environment.* New York: Routledge.

Hillocks, Jr., G. (2016). The territory of literature. *English Education, 48*(2), 109–126.

Iser, W. (1972). The reading process: A phenomenological approach. In D. Lodge (Ed.), *Modern criticism and theory: A reader* (pp. 211–228). Essex: Longman.

Jameson, F. (1991). *Postmodernism, or the cultural logic of late capitalism.* Durham, NC: Duke University Press.

Jay, P. (2010). *Global matters: the transnational turn in literary studies*. Ithaca, NY: Cornell University Press.

Jollimore, T., & Barrios, S. (2006). Creating cosmopolitans: The case for literature. *Studies in the Philosophy of Education, 25*(5), 363–383.

Le Guin, U. K. (2015). The ones who walk away from Omelas. In U. K. Le Guin (Ed.), *The wind's twelve quarters and the compass rose* (pp. 254–262). London: Orion.

Lu, C. (2000). The one and many faces of cosmopolitanism. *Journal of Political Philosophy, 8*(2), 244–267.

Mehta, P. B. (2000). Cosmopolitanism and the circle of reason. *Political Theory, 28*(5), 619–639.

Noddings, N. (2003). *Caring: A feminine approach to ethics and moral education*. Los Angeles: University of California Press.

Nussbaum, M. C. (1997). *Cultivating humanity: A classical defence of reform in liberal education*. Cambridge, MA: Harvard University Press.

O'Brien, E. (2016). *The little red chairs*. New York: Little, Brown and Company.

O'Byrne, D. J. (2003). *The dimensions of global citizenship: Political identity beyond the nation-state*. London: Frank Cass.

Posner, R. A. (1997). Against ethical criticism. *Philosophy and Literature, 21*(1), 1–27.

Pratt, M. L. (1991). Arts of the contact zone. *Profession*, 33–40.

Robbins, B. (1998). Introduction, part I: Actually existing cosmopolitanism. In P. Cheah & B. Robbins (Eds.), *Cosmopolitics: Thinking and feeling beyond the nation* (pp. 1–19). Minneapolis: University of Minnesota Press.

Rosenblatt, L. M. (1994). *The reader, the text, the poem: The transactional theory of the literary work*. Cardondale: Southern Illinois University Press.

Said, E. W. (2002). *Reflections on exile and other essays*. Cambridge, MA: Harvard University Press.

Spivak, G. C. (2003). *Death of a discipline*. New York: Columbia University Press.

Vinz, R. (2000). Cautions against canonizing an(other) literature. In R. Mahalingam & C. McCarthy (Eds.), *Multicultural curriculum: New directions for social theory, practice, and policy* (pp. 127–154). New York: Routledge.

Walkowitz, R. L. (2006). *Cosmopolitan style: Modernism beyond the nation*. New York: Columbia University Press.

Williams, B. (1985). *Ethics and the limits of philosophy*. Cambridge, MA: Harvard University Press.

2

'THE DRESS OF THOUGHT'

Analysing literature through a linguistic lens

Debra Myhill and Annabel Watson

Introduction

For teachers of English/Language Arts, developing students' literary responses to texts is a core aspect of their teaching: indeed, in the UK, developing literary responses to texts is frequently at the heart of an English teacher's identity. Most secondary English teachers in the UK enter their careers as English teachers with an English Literature degree (Shortis and Blake 2010); they are enthusiastic readers and value reading; and they are very comfortable leading discussion about texts and supporting their analysis. However, because of this dominant entry route, far fewer English teachers recognise the potential of linguistic analysis or are comfortable teaching from this perspective. In general, literature teachers are very at ease introducing a wide range of literary metalanguage for analysing text: indeed, this is often perceived as an important induction into the discourse of literary criticism. However, teachers are less likely to draw on linguistic meta-language or to explore how linguistic choices are part of authorial crafting and shaping of text. Indeed, many teachers hold epistemological stances which eschew any use of grammar or grammatical terminology in their teaching of text, whilst at the same time attributing epistemic value to the use of literary meta-language (Wilson and Myhill 2012). Yet, the relationship between what we say and how we say it is as much about linguistic decision making as it is about figurative language choices. Samuel Johnson (1817:39) described language as '*the dress of thought*', drawing attention to this intrinsic relationship between the message and how it is communicated verbally.

This lacuna in the English teacher's repertoire is almost certainly attributable to the general avoidance of linguistics, or grammar, in the English curriculum in many Anglophone countries for nearly 50 years. The debate about the place of grammar in the English curriculum is regularly re-ignited—not least currently in England where primary school students now have to take a national test in grammar at ages 7 and 11—and has been well-rehearsed elsewhere (Braddock et al. 1963; Hillocks 1984; Myhill and Watson 2014). In this chapter, we hope to move this debate beyond polarised expressions for and against grammar, and instead consider how linguistic analysis of text can support young people's interpretations and critical engagement with literature. Over the past 10 years, a sequence of cumulative research studies conducted in the *Centre for Research in Writing* at the University of Exeter have explored the linguistic structures evident in students' writing (Myhill 2009); metalinguistic understanding of writing (Myhill et al. 2011); the effectiveness of explicit teaching of grammar in context on students' writing (Myhill et al. 2012); and the nature of dialogic metalinguistic discussion about writing (Myhill et al. 2016). Drawing on these studies, this chapter will illustrate the complementarity of literary and linguistic approaches to literature, and signal the social semiotic affordances of close engagement in the teaching of literature with how language makes meaning.

The relationship between grammar and text

Our consideration of the relationship between grammar and written text, and of how language makes meaning draws on Halliday's extensive thinking about this relationship (Halliday 2003, 2004). In contrast to conceptualisations of grammar as principally concerned with learning grammatical rules and the correction of errors, Halliday regards grammar as a resource, '*a meaning-making system through which we interactively shape and interpret our world and ourselves*' (Derewianka and Jones 2010:9). Halliday was interested in language in context and how the grammatical choices we make in different contexts for different social purposes establish subtly different ways of making meaning. At its core, writing is fundamentally about making choices and decisions: as Kellogg notes, '*All writers must make decisions about their texts*' and in this decision making they have to grapple with '*the problem of content—what to say—and the problem of rhetoric-how to say it*' (Kellogg 2008:2). These choices can be *explicit* or *implicit* choices: as we become more expert at writing, more and more choices become implicit and internalised, but equally other choices become the focus of explicit attention. Literary analysis focuses on writers' choices in terms of such features as imagery, plot structures and rhetorical devices whereas linguistic analysis focuses on writers' lexical, syntactical and textual choices.

The pedagogical approach we have developed is informed by this conceptualisation of grammar and language as a semiotic resource and is based upon four key principles (Jones et al. 2013): (1) **making a link** between the grammar being introduced and how it works in the writing being taught; (2) explaining the **grammar through examples**, not lengthy explanations; (3) building in **high-quality discussion** about grammar and its effects; and (4) using examples from **authentic texts** to links writers to the broader community of writers.

The principal focus of our series of studies has been on the teaching of writing, rather than the development of responses to texts. These pedagogical principles build upon the ways in which a focused engagement with reading texts can be converted into more 'writerly' engagement with written texts and thus bring together in symbiosis the study of reading and writing, exploring the reader-writer relationship (Langer and Flihan 2000). The use of authentic texts as models for young people's own writing is critically important because it considers texts written for genuine social purposes not for school tests, and thus it avoids formulaic prescriptions of how a particular text should be shaped. 'Real' writers break rules and create hybrid genres! So authentic texts provide a fertile ground for exploring the choices writers make and how grammatical choices in a particular text in a particular context are creating meanings. In this way, the teaching of writing is constantly linked to rich reading experiences. The teaching approach analyses reading texts from a linguistic perspective to show students how texts are constructed and how meanings are shaped, and students are inducted into the repertoire of choices that 'real' writers use and then invited to choose from that repertoire in their own writing. Through these studies we became aware, and our participant teachers also reported to us, that not only was this approach improving students' writing, but it was also supporting their responses to text.

Some literary examples

In this section, we will explore in a little more detail, with some explanatory examples, how approaching texts from a linguistic perspective can offer insights and understandings complementary to a literary approach and thus potentially enrich students' responses to texts. The first example is from the opening of Dickens' *A Christmas Carol*. It provides naturally rich text for discussing narrative hooks and the first characterisation of Scrooge, as well as the simile *'as dead as a door-nail'* emphasising Marley's decease:

> Marley was dead: to begin with. There is no doubt whatever about that. The register of his burial was signed by the clergyman, the clerk, the undertaker, and the chief mourner. Scrooge signed it: and Scrooge's name was good upon 'Change, for anything he chose to put his hand to. Old Marley was as dead as a door-nail.
>
> from Dickens—*A Christmas Carol*

However, it has rich linguistic potential too. The very short initial main clause, *'Marley was dead'* establishes directly a key narrative point, which is instantly undermined by the infinitive clause, *'to begin with'*, raising doubt and creating the narrative hook. The third sentence uses a passive voice which foregrounds the burial register which proves his demise and allows Dickens to end the sentence with the list of officials who have signed, underlining its veracity. A rich discussion might be stimulated by further discussion of this passive sentence and the different effect of writing it in an active voice. The final single clause sentence, with its simile, closes the paragraph as it begins, expressing the certainty of Marley's death through its direct statement and use of the verb 'to be' as the only verb.

Another example is Wilfred Owen's poem, *Dulce et Decorum Est*, a commonly taught poem in UK classrooms. The whole poem has many linguistic aspects worth comment, but let us look closely at the final stanza.

> If in some smothering dreams you too could pace
> Behind the wagon that we flung him in,
> And watch the white eyes writhing in his face,
> His hanging face, like a devil's sick of sin;
> If you could hear, at every jolt, the blood
> Come gargling from the froth-corrupted lungs,
> Obscene as cancer, bitter as the cud
> Of vile, incurable sores on innocent tongues,
> My friend, you would not tell with such high zest
> To children ardent for some desperate glory,
> The old Lie: Dulce et Decorum est
> Pro patria mori.

This stanza is a single sentence, itself a point not often noted. The main clause is delayed until the end of the stanza (*you would not tell, with such high zest to children ardent for some desperate glory, the old Lie*) and is preceded by two long subordinate 'if' clauses. The reader has to wait for the key point of this sentence, and before arriving at that point, the reader is drawn into a very sensory invitation to imagine the soldiers' experience, elaborated in the subordinate 'if' clauses. The direct address to the reader through the pronoun 'you' and the use of the modal verbs 'could' in the subordinate clauses builds up to the use of 'would' in the main clause positions the reader not only to imagine the scene but to agree with the poet's stance—if *you could* see all this, then *you would* not be tempted to tell the old lie. Teachers could also initiate a discussion about the choice to capitalise the noun 'Lie' in the main clause, and the use of the colon to precede the statement of the Latin epithet.

An empirical study investigating whether a linguistic approach to the teaching of reading improves student outcomes

Building on our earlier studies which had demonstrated that explicit attention to linguistic features of writing could improve students' writing (Jones et al. 2012; Myhill et al. 2012), and cognisant of our own and teachers' impressions that this approach was strengthening responses to texts, we were interested to investigate empirically if there was a complementary benefit to students in terms of their capacity to respond to and analyse reading texts. Because, as noted earlier, the pedagogical approach used authentic texts as models to enable writers to think about the choices professional writers made, the teaching focused as much on reading texts as on students' own writing. We developed a study, funded by Pearson, which focused on the national examination for English for 15- to 16-year-olds (General Certificate of Secondary Education: GCSE). One paper in this examination included a reading comprehension test based on a non-fiction text in which marks were awarded for analysis of the text. The research question informing this study was: *does explicit teaching of contextualised grammar at KS4 improve pupils' attainment in reading and writing non-fiction?*

The research was a quasi-experimental pre and post-test design with 308 students, aged 14 to 15 forming the sample, drawn from twelve classes in four schools. From this an intervention group of 161 students and a comparison group of 147 was created. A nine lesson teaching unit of work was developed for the intervention group, which addressed the assessment objectives of the GCSE examination, with a particular focus on building understanding of a repertoire of linguistic and grammatical structures, and on moving from analysis of patterns in real texts to use of these patterns in students' own writing, with consideration of purpose and effectiveness throughout. A range of non-fiction texts were used, both from print and digital sources, and included newspaper and magazine articles and online newspaper editorials. The teaching unit included lesson plans, resources and Powerpoint materials. The comparison group simply taught as usual to the same GCSE assessment objectives. The pre and post-test measures, which were blind-marked by independent markers, used an adapted version of a sample GCSE non-fiction examination paper. The reading questions examined inferential comprehension and information retrieval, and language analysis; the writing question evaluated overall composition, and sentence structure, punctuation and spelling.

The intervention

The teaching intervention was a 3 week teaching unit, focussing on non-fiction and setting out to develop both students' responses to non-fiction texts and their capacity to write them. The purpose of the teaching unit was:

> to develop students' ability to analyse non-fiction texts in detail, and to write their own. There is a particular focus on building understanding of a repertoire of linguistic and grammatical structures, and on moving from analysis of patterns in real texts to use of these patterns in students' own writing, with consideration of purpose and effectiveness throughout.

The Assessment Objectives it addressed were taken from the national GCSE examination assessment objectives, with a particular focus on those objectives for which linguistic knowledge and understanding might be useful:

Reading

AO2iii Explain and evaluate how writers use linguistic, grammatical, structural and presentational features to achieve effects and engage and influence the reader.

Writing

AO3ii Organise information and ideas into structured and sequenced sentences, paragraphs and whole texts, using a variety of linguistic and structural features to support cohesion and overall coherence.

AO3iii Use a range of sentence structures for clarity, purpose and effect, with accurate punctuation and spelling.

In line with the pedagogical principles of the research approach, the teaching unit made use of several authentic texts: an extract from *The Zombie Survival Guide* by Max Brooks; a magazine article, *Astronaut Hibernation*, by Will Gater from *Focus Magazine* (January 2014); a newspaper article, *Demon of Dartmoor*, from the *Daily Mail* (29 July 2007); and Mary Shelley's article, *On Ghosts*. The unit begins with a playful exploration of headlines, using a range of headlines from different sources, and looking especially at the common structure of noun–verb–preposition–noun:

PILOT TURNS BACK AFTER SNAKE POPS OUT OF DASHBOARD
KILLER SWAN BLAMED FOR MAN'S DROWNING
NY COUPLE WEDS IN SHARK TANK

Students then generate their own random headlines using a Headline Generator, a table with headings supporting their linguistic understanding of this possible structure. They then discuss their headlines and consider their effectiveness, reflecting on whether the headline communicates clearly who did what and what happened, and whether they convey strange or shocking images and have unusual juxtapositions of words. Later in the unit of work, students explore, for example, how descriptive detail, through well-chosen nouns, verbs and adjectives can create an impression of a character. They look closely at these noun phrases, describing the Demon of Dartmoor in the *Daily Mail* newspaper article, and discuss how these visual descriptions position the reader to see the dog in a particular way:

- a four-legged fiend with glowing eyes and a blood-curdling howl
- a thick, shaggy coat
- rounded ears
- large front limbs which would be powerful enough to tear human flesh
- a pack of spectral dogs
- a phantom pack of black hunting dogs with glowing red eyes
- demonic hounds.

The teaching unit opens up multiple opportunities for students to actively discuss how the linguistic constructions are working in the text, in line with the pedagogical principle emphasising the importance of rich discussion. For example, in one lesson the class is considering noun phrases in Mary Shelley's 'On Ghosts' which convey emptiness and isolation, and contrasts and juxtapositions they evoke. The lesson plan invites the teacher to initiate exploratory discussion of the linguistic choices, which is followed by an individual task reflecting on their own writing and its linguistic choices. This is consolidated with a final paired discussion task in which students articulate their decision making and its purposes to a peer:

Whole class: feedback from pairs/groups, using ppt 5–7 as prompts if necessary. Focus discussion on the effect of these features (using the prompts on the slides). Aim for a genuinely exploratory discussion of effects which might touch on the sense of isolation, loneliness, stillness being suddenly interrupted by movement, sense of being alive and being dead, beauty and fear.

Individuals: (ppt 7) look at the description you wrote at the start of the lesson. Add another paragraph, experimenting with building up chains of words and phrases which evoke loneliness and emptiness and/or with using contrasts in your writing. (If necessary, use resource 4.3 to help students to build a word bank for loneliness and a concept bank for contrasts before starting this activity).

Pairs: (ppt 8) read your whole passage to a partner and explain how you were using words and phrases effectively—what atmosphere were you trying to create and how did your choice of words help to create that atmosphere?

The results

From the initial sample of 308 students, 240 students (comparison group $n = 116$; intervention group $n = 124$) took both the pre and post-test. The basic descriptive statistics reveal that the pre-test scores for both groups were broadly similar, but the intervention group improved their result in the post test (Table 2.1).

It is important, however, to note the variable performance at class level which lies behind these data. In both intervention and comparison groups, some class means showed negative gain scores in either the reading or writing post-test: and

TABLE 2.1 The mean scores of the two groups—pre and post-test

Group	Focus	Number	Pre-test score: mean	Post-test score: mean	Gain score
Intervention	Reading	124	4.1	4.6	0.5
	Writing		10.6	11.1	0.5
Comparison	Reading	116	3.8	3.4	−0.4
	Writing		10.2	9.4	−0.6

one comparison group class scored worse on both tests at the post-test. These differences may signal the significance of the teacher and the way they implemented the intervention, or signal contextual differences around the taking of the tests (such as the fact that the post-test happened so close to the end of term). They are a salient reminder that any intervention is not an isolated phenomenon, but one influenced by how teachers manage the intervention in their own classes. The results could also have been due to less committed attitudes to the post-test in the comparison group, as they had not received any intervention.

Following this, an analysis of covariance (ANCOVA) was undertaken to consider the significance of the results. ANCOVA was used because the data are nested in classes, and because, as a robust test, it controls for the covariate, removing some of the treatment effect which reduces the chance of a significant result. The ANCOVA analysis found statistically significant results for both reading and writing in the intervention group (reading: $p < 0.001$; writing: $p = 0.02$). However, as noted above, caution is needed in generalising too quickly from this data, particularly because the comparison group's mean declined at the post-test. A more detailed analysis of the sub-scores for the reading test teases out a little more how the two groups performed and provides more robust evidence of the impact of the attention to linguistic characteristics of text on reading comprehension. The reading paper had two questions which focused on inferential comprehension and information retrieval, while three questions required language analysis and the use of quotation as evidence. This revealed a clear, statistically significant difference in the language analysis responses, but non-significant results for inferential comprehension and retrieval (Table 2.2).

These results are important because the intervention did *not* address the development of skills of literal and inferential comprehension, but it *did* focus on language analysis and more precise metalinguistic understanding of how different linguistic structures shape meanings and effects in text. These results support a conclusion that direct and explicit teaching of grammar-meaning relationships in written text can support students' confidence in responding to how texts are shaped and constructed. We are conscious that the study is small and the intervention period very short so further research would be helpful in establishing how generalisable these data are, but these data are promising signs of the potential benefits of supporting students in making linguistic responses to texts.

TABLE 2.2 ANCOVA significance results for individual reading questions

Question	Focus	Statistical significance of group
1	Comprehension and retrieval	$p = 0.198$ *Non-significant*
2a	Comprehension	$p = 0.662$ *Non-significant*
2b	Language analysis	$p = 0.007$ *Significant*
3	Language analysis and quotation selection	$p = 0.019$ *Significant*
4	Language analysis	$p = 0.006$ *Significant*

Conclusion

This chapter set out both to argue and to illustrate how integrating linguistic perspectives within standard literary approaches to the study of texts offers a valuable opportunity to develop students' understanding of the social semiotic affordances of language and to explore how language makes meaning. The argument is theoretically founded on Halliday's conceptualisation of grammar as a functionally oriented system in which social meanings are communicated in context, and thus where grammatical choices become salient in shaping text. It is not a prescriptive conceptualisation of grammar which seeks to eradicate grammatical errors from students' writing nor is it intended to induct learners into accepted norms for writing. Rather it sets out to enrich students' knowledge about language: to develop their metalinguistic understanding of the linguistic selections that writers have used to create text and to enable them to see the connections between writers' choices and their rhetorical intentions for the text.

Pedagogically, the key argument of this chapter—that there is benefit in integrating linguistic perspectives into the study of texts—is founded on a series of research studies which have investigated the development of metalinguistic understanding (Myhill 2011), the value of explicit teaching of grammatical choices within the teaching of writing (Myhill et al. 2012) and the importance of rich dialogic talk about texts (Myhill et al. 2016). The four pedagogical principles (making connections between grammar choices and text effects; using grammatical examples not lengthy grammatical explanations; using authentic texts; and enabling rich discussion) which underpin this approach have also been adopted to develop students' responses to texts and empirically investigated with promising results.

This is a new field of enquiry, both empirically and pedagogically, and we are keen to avoid making any sweeping generalisable claims which do not take full account of the emergent nature of this body of research and the complexity of classroom environments. Although there have been a series of studies and meta-analyses which have found no evidence of any beneficial link between de-contextualised teaching of grammar and improving writing, there are very few empirical studies beyond our own which demonstrate a positive effect of embedding explicit attention to grammar and its rhetorical or communicative effects within the teaching of writing. Similarly, there are no studies that we are aware of which explore the development of higher-level comprehension through explicit attention to the linguistic, as well as the literary, aspects of text. At the same time, whilst our cumulative set of studies is showing beneficial impact for this approach, we are also aware from our own data that teachers' subject knowledge of grammar remains a significant issue (Myhill et al. 2013), both at the foundational level of confidence with the conceptual terminology of grammar but also, and importantly, their ability to see texts through a linguistic lens and be able to notice linguistic structures to draw attention to within the teaching of reading or writing. Likewise, the skill of managing high-quality rich discussion about linguistic choices makes high demands of teachers' pedagogical capacities, particularly if there is also a lack of confidence with grammatical concepts. Looking ahead, our hope is that this chapter stimulates both empirical and pedagogical attention to the opening up of students' metalinguistic knowledge about texts, recognising the complementarity of linguistic and literary insights and avoiding the unhelpful binary oppositions of the pro-anti grammar debate.

References

Braddock, R., Lloyd-Jones, R. and Schoer, L. (1963) *Research in Written Composition*. Urbana, IL: National Council of Teachers of English.

Derewianka, B. and Jones, P. (2010) From traditional to grammar to functional grammar: bridging the divide. *NALDIC Quarterly*, Special Issue 8(1), 6–15

Dickens, C. (2004) A Christmas carol: A ghost story of Christmas [ebook/46] Project Gutenberg. www.gutenberg.org/files/46/46-h/46-h.htm. Accessed 30.01.17.

Halliday, M.A.K. (2003) Introduction: On the 'architecture' of human language. In J. Webster (ed.) *On Language and Linguistics: Volume 3 in the Collected Works of MAK Halliday*. London and New York: Continuum, pp. 1–29.

Halliday, M.A.K. (2004) Three aspects of children's language development: Learning language, learning through language, learning about language. In J. J. Webster (ed.) *The Language of Early Childhood*. New York: Continuum, pp. 308–326

Hillocks, Jr., G. (1984) What works in teaching composition: A meta-analysis of experimental treatment studies. *American Journal of Education*, 93(1), 133–170.

Johnson, S. (1817) *The Lives of the English Poets 1779–1781* (Abraham Cowley) Everyman's Library #770, Volume 1. London: J. M. Dent & Sons, Ltd., pp. 39–40.

Jones, S., Myhill, D.A., Watson, A. and Lines, H.E. (2013) Playful explicitness with grammar: A pedagogy for writing. *Literacy*, 47(2), 103–111.

Kellogg, R. (2008) Training writing skills: A cognitive developmental perspective. *Journal of Writing Research*, 1(1), 1–26.

Langer, S. and Flihan, S. (2000) Writing and reading relationships: Constructive tasks. In R. Indrisano and James R. Squire (eds) *Writing: Research/Theory/Practice*. Newark, DE: International Reading Association.

Myhill, D.A. (2009) Becoming a designer: Trajectories of linguistic development. In: R. Beard, D. Myhill, J. Riley and M. Nystrand (eds) *The Sage Handbook of Writing Development*. London: SAGE, pp. 402–414

Myhill, D.A. (2011) 'The ordeal of deliberate choice': Metalinguistic development in secondary writers. In V. Berninger (ed.) *Past, Present, and Future Contributions of Cognitive Writing Research to Cognitive Psychology*. New York: Psychology Press/Taylor Francis Group, pp. 247–274

Myhill, D.A., Jones, S.M., Lines, H. and Watson A. (2012) Re-thinking grammar: The impact of embedded grammar teaching on students' writing and students' metalinguistic understanding. *Research Papers in Education*, 27(2), 1–28.

Myhill, D.A., Jones, S.M. and Watson, A. (2013) Grammar matters: How teachers' grammatical subject knowledge impacts on the teaching of writing. *Teaching and Teacher Education*, 36, 77–91.

Myhill, D.A., Jones, S.M. and Wilson, A.C. (2016) Writing conversations: Fostering metalinguistic discussion about writing. *Research Papers in Education*, 31(1), 23–44.

Myhill, D.A. and Watson, A. (2014) The role of grammar in the writing curriculum: A review. *Journal of Child Language Teaching and Therapy*, 30(1), 41–62.

Shortis, T. and Blake, J. (2010) *Who's Prepared to Teach School English? The Degree Level Qualifications and Preparedness of Initial Teacher Trainees in English*. London: CLIE.

Wilson, A.C. and Myhill, D.A. (2012) Ways with words: Teachers' personal epistemologies of the role of metalanguage in the teaching of poetry writing. *Language and Education*, 26(6), 553–568.

3

EXPLORING AND ANALYZING LITERATURE THROUGH MULTIMODAL COMPOSITION

Blaine E. Smith

Multimodal composing involves the skillful interweaving and layering of modes—including visuals, sounds, movement, and text—to create a synergistic message. In digital products like videos, websites, and soundscapes, the interaction between modes is important and the unique assemblage of different modes communicates a message that no single mode communicates on its own (Jewitt, 2009; Kress, 2010). As described by Hull and Nelson (2005), 'multimodality can afford not just a new way to make meaning, but a different kind of meaning' (p. 225).

This chapter examines the new and different kinds of meaning adolescents make when exploring and analyzing literature through multiple modes in digital environments. In particular, I will present findings from an urban Grade 12 Advanced Placement Literature and Composition class that participated in a multimodal literature unit. Drawing upon students' products and perspectives, I will illustrate how they were able to construct multidimensional thematic analyses, immerse themselves into the narrative world of *The Things They Carried* (1990), and make multiple intertextual and personal connections to the novel. This chapter will conclude with a discussion of the implications for integrating multimodal literary analysis into the English Language Arts (ELA) classroom.

Conceptual framework and literature review

This study is broadly situated within social semiotics (Kress, 2003, 2010) and multi-literacies (1996) frameworks, which are based on the assumption that various modes (e.g., visuals, text, sound, movement) are integral in meaning making. Social semiotics elucidates how different modes are imbued with different meaning potentials that are shaped by material and sociocultural factors (Kress,

2010). A mode carries with it specific communicative affordances and possibilities for constructing meaning, which also interact and contribute to the constructed multimodal message (Van Leeuwen, 2005). These affordances of a mode offer potentials that make it better for certain communicative tasks than other modes (Kress, 2003). For example, a student might be able to express characterization visually and aurally in ways that are not possible through writing alone. Furthermore, the layering of multiple modes offers potentials for compositions where co-occurring modes build upon one another in rich and generative ways (Jewitt, 2009).

Research in secondary ELA classrooms describes how multimodal projects offer multiple points of entry (Jewitt, 2009; Smith, 2016) for students to explore and express their identities (Honeyford, 2014; Pacheco & Smith, 2015). However, only a few studies (Oldaker, 2010; Pantaleo, 2011; Tan & Guo, 2009) have closely examined how secondary students analyze literature through multimodal compositions. Jocius (2013) found that Grade 12 students learned literary devices through creating digital videos and multimodal PowerPoint presentations. Similarly, Bailey (2009) illustrated how Grade 9 students 'learned literary elements, poetic devices, rhetorical elements, and used reading and writing strategies in ways that previous classes never had before' through multimodal projects connected to literature (p. 230). This emerging work points to the pedagogical potential for integrating digital literacies in the ELA curriculum for supporting literary analysis and response.

Methods

The setting and participants

This study was conducted in a Grade 12 Advanced Placement Literature and Composition class at an urban magnet high school in a major mid-South city in the United States. The composition of the school population was 76% Black, 18% White, 5% Hispanic, and 1% Asian, with 67% of the students participating in the free/reduced price lunch program.

Through purposeful sampling (Patton, 1990), three pairs of focal students who selected each other to work with during the unit were chosen for in-depth analysis of their multimodal compositional processes, products, and perspectives. In consultation with the teacher (Mrs. Buchanan; all names pseudonyms) focal pairs were identified who varied in literacy abilities, technology experience, out-of-school interests, and class engagement.

Literature and multimodal response unit: the Things They Carried

Three central multimodal compositions were connected to the anchor text, *The Things They Carried* (O'Brien, 1990), for the 7-week literature and multimodal response unit. A collection of related short stories, O'Brien's acclaimed work presents different perspectives from a platoon of American soldiers during the Vietnam War. Major themes in the novel include physical and emotional burdens and truth and fiction in storytelling.

Mrs. Buchanan set aside ample class time for students to work on their projects across the 18-day unit. Ten in-class composing workshops included 3 days for the informational webpage, 5 days for the hypertext literary analysis, and 2 days for the audio letter.

Multimodal project #1: informational webpage

Students designed an informational webpage on a chosen topic related to the Vietnam War or American culture during that time period. Using Weebly, an online tool that allows users to easily create websites (www.weebly.com), they were asked to combine artifacts of research (images, videos, songs, primary documents) with a written synthesis of multiple sources to explore and explain relevant historical phenomena. Each student webpage linked to an overarching class website on the literature unit and was made public on the Internet.

Multimodal project #2: hypertext literary analysis

For the second multimodal project, students created a hyperlinked PowerPoint that analyzed the multiple layers of meaning in passages from the novel. The class was challenged to expand their literary analysis skills to a nonlinear and multimodal format that provided more freedom and creativity in their response. Each student pair selected a chapter from the novel and included key passages on PowerPoint slides. Specific sections of text were hyperlinked from these passages to other slides where students explored key words and phrases, literary devices, intertextual connections, questions, and personal reactions. The hypertext literary analysis also included a culminating synthesis slide—what Mrs. Buchanan referred to as a 'multimodal theme statement.' Here, students represented their understanding of a theme from their chapter with a summary statement, connected visual(s), and audio.

Multimodal project #3: audio letter

The final product was an audio letter from a character in the novel. Students used Audacity audio software to record soundscapes that layered voice narration, music, and sound effects to express a character's physical and emotional experiences during the war. This assignment required that students utilize their knowledge of the novel to speak convincingly in the character's voice and tell an 'authentic story.' Students chose an image to accompany the soundscape and their final product was posted on the class website.

Scaffolded digital writer's workshop

Throughout the literature unit, the class participated in a scaffolded digital writer's workshop (Dalton, 2013) designed to support students in seeing themselves as 'designers' (New London Group, 1996) and understanding how multiple modes can be used for expression and communication. This workshop model also focused on developing a supportive class community where students shared their work and relied on one another as resources.

The workshop followed a sequence to scaffold the composing process (Table 3.1). First, when introducing a project, Mrs. Buchanan demonstrated *why* and *how* a multimodal project was created, providing teacher created and real-world examples that made clear the various design decisions a composer could make. Second, students had the choice to work individually or collaboratively during workshop time, and were encouraged to share strategies and resources. Third, students shared their work both in class (e.g., whole-class presentations, gallery walks, peer workshops) and with a wider audience (e.g., class website and culminating presentation for administrators, peers, and community members). Lastly, students submitted typed reflections with each of their final projects where they addressed specific questions aimed at uncovering their composing process, collaborations, and design decisions.

TABLE 3.1 Schedule of in-class multimodal workshops[a]

Informational webpage workshop		
Day 1	*Introduction and demonstration:*	• Presentation and discussion about multimodal composition
		• Mrs. Buchanan demonstrated features of the Weebly tool
		• Mrs. Buchanan presented an example of Vietnam-era Weebly she created with explanations of her process and design decisions
		• Students analyzed websites and discussed their effectiveness
		• Students choose webpage topics and partners
	Create:	• Students began creating informational webpages
Day 2	*Demonstration:*	• Mrs. Buchanan demonstrated importing and editing media in Weebly
		• Student (Adrianna) demonstrated how to change font style and color in Weebly by using html code
	Create:	• Students collaboratively worked on their webpages

Day 3	Share:	• Peer workshop of in-process work at the beginning of class • Students who had completed their webpage presented at the end of class (the rest presented on the following day)
	Create:	• Students collaboratively worked to complete their webpages
	Reflect:	• Students were assigned a metanarrative reflection to submit with final product

Hypertext literary analysis workshop

Day 1	Introduction and demonstration:	• Mrs. Buchanan presented a hypertext literary analysis example she created for a poem with an explanation of her process and design decisions • Mrs. Buchanan presented other student examples • Mrs. Buchanan demonstrated hyperlinking in PowerPoint
	Create:	• Students chose partners and chapter to analyze • Students began creating their hypertext literary analyses
Day 2	Demonstrate:	• Mrs. Buchanan showed the hypertext analysis she created for a chapter from *The Things They Carried*, she described her process and design decisions
	Create:	• Students collaboratively worked on their hypertext analyses
Day 3	Create:	• Students collaboratively worked on their hypertext analyses
Day 4	Demonstrate:	• Mrs. Buchanan demonstrated how to create a multimodal synthesis slide
	Share:	• Students discussed ideas for their multimodal synthesis slides
	Create:	• Gallery walk of students' in-process work at the end of class • Students collaboratively worked on their hypertext analyses
Day 5	Demonstrate:	• Mrs. Buchanan provided a mini-lesson on technical skills students identified as wanting to learn in the prior session (e.g., collaging and editing images and recording voice narration in PowerPoint)
	Create:	• Students collaboratively worked on their hypertext analyses
	Reflect:	• Students were assigned a meta-narrative reflection to submit with final product

(Continued)

Audio letter workshop		
Day 1	*Introduction and demonstration:*	• Class listened to authentic audio letters from Vietnam soldiers
		• Class watched/listened to radio and TV commercials and discussed how sound was used in storytelling
		• Mrs. Buchanan demonstrated how to use Audacity
	Create:	• Students chose partners and began to work on audio letter
Day 2	*Demonstrate:*	• Student (Pete) presented a mini-lesson on how to mix multiple audio tracks in Audacity
	Create:	• Students collaboratively worked on their audio letters
	Reflect:	• Students were assigned a meta-narrative reflection to submit with their final product
Final presentation	*Share, reflect and respond:*	• Students presented their work and explained their compositional choices to the class, principal, administrators, and 11th grade peers
		• Students responded to questions and feedback
		• Informational webpages and audio letters are published on class website

a   The class met alternating days for 85-minute periods. The schedule does not include instruction that occurred on non-workshop days (e.g., discussions, practice writing exams, lectures, etc.)

Data collection and analysis

A variety of data from different perspectives and sources were collected in order to examine students' multimodal literary analyses.

- *Computer screen recordings*: during in-class workshops, focal pairs used research laptops with Camtasia software to record their screen movement and conversations.
- *Video observations*: focused observations (Patton, 1990) of the three focal pairs were conducted via videotaping and taking field notes.
- *Design interviews*: students participated in 30-minute semi-structured design interviews (Dalton et al., 2015) after each of their three multimodal products were completed. The purpose of these interviews was to learn more about students' prior and current experiences with technology and perspectives on their compositional processes and products.

- *Artifacts and materials*: Along with their final compositions that each focal pair submitted together, artifacts related to their multimodal projects and process (e.g., graphic organizers, reflections, and notes) were collected.

Based on Grounded Theory (Strauss & Corbin, 1998), screen capture data, video observations, interview transcripts, and written student reflections were iteratively analyzed. This process of disassembling and reassembling the data involved several rounds of open coding across these data sources to distinguish initial themes in students' multimodal composing processes and products. Comparative case analysis (Stake, 2006) involved analyzing the individual themes and patterns for each case of focal pairs and then employing axial coding (Strauss & Corbin, 1998) once again to generate overall themes across all three focal pairs. This process required not only looking for similarities, but also noting unique differences amongst pairs and for each multimodal project.

Findings

Comparative analysis revealed how students leveraged their multimodal projects to create multidimensional thematic analyses, immerse themselves in O'Brien's narrative world, and make multiple intertextual and personal connections to the novel. It is important to note that these findings are not discrete—students were often able to achieve all three effects within the same composition. In the following, each multimodal literary analysis theme is described with student examples.

Multidimensional thematic analyses

Through layering visuals, text, sound, and movement, students created multimodal analyses that explored important themes from the novel. Different modes communicated different aspects of the theme, which constructed generative multimodal compositions that required a reader/viewer to traverse across modes to construct meaning. These instances of multidimensional thematic analyses were particularly evident in their hypertext projects, where students combined abstract modes (e.g., images and music that connected to the overall theme) with plot-specific modes (e.g., quotes, images, and sounds directly from the novel) to create complex interpretive spaces.

Evelyn and Catie's hypertext analyzed the themes of perception and truth in storytelling. One of the most striking examples of this theme was seen in a slide Evelyn created where she collaged abstract visuals to enhance the following quote:

> Rights spills over into wrong. Order blends into chaos, love into hate, ugliness into beauty, law into savagery. The vapors suck you in, you can't tell where you are, or why you're there, and the only certainty is ambiguity.
>
> *(O'Brien, 1990, p. 86)*

Evelyn layered three 'surreal' images that thematically connected to the idea of elements 'spill[ing] over' into each other and one's perception being challenged. She also placed a picture of a machine gun centrally where all of the images converged in the middle of the PowerPoint slide. Evelyn explained that she liked the ambiguity in the pictures and 'not being able to tell' what they represented, which emphasized the central theme of the quotation (hypertext analysis interview). Other students also created this analytic effect by juxtaposing visuals and songs to key quotations or themes in the novel.

Across the multimodal projects, there was variation in how students leveraged different modes to construct their multidimensional analyses. They described differing textual and visual modal preferences (Smith, 2016). For example, two pairs of students fore-fronted the visual aspects of their projects to represent themes. Marcus and DeShawn—who exhibited a visual modal preference—explained how they felt they could convey their 'vision of the story much better by using pictures' (Marcus, hypertext written reflection). Conversely, Evelyn and Catie described writing first and then used other modes to support their textual analysis. The multimodal projects offered students flexibility in how they orchestrated and accentuated multiple modes to analyze themes.

Immersion into the narrative world

Students also used their multimodal compositions as conduits into the narrative world of *The Things They Carried*. Multiple modes were used to develop a multisensory experience indicative of the novel's context, tenor, and experiences of characters. Through their immersion, students were able to experiment with different points of view to develop a nuanced understanding of characterization.

Students aimed at providing an 'authentic' experience for their audience by recreating the senses that characters experienced in the novel. To meet this goal, they incorporated the diegetic sights (e.g., the 'muck' where soldiers made camp) and sounds (e.g., machine guns, 'spooky' music, and sounds from nature) to transport their audience into O'Brien's narrative world.

Along with immersion into the context of the novel, students also used their multimodal compositions as a means to inhabit different character points-of-view. Within their hypertext literary analyses (ranging from 12 to 16 PowerPoint slides), students often traversed different character perspectives while also reemerging to critically analyze the text and even pose questions to O'Brien about his rhetorical choices (e.g., 'Why did you choose to make the most religious person of the group endure the worst death imaginable?').

Students' immersion into the experiences of characters was particularly evident with the audio letter assignment, which required them to speak convincingly through a character's perspective and tell an 'authentic story.' Adrianna and Kaila used their audio letter to develop the peripheral story of a main character's (Kiowa) wife who sent letters from home while he was in Vietnam. Organized in an epistolary style, their project gave a female perspective of the effects of Kiowa's 'dark and disturbing' death on others. Their final audio letter (Table 3.2) posted on the class webpage included an artistic image of a silhouetted man's head bowed while holding 'prayer beads.' Adrianna explained they selected that image to 'represent Kiowa' because 'he was very religious' (audio letter interview). The aural component of their project involved the layering of two songs, a recorded sound effect of an infant giggling, Kaila's voice sobbing, and voice narration of Adrianna and their classmate, Pete, who provided the voice for Kiowa. Kaila explained their sound selections:

> The first song is 'What the World Needs Now is Love' and it sort of represents how she was feeling. She wanted the love from Kiowa but he was over there in that really dark, desolate, loveless place. And then it switched to the soft piano and the baby giggling and that was to represent that she had just had the baby. He was away from the baby and he couldn't be there, but the baby was still laughing because that's what babies do, they laugh. And then the sad piano at the end was because he died.
>
> *(Audio letter interview)*

When reflecting on the audio letter assignment, Adrianna and Kaila described how the process made them gain more empathy for Kiowa and what he experienced as a soldier. Kaila explained, 'I think with this audio we really had something that helped us and other people feel when reading the story.' Similarly, Adrianna believed the project seemed 'more real' than writing: 'with the audio letter you can include other people's voices instead of just telling a story flat on paper.' By integrating sounds and visuals with their writing, students were able to create sensory experiences evocative of the narrative world and experiment with different points of view.

Connecting to literature through links and multiple modes

Students also made a variety of connections to literature by working with multiple modes in digital environments. These linkages occurred on different levels—including creating intertextual and historical connections to the novel, infusing their interests and popular culture, and emotionally relating to characters.

Students purposefully used hyperlinks and media to situate *The Things They Carried* within the surrounding cultural and political context of the Vietnam War era. These connections were achieved by incorporating historical images and video clips—including Vietnam protests, battle footage, and the effects of Agent Orange. In addition, aural associations were made by infusing music that emphasized dissenting viewpoints during that time. Students also incorporated hyperlinks that intertextually connected the novel to other influential texts and movies dealing with similar themes.

TABLE 3.2 Multimodal transcript of Adrianna and Kaila's audio letter

Time	Music	Sound effect	Voice narration
00:00			[Adrianna's voice] March 1st
00:01	['What the World Needs Now is Love' by Dionne Warwick] What the world needs now, is love sweet love. It's the only thing that there's just too little of.		Dear Kiowa, Your letter depresses me. The war sounds worse than I thought it would be. I can't believe you've only been there a month and you're already talking about dead Charlie and humping around. You sound like you're in a lot of pain. I don't blame you. From what I've heard from Martha, Jimmy says it's hard out there. You don't talk about it much though; that's why you'll make it out. You're strong. God loves you. I love you. Please be careful, Dahlia
00:22	What the world needs now is love sweet love. No, not just for some but for everyone.		September 12 Dear Kiowa, I know I haven't been writing. That's my fault because the baby is hard to manage by yourself. Rozene is a sweet girl. Our daughter is perfect just like you. I've been showing her pictures of you.
00:33	['Sparrow' by Miika 153]	Baby giggling	She laughs every time she sees your face. She doesn't even really know you and she misses you as much as I do. There is a picture of us in this letter. I thought you'd want to see us. I also put in her first pair of socks. They are a good luck charm for you to come home safely. Please do. Be safe my love, Dahlia

00:49	[*Same song but started at a different section*]
	October 18
	Dear Kiowa,
	Your mother came by to visit to see Rozene. She sends her love though I know that might not mean much in the loveless place you're in. Dwelling on Lavender for this long isn't healthy. You know it wasn't your fault. Be safe while you're moving through the hole you're in. I was reading an article and they said the muck over there can pull you under. Don't let yourself be pulled.
01:10	[*Pete's voice*] Ma'am there's a telegram for you.
01:14	[*Adrianna's voice*] Dead?
01:16	[*Kaila's voice*] Sobbing
01:23	He, he, he, he can't be dead.
01:25	Sobbing
01:33–01:36	[*Pete's voice*] I'm sorry miss. He was a great soldier.

TABLE 3.3 Pop culture connections during DeShawn and Calvin' composing process

---

Informational website on Vietnam-era weapons and war tactics

- Included image in website banner from video game set in Vietnam (Call of Duty: Black Ops)
- Included YouTube 'teaser' video of weapons for a video game set in Vietnam (Battlefield 2)
- Included 'Rap' mash up audio of all of the weapon sounds from a video game (Battlefield 2) set in Vietnam

Hypertext literary analysis of chapter 'in the field'

- Searched for scene from the movie *Joe Dirt* on YouTube
- Included image of pop singer Rhianna to represent a character (Billie)
- Include the song 'Billie Jean' by Michael Jackson to connect to character

Audio letter from Kiowa, soldier who drowned in excrement pit

- Voice narration included lyrics from the hip hop song 'Headlines' by Drake
- Search for instrumental version of the rap song 'Pop that Trunk' by Yelawolf
- Include instrumental version of the hip hop song 'President Carter' by Lil' Wayne
- Search for a 'bomb explosion sound effect' on YouTube from a specific episode of the anime television series Dragon Ball Z

In accord with other research (Bailey, 2009; Honeyford, 2013), pop culture connections also served as an entry point for students while multimodal composing. This theme was evident throughout their processes and in their final projects. For example, De Shawn and Marcus constantly integrated their knowledge of video games, movies, rap and R&B music, and anime when composing (see Table 3.3 for a complete list of pop culture connections during their process). DeShawn explained that having the ability to draw from their out-of-school interests and experiences contributed to their enjoying the multimodal projects because they 'reflected [their] personality and it showed [their] creative side' (webpage interview).

Finally, all focal pairs explained how the multimodal projects allowed for them to emotionally connect with the novel in personal ways. In interviews and written reflections, students explained they picked their chapter for the hypertext literary analysis because of their emotional reactions while reading. Catie described their chapter as 'the most heartfelt' of the book, and Evelyn said she was drawn to the 'really vivid' story because of the multitude of emotions she experienced while reading it, which she wanted to convey to others (hypertext interviews). In addition, students described how the flexibility to use multiple modes allowed them to forge deeper affective connections than with words alone. Adrianna believed collaging and editing images helped her to convey the mental state of characters in new ways:

This [hypertext analysis] was different because it was a lot easier to express exactly what I thought because I'm not, I mean I'm good with words, I just don't know what to say sometimes. The pictures help because they exactly describe the emotion I was looking for.

(hypertext analysis interview)

Similarly, Kaila viewed the advantages of multimodal projects for expressing her feelings:

You got to really express what you felt about the book and with writing you can express yourself, but not in colors and everything. Blank ink, that's not really going to do anything. When you really want to express yourself, something like this [hypertext literary analysis] is amazing because other people really see how you feel. Not everybody is good at writing, so if you're not good at writing and you write an essay, nobody is going to get what you felt. They're just going to be like 'oh this isn't that great.' But if you're good at something like this and you do it, people are going to be like 'wow!'

(hypertext analysis interview)

Discussion and implications

Multimodal composing offered adolescents new and different ways to analyze literature. Findings from this study reveal how students layered modes to create multidimensional thematic analyses of *The Things They Carried*. They were able to immerse themselves into O'Brien's narrative world and explore multiple points of view. Students also leveraged the affordances of the digital projects to make a variety of intertextual and personal connections. By choosing from a multimodal palette of visuals, sound, movement, and text, students had flexibility to orchestrate modes in individualized and complex ways.

Moving forward, more research is needed that examines the semiotic potential multiple modes possess for representing and learning content. In particular, how student understanding is revealed, travels, and transforms across modalities. Similar to research on writing-to-learn, which explores how writing serves as a tool for thinking, researchers need to consider the pedagogical potential of *multimodal composing-to-learn*. Focusing on the learning opportunities would aid in transitioning multimodal projects from being viewed as merely an engaging activity, to becoming a more integral part of the curriculum. Especially in the results-based environment of today's schools, research examining the relationship between print-based writing and multimodal composition would be beneficial.

The findings from this study also have implications for the integration of multimodal literary analysis in the secondary ELA classroom. First, when considering the semiotic potential various modes have for analyzing literature, it is important for teachers to take advantage of the uniqueness of multimodal meaning-making (Dalton, 2013) and not revert to print-based scaffolding practices (e.g., requiring students to write first or overly constricting the composing process). As demonstrated in these findings, the freedom for students to traverse and combine modes allowed for them to explore literature in personal and meaningful ways. Second, just as it is vital to explicitly teach students different techniques for expanding their written craft, students can also benefit from explicit instruction (New London Group, 1996) that helps them learn how to capitalize on the semiotic power of modes and learn different ways to orchestrate modes for different rhetorical effects. Finally, students need time to reflect upon their multimodal compositions (Smith & Dalton, 2016). Not only will this promote the intentional use of modes, but these insights into students' design decisions also help teachers uncover the multimodal connections to literature when assessing student work.

References

Bailey, N. M. (2009). 'It makes it more real': Teaching new literacies in a secondary English classroom. *English Education, 41*(3), 207–234.

Dalton, B. (2013). Multimodal composition and the Common Core State Standards. *The Reading Teacher, 66*(4), 333–339

Dalton, B., Robinson, K., Lavvorn, J., Smith, B. E., Alvey, T., Mo, E., Uccelli, P. & Proctor, C. P. (2015). Fifth-grade students' multimodal compositions: Modal use and design intentionality. *Elementary School Journal, 115*(4), 548–569.

Honeyford, M. A. (2013). The simultaneity of experience: Cultural identity, magical realism and the artefactual in digital storytelling. *Literacy, 47*(1), 17–25.

Hull, G., & Nelson, M. (2005). Locating the semiotic power of multimodality. *Written Communication, 22,* 224–261

Jewitt, C. (2009). *The Routledge handbook of multimodal analysis.* New York: Routledge.

Jocius, R. (2013). Exploring adolescents' multimodal responses to *The Kite Runner*: Understanding how students use digital media for academic purposes. *Journal of Media Literacy Education, 5*(1), 310–325.

Kress, G. (2003). *Literacy in the new media age.* London: Routledge.

Kress, G. (2010). *Multimodality: A social semiotic approach to contemporary communication.* New York: Routledge.

New London Group. (1996). A pedagogy of multiliteracies: Designing social features. *Harvard Educational Review, 66,* 60–92.

O'Brien, T. (1990). *The things they carried.* Boston, MA: Houghton Mifflin Harcourt.

Oldaker, A. (2010). Creating video games in middle school language arts classroom: A narrative account. *Voices from the Middle, 17*(3), 19–26.

Pacheco, M. B. & Smith, B. E. (2015). Across languages, modes, and identities: Bilingual adolescents' multimodal codemeshing in the literacy classroom. *Bilingual Research Journal, 38*(3), 292–312.

Pantaleo, S. (2011). Warning: A grade 7 student disrupts narrative boundaries. *Journal of Literacy Research, 43*(1), 39–67.

Patton, M. Q. (1990). *Qualitative evaluation and research methods* (2nd ed.). Newbury Park, CA: Sage Publications, Inc.

Smith, B. E. (2016). Composing across modes: A comparative analysis of adolescents' multimodal composing processes. *Learning, Media & Technology*. doi:10.1080/17439884.2016.1182924.

Smith, B. E. & Dalton, B. (2016). 'Seeing it from a different light': Students' video reflections about their multimodal compositions. *Journal of Adolescent & Adult Literacy*, *59*(6), 719–729.

Stake, R. E. (2006). *Multiple case study analysis*. New York: Guilford Press.

Strauss, A., & Corbin, J. (1998). *Basics of qualitative research: Techniques and procedures for developing grounded theory* (2nd ed.). Thousand Oaks, CA: Sage.

Tan, L., & Guo, L. (2009). From print to critical multimedia literacy: One teacher's foray into new literacies practices. *Journal of Adolescent & Adult Literacy*, *53*(4), 315–324.

Van Leeuwen, T. (2005). *Introducing social semiotics*. London: Routledge.

4

LONDON IN SPACE AND TIME

Peter Ackroyd and Will Self

Andrew Green

Introduction

Place and space are fundamental aspects of literary texts. The interaction between writers' and readers' constructions of 'place' and 'space' and the connection of the literary constructions to real locations are fascinating issues for teachers and students alike to consider. Authors', teachers' and students' personal experiences (or the lack of such experiences) breed assumptions and expectations that fundamentally shape how place and space are received and approached in personal reading and in the classroom.

Urban space and theories of spatiality create particular pedagogic challenges but also offer great potential richness. How, for example, is the city to be understood as place? Does 'place' change over time? Is it, in other words, a purely physical concept, or does it also comprise social and spiritual elements? Are cities comprehensible as 'place', or is 'space' a more useful conceit? What shapes urban environments and how do they develop through time? These are not solely geographical or urban development problems, but also inform literary studies. How, for instance, do literary representations respond to and shape perceptions of the urban topos, and what are the respective roles of writers, readers, teachers and students in constructing the meaning of 'place' and 'space' through literary texts?

Notions of pedagogy have developed to embrace the idea of spatial turn (Charlton *et al.*, 2011; Wyse *et al.*, 2011). When students read—and write—about the city they become personal constructors of urban spatiality. In contradistinction to the rhetoric of globalisation, therefore, which tends to minimise the importance of 'place' (Cresswell, 2004; Kostogriz, 2006), students often encounter the urban environment as locality. Self and Ackroyd insist upon the importance and the unique nature of 'place' and 'space' in the city, and as such provide a rich source for developing students' understanding of the interaction between people and places.

Reading and writing: constructions of the city

Reading and writing are integral processes through which learners interpret and create the world around them (Bavidge, 2006; Leander & Rowe, 2006). As students explore the purposes and social functions of literature, they need also to consider how this reflects upon recreations and perceptions of space and place. The actual world, the world as it is represented in literary texts and the ways in which these two related realities are recreated within a third space—the space of reception—are substantially different (Bakhtin, 1981). Time-space/place connections encoded at the point of writing and those decoded at the point of reading may differ substantially. Teachers are influential in creating the conditions—through both reading and writing—within which students can explore this hiatus as they develop personal responses to texts and 'space'. Ackroyd and Self are self-consciously aware of this hiatus and use it to considerable effect.

Classrooms are, therefore, 'spaces' in their own right where students and teachers collaborate with writers in actualising textual visions. Larkin comes close to defining this in 'The Pleasure Principle' when he refers to 'the recurrent situation of people in different times and places setting off the device [the literary text] and re-creating in themselves what the poet felt when he wrote it' (1983: 81). In this the classroom is best conceived not as a fixed and unchanging entity, but as a process (Wyse *et al.*, 2011)—a locus of multiple and constantly changing interactions which dynamically shape textual meaning. If Eaglestone (2001: 7) is correct in asserting that learners are 'natural theorists', then engaging with the 'process' of producing 'place'/'space' as part of meaning-making is central to students' development (see Figure 4.1).

Variations on Figure 4.1 provide a useful resource in the process of studying literary texts, encouraging students to explore the shifting balance of meaning-making. It makes explicit the multiple 'dialogues' that go into creating possible interpretations. By locating where different types of 'meaning' lie and when these meanings become useful, students actively interrogate their processes as readers and as students of literature. Naturally, such an approach opens fertile ground in exploring the creation and reception of urban space. Holloway and Kneale (2000) envisage just such a Bakhtinian dialogic in the construction of the city, and Massey (2005) suggests that it is through such intimate interactions and not only through larger political, social, physical and economic gestures that conceptualisations of urban 'space' are shaped.

It is also useful to consider whether classrooms are liberating or limiting reading and meaning-making 'spaces'. Urban space can be used to provide opportunities for *in situ* reading. Using textual locations (e.g. visiting Nicholas Hawksmoor's churches when reading *Hawksmoor*) immerses students in the 'place' of the literary text and its locational realities. As Charlton *et al.* (2011: 71) argue, '[b]eing socially constructed, place, identity and literacy are open for reconstruction'. By engaging students with their identities as readers of place alongside the methods of artistic representation authors employ in the very places they represent,

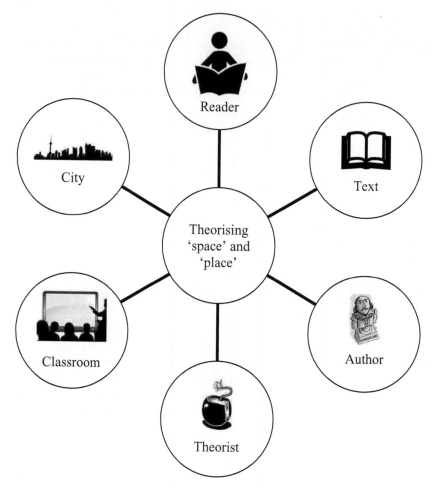

FIGURE 4.1 Theorising 'place'/'space' (developed from Atherton, Green, & Snapper, 2013: 128).

teachers can create rich reading and learning environments. By taking literary texts to the places and spaces they represent, teachers can encourage students to deepen their understandings of urban space and of themselves as consumers and co-constructors of literary meaning.

Constructions of urban space

Massey (2005: 9) has observed that space 'is always in the process of being made. It is never finished; never closed'. Writers and other creative artists play a central role in building perceptions and understanding of the urban environment. When they take on the recreation of the city they do not simply adopt or reflect urban space, but become 'makers' of it. In the case of London, writers enter an evolving and centuries-old literary dialogue within which the 'space' of the city is (re)negotiated and (re)constructed. Self and Ackroyd work within the continuum of London literature, writing of a London that has already been envisaged and shaped in the cultural imagination by countless other authors. Literary works, in other words, function in as creators of a particular brand of urban space. As Dolezel (1998: x) observes, 'fictional constructs deeply influence our imaging and understanding of reality'. Ackroyd's and Self's relation to previous literary (and other) manifestations of the city is not simply an ontological proposition, but is also essentially epistemological. Writing and reading function together to forge a response to the possibilities of space and place, shaping emergent personal narratives of place (Gulson & Symes, 2007). These subjective narratives offer powerful pedagogic moments allowing students to deepen their relations to the space/place of the city and also to enhance their comprehension of themselves as readers.

Text is a significant means by which the world is represented and by which children are often taught to interpret the world (Charlton *et al.*, 2011), and Sheehy and Leander (2004) see interpretive reading as active engagement with other space-times. Within this dynamic process, students and teachers draw upon personal imported senses of space and place. Readers' knowledge (or lack of knowledge) of particular locations and attitudes towards and responses to texts, is active in the creative function. Readers draw upon three levels of meaning in relation to place/space when they approach literary texts:

- factual realities—place as it exists and/or existed in the real world;
- space/place in narrative—place as reproduced and used (for social/political/ pedagogic functions) by the author; and
- space/place as it exists (or not) within the reader's knowledge—place as lived experience.

The co-existence of these multiple layers of space/place within heteregeneous classrooms provides a wealth of pedagogic opportunity and challenge for exploring personal, spatial and literary understanding. Place/space, identity and time are fundamentally inter-related (Massey, 2005) within the literary text *and* within the pedagogic space and can be utilised to frame students' approaches to text, drawing on personal, social, public and cultural narratives (Somers, 1994).

Both Ackroyd and Self explore the intrinsic relationship between identity, space and time. The historical 'presence' of place and the ubiquitous presence of words (contemporary and historical) within urban space are significant means by which both explore the city. Ackroyd pursues this most strikingly in *Hawksmoor* and *The House of Dr Dee*. Speaking of *Hawksmoor* he observes, '[t]he language of the eighteenth century still exists in countless books and documents as well as in the language we speak every day. It may look different, but it still exerts influence, as my novel shows'. The language of the city and the language of the past, in effect, become lenses through which to read the contemporary city.

Self and Ackroyd are both clear about the importance of such connections in artistically creating place and in understanding the nature of London. Works such as *Hawksmoor*, *The House of Dr Dee* and *Umbrella* bring together inter-connected individual stories which project understandings of urban space. Through the interaction of these stories *of* place (London) *in* place (the classroom), we approach Featherstone's (1995) conception of how plural subjectivities interact with multiple identities of place.

The urban environment of *Umbrella* is a place of intimate connection (Massey, 2005). For Self, the city becomes a space where he can experience 'a very intense communion … with other people's minds'. His city is primarily a place of relational creativity where 'you can meet people whether they are existent or non-existent or inexistent'. The literary text thus functions as a creative and dialogic extension of the urban environment. A good example of this is Self's exploration of mental illness—the city as metaphor for such states, and mental illness as the shaper of response to the city—and he sees in the topography of London an analogue for the mental disturbance and reconstruction of his characters. In this Self emerges from a long urban artistic tradition, going back through Virginia Woolf, Wilkie Collins and Charles Dickens to William Hogarth (see Figure 4.2), Henry Fielding and beyond.

Illegality and narcotics are also powerful motifs for Self. Like mental illness, they represent destabilising forces at work in the city, representing the

FIGURE 4.2 *The Rake's Progress*, Plate VIII 'Scene in Bedlam' (William Hogarth, 1763).

relationship between continuity and disjunction. Self's London, however, is not all subversion and psychosis—except in so far as these may be taken as inherent in the 'nature' of the city. He confessedly depends upon urban and literary continuity manifested in his 'growing interest in psychogeography'. By this he seems to mean something rather distinct from the quasi-spiritual 'spirit of place' invoked by Ackroyd, or the urban arcana so favoured by Sinclair. He goes on to explain at greater length:

> It is about the nature of places and their influence. For me that is quite political. It is very much connected with a personal sense of alienation, particularly from London—the city where I was born and have lived all my life—and a sense of the city as a kind of economic and cultural artefact. It is an attempt to understand its physical geography and topography and the shapes that exist beneath its streets.

This partially relates to Gottdiener's (1994) emphasis on the sociospatial nature of urban space, particularly the role of political economy as a shaping imperative upon the city and its inhabitants. Asked if *Umbrella* is as much a project in making sense of himself as it is an attempt to elucidate the nature of London, Self initially demurs, 'No, as a person, as somebody who lives in the city in the 21st century and feels alienated from it'. He is open to the suggestion, however, and approaches how the city and isolation are prerequisites for writers of urban 'space'—'Maybe you're right, though. Maybe it *is* connected with being a writer, which is an isolated occupation, so maybe that sense of alienation is connected with what I do for a living'—and pursues this Durkheimian anomie (1893, 1997) to draw on the kinds of deterministic economic forces Gottdiener (1994) envisages:

> Psychogeography emerged from a group of French Marxists—the 'situationists'—who saw the city and the ways we move around it as being determined by economic imperatives. These control our movements and emotions—we go to one place to work, another to shop, another to be entertained and another to live. That kind of way of being in the city is inherently alienating and controlling—any commuter on the tube, the trains, the buses or in a 100 mile traffic jam on the M25 understands that.

Charlton *et al.* (2011: 65) consider the 'power-geometries' that go into the construction of place and 'the connections between places'. This resonates with Self's vision of London as an atomising spatial imperative shaping space/place and its inhabitants, creating functionally differentiated 'sectors'. This takes us back to *Umbrella*'s focus on psychosis and its treatment and a London constructed as a vast yet claustrophobic mental 'space'—a disturbingly brown, Hogarthian asylum. Self pursues the genesis of this metaphor at length:

> Over the years as I read and thought about London, I became very interested in modernity as a phenomenon. For me, London was at about its most

modern in 1905. All the things we think of as being the contemporary city were effectively in place by then—a deep level electric tube system, instant messaging via pneumatic tubes connecting loads of businesses, telephones, stock market quotes coming in from Wall Street and the Bourse in Paris instantaneously. It was also a huge port in a way that it isn't any more. If you want to look at it that way, the city has retreated from that over the last hundred years in some ways. I was very interested to try to capture the changing city. In Edwardian times if you took any square acre of London you would have found at least four centuries of housing existing. It was a very textured and multi-layered city. That richness was lost in the inter-war period. It wasn't the Blitz, it was development in the 20s and 30s that did for it. I didn't feel that anyone had quite dealt with that in a way that I found worked for me in fiction, so *Umbrella* is my attempt to dig out the layers. The asylum, individual pathology and illness in some way encode social, cultural and economic change.

London and narrative construct

Umbrella's narrative methods relate intrinsically to notions of the city. Although he disingenuously eschews the idea that the novel's epigraph from *Ulysses* is setting up a deliberate Joycean parallel, Self discusses his narrative method in terms that warrant debate in the classroom:

> Some people have referred to the narrative as stream of consciousness, but stream of consciousness is a very slippery customer. I guess I'd say the book is written in what Kafka critics call a monopolised narrative with stream of consciousness frills. I mean what is the content of our consciousness? It's seldom verbal. It's often intensely imagistic or sensory, and how do you put those things into words? So there is always compromise. I use the continuous present, which I think is perhaps more important. The subject of modernity seemed to demand the continuous present. It reflected what I wanted to explore through linked consciousnesses over time.

Self sees his use of the continuous present to represent the city as a means of superseding time. Space is thus conceived in Masseyan terms as a locus for multiplicity—a realm 'of coexisting heterogeneity' (Massey, 2005: 9). The proliferating voices, places and languages of London serve a representational function that is forever 'present'. In this sense Self's project relates to the work of Peter Ackroyd, 'I was very concerned to present that idea of the transcendence of time, which writers like Ackroyd do in *Hawksmoor*. Those were emotional decisions about how I wanted to tell this particular story'. In this sense *Umbrella*, whilst 'inflected by and influenced by the high modernists like Joyce and Woolf', is fundamentally and self-consciously representational, not simply a programmatic response to previous literary representations of the city. This said, however, reading *Umbrella* alongside works such as *Ulysses*, *The Waste Land* and *Mrs Dalloway* provides a stimulating means of developing students' reading of literary urban space.

London is almost a character in Peter Ackroyd's fiction, biographies and historico-cultural writings—*London: The Biography*, *Thames: Sacred River* and *London Under*. Thrift (1996) suggests that cities are inhuman or trans-human entities, and Ackroyd's vision of the quasi-spiritual powers of the city relates to such a conception. This emerges particularly strongly in *London: The Biography* (2001: 779) where he observes, 'London goes beyond any boundary or convention. It contains every wish or word ever spoken, every action or gesture ever made, every harsh or noble statement ever expressed. It is illimitable. It is Infinite London'. Such a vision may emerge from Ackroyd's peculiar Catholic-inflected spirituality. Onega (1997: 208) sees Ackroyd's delineation of London as 'a mystic centre of power'. The arcane spiritual yearnings of Mirabilis and Nicholas Dyer (*Hawksmoor*) and of John Dee (*The House of Dr Dee*) chime with the monadic mysticism of Soja's (1989) vision of urbanity, and these provide interesting theoretical perspectives from which students may explore the urban environment.

However, Ackroyd's London is not merely spiritual. When asked to explain how London is 'illimitable' and 'infinite', he defines it in more earthly terms that echo yet also move beyond Thrift's essentially political paradigms and Self's emphasis on London's political, commercial and temporal imperatives:

> London is a city of so many aspects and times. It is a city that has changed beyond recognition, but that has also retained a distinct nature. It is a dark city of trade and money, a place often built on hardness and self-interest. It is a place that casts shadows over time. These shadows live in the fabric of the city, and sometimes these shadows emerge to exert their influence on people and places. London is like an echo chamber where elements of the past and the present coexist, creating a complex music of the city.

The rich image of a city 'that casts shadows over time' seeks to deny neither the force of time nor the force of place, but seems rather to realign them in our imaginations, and reflects Charlton *et al.*'s (2011) emphasis upon the importance of allowing students' personal lived experiences of the city to interact with literary reconstructions.

Both Ackroyd and Self are engaged in what Massey (2013) terms 'spatialisation of time'. *Hawksmoor* evokes this through Dyer's construction of a spiritual map on the face of 18th century London to create a door into eternity. Similarly, Dee's quest for the entrance to a mythical eternal city beneath Elizabethan London creates firm connections between the realms of space and time. Ackroyd expresses the belief that there is a 'territorial imperative' of the city, 'a kind of 'spirit of place' or *genius loci*' that embodies 'certain historical continuities and imperatives which continue to exert their influence'. Using the city itself as a location for reading with students may prove a powerful pedagogic method in eliciting this influence and in considering how space and place shape both writing and reading.

Literary layers

Ackroyd has frequently sought to explore the nature of London through the lives of its writers and other artists, both fictional and real. He observes that '[t]he layers of the past … are often best captured through the lives of artists and the ways they sought to represent the city'. In *Eliot, Dickens, Blake, More* and his other biographies, Ackroyd builds bridges to the past not through the authors' lives, works and urban environments, but also through their written styles. Ackroyd recreates their preoccupations and inflections within his own writing, thus dramatising both his characters and the city they inhabit. By entering into their language-worlds, Ackroyd lends a peculiar power to his urban project as language and place interact. Given this emphasis on the relation between language, place and art, it is significant that Ackroyd does not draw a distinction between his fictional and non-fictional writings:

> I see all my writing as being of one piece—fiction, biography and the more historical books like *London, Thames* and *Albion*. They are all part of the same process and I hope that they work together as sequence. I think that the distinction between fiction and biography is more or less artificial. Both depend strongly on character and narrative and are about the building of convincing representations. Biography is not only the study of a person, it is also the study of period and place.

In *London: The Biography* and *Thames: Sacred River*, he 'was looking to discover continuities so that the story of the city and the river could be reanimated'. His purpose is to that extent historical, as he goes on to suggest:

> I wanted to create an organic whole out of the city and the river and through them to tell a different story. For me, I suppose, it was trying to write a different form of cultural history. I think they are innovative in creating a different form of genre related to fiction, biography and history that draws together threads of the city's and the river's existence across time. The same process was at work in *Albion*, which looks at the particularities of English cultural heritage.

By encouraging students to explore the potential of different genres and by exploring how and where genres blur, both in the act of reading and in the act of writing, teachers can engage their students in high-concept thinking about both the nature of literature and the nature of urban space.

Conclusion

Paradigms of literary study in the senior years of schooling need to evolve to encourage students to engage subjectively with a range of critical and theoretical agendas and how these function in literary representation and critical response. Scholes (1985: 153) observes the fundamentally 'political' nature of such processes, asking his readers to consider:

> who [what and where] is represented, who does the representing, who [what and where] is object, who [what and where] is subject—and how do these representations connect to the values of groups, communities, classes, tribes, sects and nations?

Teachers and students approaching literary representations of urban space benefit from bringing such questions to bear on the texts they study. Pedagogies that actively require students to utilise their own lived experiences of the city in their readings of urban texts engage them in critical dialogue not only with literary representations of the city, but also with themselves and learners and readers and with the city itself.

Self and Ackroyd use the act of literary creation to delve for the shapes that exist within and beneath the streets of London, seeking to make sense of how the city continually 'reshapes' itself. The historical, vocal, linguistic, temporal and spatial echoes that resound through the pages of their work encode their perceptions of the influence of place, and all of these emerge from a powerful pedagogical impulse that connects both ontological and epistemological dimensions of their subject. The literature classroom offers an exciting space within which such impulses can be explored. As students subject literary reconstructions of the city to theories of urban space and their own lived experiences of the city through mediated acts of reading and writing, they bring personal subjectivities to bear in newly theorised and powerful ways. In so doing, as this paper has argued, they become more informed as co-constructors both of the urban environment and of their own learning.

References

Ackroyd, P. (1985). *Hawksmoor*. London: Hamish Hamilton.

Ackroyd, P. (1990). *Dickens*. London: Sinclair-Stevenson.

Ackroyd, P. (1993a). *The house of Dr Dee*. London: Hamish Hamilton.

Ackroyd, P. (1993b). *T.S. Eliot*. London: Penguin.

Ackroyd, P. (1995). *Blake*. London: Sinclair-Stevenson.

Ackroyd, P. (1999). *Thomas more*. London: Vintage.

Ackroyd, P. (2001). *London: The biography*. London: Vintage.

Ackroyd, P. (2002). *Albion*. London: Chatto & Windus.

Ackroyd, P. (2008). *Thames: Sacred river*. London: Vintage.

Ackroyd, P. (2012). *London under*. London: Vintage.

Atherton, C., Green, A., & Snapper, G. (2013). *Teaching literature 16–19*. London: Routledge.

Bakhtin, M. (1981). *The dialogic imagination: Four essays* (M. Holquist, Ed., C. Emerson & M. Holquist (Trans.)). Austin: Texas University Press.

Bavidge, J. (2006). Stories in space: the geographies of children's literature. *Children's Geographies, 4*(3), 319–30.

Charlton, E., Wyse, D., Cliff Hodges, G., Nikolajeva, M., Pointon, P., & Taylor, L. (2011). Place-related identities through texts: Interdisciplinary theory to research agenda. *British Journal of Educational Studies, 59*(1), 63–74.

Cresswell, T. (2004). *Place: A short introduction.* Oxford: Blackwell.

Dolezel, L. (1998). *Heterocosmica: Fiction and possible worlds.* Baltimore, MD: Johns Hopkins University Press.

Durkheim, E. (1893, 1997). *The division of labour in society.* London: The Free Press.

Eaglestone, R. (2001). Active voice! *English Association Newsletter, 166,* 6–7.

Eliot, T. S. (2002). *The waste land and other poems.* London: Faber.

Featherstone, M. (1995). *Undoing culture.* London: Sage.

Gottdiener, M. (1994). *The social production of urban space* (2nd ed.). Austin: University of Texas Press.

Gulson, K. N., & Symes, C. (2007). Knowing one's place: Space, theory, education. *Critical Studies in Education, 48*(1), 97–110.

Holloway, J., & Kneale, J. (2000). Mikhail Bakhtin: Dialogics of space. In M. Crang & N. Thrift (Eds.), *Thinking space* (pp. 71–88). London: Routledge.

Joyce, J. (2011). *Ulysses.* London: Penguin Modern Classics.

Kostogriz, A. (2006). Putting 'space' on the agenda of sociocultural research. *Mind, Culture, and Activity, 13*(3), 176–190.

Larkin, P. (1983). The pleasure principle. In *Required writing: Miscellaneous pieces 1955–1982* (pp. 80–82). London: Faber and Faber.

Leander, K. M., & Rowe, D. W. (2006). Mapping literacy spaces in motion: A rhizomatic analysis of a classroom literacy performance. *Reading Research Quarterly, 41*(4), 428–460.

Massey, D. (2005). *For space.* London: Sage.

Massey, D. (2013). *Landscape/space/politics: An essay.* Retrieved July 26, 2013 from http://thefutureoflandscape.wordpress.com/landscapespacepolitics-an-essay/.

Onega, S. (1997). The mythical impulse in British historiographic metafiction. *European Journal of English Studies, 1*(2), 184–204.

Scholes, R. (1985). *Textual power: Literary theory and the teaching of English.* New Haven, CT: Yale University Press.

Self, W. (2012). *Umbrella.* London: Bloomsbury.

Sheehy, H., & Leander, K. (Ed.) (2004). *Spatialising literacy research and practice.* New York: Peter Lang.

Soja, E. (1989). *Postmodern geographics: The reassertion of space in critical social theory.* London: Verso.

Somers, M. R. (1994). The narrative constitution of identity: A relational and network approach. *Theory and Society, 34*(1), 41–55.

Thrift, N. (1996). *Spatial formations.* London: Sage.

Woolf, V. (2002). *Mrs Dalloway.* London: Penguin Modern Classics.

Wyse, D., Nikolajeva, M., Charlton, E., Cliff-Hodges, G., Pointon, P., & Taylor, L. (2011). Place-related identity, texts and transcultural meanings. *British Educational Research Journal, 38*(6), 1–2.

5

BEYOND THE PERSONAL AND THE INDIVIDUAL

Reconsidering the role of emotion in literature learning

Amanda Haertling Thein

What is the role of emotion in literature learning and instruction? This question has been explicitly and implicitly considered in scholarship on the teaching of literature since the late 1800s, when English came into its own as an academic discipline.

In the early decades of the 20th century, the New Critics aimed to develop objective methods for studying literature by separating emotion from literary criticism (Richards, 1929). For instance, Ransom (1937) explained that literary study and criticism should be concerned with the text as an aesthetic object and not with its effects:

> It is hardly criticism to assert that a proper literary work is one that … causes some remarkable psychological effect, such as oblivion of the outer world, the flowing of tears, visceral or laryngeal sensation, and the like; or one that induces perfect illusion, or brings us into spiritual ecstasy; or even one that produces a catharsis of our emotions.
>
> *(p. 597)*

Further, Wimsatt and Beardsley (1949) made the case that emotional responses to texts constituted interpretive error that made objective criticism impossible—a concept known as the 'affective fallacy.' In short, the New Critics saw emotion as a distraction to literature study and something to be avoided or ignored—a view that permeated literature pedagogy in secondary schools through much of the 20th century.

In response to New Critical approaches to literature pedagogy, reader response (Rosenblatt, 1978) and personal growth (Dixon, 1975) models of literature pedagogy emerged in the second half of the 20th century. These approaches—particularly as they have been taken up in textbooks and curriculum guides—center on literature study as a means for personal growth and moral development.

In these approaches to literature pedagogy, teachers often attempt to evoke emotional responses in an effort to generate student interest in particular themes or topics. Emotion, in this view, is something that is invited into the literature classroom as a means to spur engagement in moral and ethical questions raised by literature.

Contemporary literature pedagogy grounded in critical literacy and sociocultural theories of reader response strives to engage students in literature study with the goal of exploring and critiquing ways that characters' identities and experiences are socially and culturally constructed and shaped via institutional and systemic power structures. Proponents of this approach to literature pedagogy have often troubled practices of evoking personal and emotional responses as a means of engaging students in literature learning, arguing that such practices might limit the ability of readers to understand how characters and situations in literature are shaped by larger social and cultural forces (Appleman, 2009; Lewis, 2000; McLaughlin & DeVoogd, 2004). In this view, emotion is something to approach with caution and to sometimes challenge given that it might lead to over-identification with personal experiences and impede critical perspectives.

In looking across this scholarship on the study of literature, emotion consistently lurks in the background as something personal and individual that can be invited into or left out of literature pedagogy depending on one's goals for literature instruction. In this chapter I draw on sociocultural theories of emotion drawn from 'Critical Emotion Studies' (Trainor, 2006) to challenge this personal, individual, and peripheral view of emotion in literature pedagogy. Instead, I argue for the centrality of emotion in literature learning. I begin by outlining various theories of emotion, explaining how theories aligned with Critical Emotion Studies move emotion from the individual to the social. Next, I detail two key ways in which a sociocultural theories emotion found in Critical Emotion Studies might change how English teachers and teacher educators think about the role of emotion in literature pedagogy. Specifically, I contend that emotion is always already a part of literature learning and that emotional rules have material implication for learning. I conclude this chapter by arguing that emotion can be disrupted and re-shaped in the interest of constructing more equitable classroom spaces that generate richer responses to literature. Further, I offer suggestions for cultivating teachers' and students' awareness of the ways in which emotion is constructed, leveraged, and mobilized.

Defining emotion

Emotion has been defined in a variety of ways across disciplinary boundaries. Ahmed (2004) suggests that these definitions can be thought of as largely fitting within two broad categories—those that view emotion as bodily sensations (Hume, 1964; James, 1890) and those that see it as cognitive and related to thought processes, judgments, and attitudes (Nussbaum, 2001; Solomon, 1995). In common, scholarship in both categories conceptualizes emotion as natural and located in the individual, while at the same time experienced universally (Boler, 1999). A multidisciplinary 'affective turn' (Clough, 2007) in the social sciences and humanities, however, has generated new theories of affect and emotion that challenge these two dominant conceptualizations of emotion.

Within this affective turn, some scholars have focused on affect theory—a line of scholarship driven by the work of philosophers such as Deleuze, Spinoza, Whitehead, and Bergson. Affect theory is concerned with affect as non-conscious, unstructured, embodied intensity (Massumi, 2002). This theorization positions affect as distinct from emotion; in Massumi's view, 'emotion and affect—if affect is intensity—follow different logics and pertain to different orders' (p. 27). Zembylas (2014) explains these differences as they are articulated in affect theory:

> Emotion signals cultural constructs and conscious processes, where affect marks precognitive sensory experience, relations to surroundings, and generally the body's capacity to act, to engage, to resist, and to connect. Hence emotion represents a form of assimilation, a closure and containment of affect within symbolic means, whereas affect is considered along the lines of a bodily intensity resistant to domestication, always evading a final structuration.
>
> *(Hook, 2011, p. 397)*

In this view, affect differs from emotion because it is asocial and not bound by discourse or language. Emotion, for affect theorists, is the result of the social, cultural, linguistic, and discursive structuring of affect—it is 'qualified intensity' (Massumi, 2002, p. 28).

Although important scholarship has begun to examine the role of affective intensities in literature learning (e.g., Leander & Boldt, 2013), Boler (2015) makes the case that the study of emotion—which might be thought of as captured affect—carries its own urgency. She explains:

> We may grant that affects, vibrating and pulsing like electricity, can pass between bodies in classroom. Yet surely of primary concern in any challenge to the recolonization of emotions and learning are the emotions, which affect theory sees as captured—named—and coded.
>
> *(p. 1493)*

Therefore, in thinking about the teaching of literature in this chapter, I ground my arguments in the work of scholars in Critical Emotion Studies (e.g., Ahmed, 2004; Boler, 1999; Trainor, 2006), who are interested in primarily in emotion rather than affect as the two concepts are defined in affect theory. I do so in an effort to shed light on the ways in which emotion structures literature learning and can be usefully disrupted.

Critical Emotion Studies, while multidisciplinary, has deep roots in Feminist scholarship on emotion—scholarship that aimed to collapse distinctions between the rational and the emotional, and to examine the politics of emotion (e.g., Tompkins, 1987). According to Trainor (2006), scholarship that falls within the broad field of Critical Emotion Studies shares in common four basic tenets:

- Emotions cannot be seen as distinct from reason. Emotions are intertwined with rational decision-making and are central to the construction of belief
- Emotions are not private, individual experiences but are, rather socially experienced and constructed
- Emotion is taught and learned at home and at school. It is an important, deeply embedded, site of social control
- Emotions are structured in ways that relate to the system of values and norms that exist in a social context

(pp. 647–648)

Following these tenets, scholars in Critical Emotion Studies have examined emotional rules (Boler, 1999; Winans, 2012; Zembylas, 2002) that determine what count as appropriate attitudes, dispositions, and affective stances in particular social contexts (especially in academia and in K through 12 education); the emotional labor (Hochschild, 1983) that is required to follow emotional rules and meet authoritative mandates and directives in certain contexts and professions (e.g., teaching); outlaw emotions (Jaggar, 1989) that can be performed in an effort to disrupt status quo, patriarchal hierarchies, and epistemologies; and the ways in which emotion circulates and comes to 'stick' to particular objects through repeated performances in particular sociopolitical moments (Ahmed, 2004).

In the sections that follow, I detail two key ways in which the scholarship in Critical Emotion Studies highlighted above allows for a reconceptualization of the role of emotion in literature pedagogy and learning.

Emotion in literature pedagogy and learning

Emotion is always, already in the literature classroom

A primary way in which sociocultural theories of emotion associated with Critical Emotion Studies reconceptualize emotion in literature pedagogy and learning is by revealing the ways in which emotion is always already a part of any social context—including the literature classroom—structuring the kinds of interactions people have, the ways in which people position themselves, and the kinds of discourses that are sanctioned. In the literature classroom, that means that emotion cannot be invited into or left out of students' literary responses. Instead, emotion—especially in the form of emotion rules (Boler, 1999; Winans, 2012; Zembylas, 2002)—always 'informs and guides our attention and the kinds of questions we choose to explore' (Winans, 2012, p. 155), fostering 'habits of (in)attention' (Boler, 1999, p. 180). Drawing on Boler (1999) and Zembylas (2002), Winans (2012) defines emotional rules as socially and culturally constructed norms for expression that are negotiated and performed in various social contexts, allowing for and constraining certain identity performances. She explains that:

Although emotion might appear to be simply an individual personal response, it is often informed by emotional rules that are negotiated by groups and enforced by individuals and groups. People are socialized within the context of various emotional rules, rules that are informed by power relations. As one responds to emotional rules, one negotiates individual and social identity.

(pp. 154–155)

Emotional rules are not pre-existing or static. Instead, emotional rules come to 'stick' in particularly social and cultural contexts as certain forms of emotion are repeatedly performed and mobilized (Ahmed, 2005).

Boler (1999) and Zembylas (2005) have both considered how emotional rules function in schools, guiding and policing expectations and experiences of students and teachers. For instance, while Boler (1999) points out that emotional rules that perpetuate status quo, white, middle-class behaviors can be traced through schools since the common schools movement, she pays particular attention to 'emotional intelligence' (Goleman, 1995) or emotional literacy programs that became widespread in schools in the 1990s. In Boler's view, these programs— which encourage the acquisition of particular emotional dispositions (empathy, self-control, delayed gratification, optimism, etc.)—illuminate ways in which schools encourage students to adopt normatively white, Protestant, masculine, middle-class identities through emotional rules disguised as neutral life skills. Likewise, Zembylas (2005) argues that teachers are often compelled to adhere to emotional rules created by curricular, policy, and administrative mandates.

Within the literature classroom, emotional rules accumulate and stick in relationship to larger emotional rules associated with schooling and in relationship to particular paradigms of literature pedagogy. For instance, New Critical and formalist approaches to literature pedagogy tend to rely on emotional rules of distance and rationality associated with technical forms of close reading that exclude lived world connections. On the other hand, personal growth and reader response approaches to literature pedagogy often forward emotional rules related to sympathy, understanding, and acceptance associated with lived world connections rather than literary analysis.

Approaches to literature instruction based in critical literacy also perpetuate certain emotional rules related to rationality, egalitarianism, fairness, and political correctness (Ellsworth, 1989; Janks, 2002; Lewis & Tierney, 2011). For instance, in a study of one 10th grade student's responses to literature in two classroom contexts (a large class discussion and a small group literature circle), Thein, Guise, and Sloan (2015) found that emotional rules related to critical literacy evoked certain kinds of responses while inhibiting others. The authors found that in the large class discussion where critical literacy was supported, the focal student, Nina, followed emotional rules of distanced rationality, egalitarianism, and political correctness in making made well-reasoned literary interpretations grounded in critical literacy practices such as perspective-taking and analyses of social and cultural power structures. However, they found that these responses did not include anger, fear, frustration, or visceral reactions to characters and situations—emotions that she did perform in her responses to literature in the space of a small group literature circle in which she and her peers disrupted the emotional rules of critical literacy. The authors argued, then, that no pedagogy—even one like critical literacy that aims to be progressive and democratic—is without emotional rules that structure what counts as appropriate and worthwhile in literature interpretation.

For English teachers, understanding emotion as always already a part of literature learning means understanding that emotion is not something that once chooses to invite into or leave out of the literature classroom, but instead is something that has a central place in the literature classroom. The choices teachers make in their approaches to literature instruction, then, matter not in whether they include emotion, but in how and what kinds of emotion they sanction, evoke, and invite.

Emotion has material implications for literature learning

In addition to being always already in the literature classroom, emotion has material implications for the kinds of literary responses students share, the uptake of those responses by teachers and classmates, and the ways in which literature interpretations are constructed. For instance, in an ethnographic study of race and literacy in a white high school, Trainor (2008) found that emotional rules that circulated in the school on the whole were reflected in the seemingly racist discourses expressed by students in their responses to multicultural literature. This school repeatedly emphasized emotional rules related to individual agency, fairness, tolerance, and positivity. In taking up these rules in the English classroom, students resisted engagement with multicultural texts that critiqued structural and institutional racism, seeing these critiques as unfair and intolerant of white people. Additionally, students' interpretations of multicultural texts were driven by these emotional rules; students read Maya Angelou's work as negative and 'whiney' and suggested that she ought to develop a more positive outlook if she hoped to succeed. Therefore, students' seemingly surface-level, racist interpretations of Angelou's work might be better understood as reflecting an adherence to emotional rules that valued positivity and individual initiative. In short, the emotional rules that circulated in the school were taken up by students in their English classroom, playing a key role in their literature engagement and learning.

Similarly, in Thein, Guise, and Sloan's (2015) previously discussed study, the authors argue that adhering to the emotional rules of critical literacy in the large class literature discussion not only structured the emotional stances students took up relative to the text, but also the kinds of discourses that were evoked in interpreting the text. The authors note that in discussing Dorothy Allison's *Bastard out of Carolina* (1993), a novel in which a young girl, Bone, is sexually abused by her stepfather Glen, Nina and her peers in her literature circle expressed anger, frustration, and even violent ideations in developing interpretations of Glen's actions. The authors explain that while this sort of interpretation would not typically be sanctioned by the emotional rules of critical literacy, it is nonetheless important given the questions it evokes:

> The excitement and joy that emerged in Nina and her peers' responses as
> they considered the idea of violence toward Glen is important. Although

short-lived in the novel, the moment when Bone's uncles nearly kill Glen is one of the only moments when *anyone* attempts to take action in ending Bone's abuse. Nina and her peers might have felt a temporary respite from the infuriating, helpless feelings they expressed in other instances as they read about the cyclical and tenacious nature of abuse and oppression depicted in this novel; imagining Glen being beaten or killed might have allowed Nina to feel agency in the face of this helplessness. Larger questions are evoked by the responses that were voiced in this excerpt and the discourses of violence that surfaced—questions related to the appeal of violence in the face of oppression, and to how both those who are oppressed and those who are empowered can feel less helpless and can work toward systemic change through nonviolent means.

(p. 217)

While the above studies illustrate how emotional rules can limit and constrain literature learning, other studies exemplify ways in which disrupting emotional rules can open up spaces for new literary engagement and interpretation. One way teachers can disrupt emotional rules is by actively resisting emotional policing of students' responses. For instance, Lewis and Tierney (2011) draw on data from a study in an urban high school to argue that when emotion—especially related to race—is intentionally *not* policed by teachers, students can mobilize emotion toward textual interpretations that move beyond the 'right and tasteful' emotions so often forwarded by literature pedagogy. In this study, the authors discuss the example of Vanessa, an African-American student who refuses to participate in a distanced, rational critique of the Disney film *Pocahontas*, and instead takes up this text toward developing a more deeply felt interpretation related to her own positioning as a young African-American woman. The authors explain:

> Personal growth models of English focus on the right and tasteful kind of affect (or feeling) and mask the ideological roots of language which emotion—when we cease to police it—has the potential to illuminate. Vanessa and Shannon mobilize emotion in their response to the discussion of *Pocahontas* because the film and the text threaten them in deeply felt ways, and in doing so, they expose and negotiate underlying ideologies about black women and speak back to their own subjectification in the face of them.

(pp. 327–328)

Lewis and Tierney's study illustrates the powerful textual interpretations students can construct when teachers resist policing students' responses via emotional rules for literature learning.

New spaces for literature interpretation and engagement can also be generated when teachers explicitly question and disrupt emotional rules. In a study of upper-elementary school girls' literature response in an afterschool book club, Thein and Schmidt (under review) found that girls sometimes brought up topics and themes that they then chose to retract when policed by their peers. For example, when a student suggested that a character in Peg Kehret's *Abduction* (2004) who had been kidnapped might be at risk of being raped, other students told her not to talk about rape, citing the topic as 'not school appropriate,' and explaining that such discussion would lead to an office referral. In response, the leader of this small group explained that rape was a topic that they *could* talk about in their book club and that they needn't worry about an office referral. Following this disruption of emotional rules, the girls eagerly shared their fears about rape, rumors they had heard about sexual violence in their neighborhood, and stories of relatives' experiences with sexual assault. This discussion led to deep engagement in the literary text, surfacing questions about the extent to which adults believe children when they report crime, and textually supported claims about the resourcefulness of children.

The studies in this section illustrate that emotion and emotional rules have clear implications for literature learning. And, they illustrate the power that disrupting emotional rules can have for developing new habits of attentions and new literary engagements and interpretations.

Implications for literature teaching and learning

I have argued in this chapter that a sociocultural view of emotion grounded in Critical Emotion Studies provides a new lens for understanding the role of emotion in literature teaching and learning. Specifically, I have made the case that this view of emotion illuminates both the constant and central presence of emotion in the literature classroom, and the material ways in which emotion and emotional rules interact with literature teaching and learning, opening spaces for certain interpretive possibilities while inhibiting others. Emotion and emotional rules, however, are not static; just as emotion and emotional rules come to 'stick' and sediment through repeated performances, so too can they be disrupted and newly mobilized. In this section, I discuss several ways that teachers can disrupt emotion and emotional rules in an effort to expand interpretative possibilities and create more democratic spaces for students to voice diverse perspectives.

In Julie Lindquist's (2004) essay on emotion, empathy, and social class in the college classroom she argues that teachers often ask students—particularly those from marginalized backgrounds—to engage in 'deep acting' in order to meet the emotional expectations of liberal empathy and tolerance so often encouraged in our literacy classrooms. Lindquist suggests that teachers need to take some of this emotional load off of students by exercising the emotional restraint and 'deep acting' necessary for students to voice their deeply held beliefs, values, and perspectives. Lindquist explains:

> Teachers should be willing to enable affective learning by doing the kind of 'deep acting' students do as a matter of course ... the paradox is that teachers must sometimes be dishonest to be most real to students, to create the

kind of environment of trust that allows emotions to be something other than commodities or distractions.

(p. 206)

While it may sound as though Lindquist is suggesting that teachers take on a sort of 'emotional labor' (Hochschild, 1983) that is false or constraining, I argue that Lindquist's suggestions are closer to what Zembylas (2005) refers to in more neutral terms as 'emotion work'—or 'the act of shaping or evoking emotion' (p. 44).

For Zembylas (2005), emotion work is different from emotional labor in as much as emotional labor is work done to meet hierarchical policy, curricular, and administrative mandates, while emotion work can be used toward positive ends including gaining agency, fostering democracy, and disrupting hierarchies. Further, Zembylas argues that teachers can engage in positive emotion work—like engaging in emotional restraint with the goal of creating new spaces for a diversity of student responses—by gaining 'critical emotional knowledge,' or an awareness of how emotion is constructed, used, and mobilized in their teaching. He explains that by 'developing an awareness of their emotional responses as a valuable source of information about one's self, and using the power of emotion as a basis for collective and social resistance, teachers can sort their experiences, their anxieties, their fears, their excitements and learn how to use them in empowering ways' (p. 41). Through gaining critical emotional knowledge teachers might become better aware of the ways that emotion and emotional rules circulate and structure literature learning in their classrooms, and develop means for leveraging emotion in ways that disrupt the status quo and generate new interpretive spaces.

Thein and Schmidt (under review) offer several suggestions for helping teachers develop critical emotional knowledge. They recommend that pre-service teachers conduct analyses of emotion and emotional rules in their fields sites, examining, for instance, the emotional rules at play in their school, classroom, and literature pedagogy; and the kinds of emotion work—both positive and negative—that teachers in their site engage in and to what effect. For practicing teachers, the authors recommend reflection on elements of their work that have been particularly emotionally difficult, such as working with a challenging student. Teachers might ask themselves questions about the kinds of emotion work they engage in when working with that student, the assumptions they have about that student, the ways in which that student might make them uncomfortable, and ways in which they might disrupt their status quo emotional practices—by sitting with discomfort and more fully revealing their own vulnerabilities—in working with that student. Similar reflection with positive elements of the teaching experience—work that feels gratifying or fulfilling—might also increase teachers' critical emotional knowledge.

Teachers can also disrupt emotional rules by helping their students develop what Winans (2012) calls 'critical emotional literacy.' Similar to Zembylas's critical emotional knowledge, critical emotional literacy is an awareness of how emotions structure and guide attentions, identities, and interpretations of literary texts and lived world situations. Winans explains, 'We need to emphasize the goal of helping students to develop a more conscious and embodied awareness of how they see and interpret the world. Doing so is vital so that students can make more conscious choices about how they negotiate their interpretive frameworks and how they live' (p. 151).

For Winans, helping students develop critical emotional literacy is far different from teaching 'emotional intelligence' (Goleman, 1995). Winans explains that in Goleman's model of emotional intelligence, people strive to learn emotional stances, attitudes, and rules that fit with accepted social norms, thus reifying social hierarchies. In Winans' model of critical emotional literacy, students learn to recognize emotion and emotional rules so that they can closely attend to the ways in which emotion structures their lives and their interpretive practices.

One strategy Winans offers is helping students to analyze emotion through the study of moments of high emotion or tension in literary texts or lived experienced. In such analyses, students examine how emotion is constructed and circulated in a given moment and what social consequences it generates. For example, a white student in Winans' class analyzed a disagreement she had with an African-American friend as well as her debriefing on this disagreement with her white roommate. Among other insights, she came to see that in debriefing with her roommate she angrily positioned her African-American friend as ungrateful for unearned financial aid. This positioning not only created a bond with her roommate, but also served to uphold emotional rules for talking about race in her white community—rules related to denial of shame and guilt for participation in a racist world. Conducting this analysis helped this student to develop an awareness of some of the ways in which emotion and emotional rules persuaded her to be complicit in problematic racial discourses.

Similar analyses of events in literary texts could be undertaken with students. For instance, students could examine the moment in *Of Mice and Men* (Steinbeck, 1994) when Lennie accidentally kills Curley's wife. Students might look at emotion experienced by Lennie in the moments leading up to the incident. What made him panic? Where did his fear come from? What about his anger? What experiences and knowledge did he have that mobilized these emotions in this moment? Students might then look at the emotion that surrounds Curley's wife. Why do the men view her with anger and disdain? What do these emotions accomplish for the men? How does she respond to that emotional positioning? To what end? Finally, students could study George, Candy, Curley, and the other men's responses to Curley's wife's death. Where does hatred and anger emerge? What social norms and emotional rules are bound up in these emotions? Where does sadness and loss emerge?

Within such an analysis of emotion, students might also examine particular objects in texts that seem to mobilize particular kinds of emotion (Lewis & Tierney, 2011) or that emotion seems to 'stick' to (Ahmed, 2004). In the case of *Of Mice and Men*, Curley's wife could herself be viewed as a 'sticky object' that emotion seems to accumulate around. Or, students might examine the narrative about buying a plot of land that George and Lennie repeatedly tell one another as an object that mobilizes emotion.

Activities in which students analyze emotion in their lived worlds and text worlds offer opportunities for students to develop critical emotional literacy and help them gain an awareness of the ways in which emotion structures their responses to literature and their interactions with others. Such an awareness has the potential to help students notice and disrupt limiting emotional rules in the English classroom and beyond.

When teachers and students gain critical emotional knowledge and critical emotional literacy, they will be in a position to work together to gain an awareness of emotional rules for literature response and interpretation that circulate in their classroom, and to disrupt those rules in an effort to open up new interpretive spaces. Disrupting emotional rules can mean changing discussion patterns by allowing students to lead discussion and to discuss texts in various partner and small group configurations. It can mean encouraging students to voice characters and explore their perspectives through role-play and writing activities. And it can also mean inviting new discourses into the literature classroom by exploring texts that break emotional rules, or text genres, modes, and media that evoke response in alternative ways (visual, auditory, etc.). Finally, and most importantly, disrupting emotional rules for literature learning means developing classroom practices wherein both the teacher and students attend to and explore a wide range of literary responses, including those that initially seem troubling, resistant, or off-base, with the goal of listening to deeper questions that such responses might evoke—questions that might reveal new and unexpected emotion that is worthy of exploration.

References

Ahmed, S. (2004). *The cultural politics of emotion.* New York: Routledge.

Allison, D. (1993). *Bastard out of Carolina.* New York: Plume.

Appleman, D. (2009). *Critical encounters in high school English: Teaching literary theory to adolescents* (2nd ed.). New York: Teachers College Press.

Boler, M. (1999). *Feeling power: Emotions and education.* New York: Routledge.

Boler, M. (2015). Feminist politics of emotion and critical digital pedagogies: A call to action. *Publications of the Modern Language Association of America, 130*(5), 1489–1486.

Clough, P. T. (2007). Introduction. In P. T. Clough & J. Halley (Eds.), *The affective turn: Theorizing the social* (pp. 1–33). Durham, NC: Duke University Press.

Dixon, J. (1975). *Growth through English: Set in the perspective of the seventies.* Oxford, United Kingdom: Oxford University Press.

Ellsworth, E. (1989). Why doesn't this feel empowering? Working through the repressive myths of critical pedagogy. *Harvard Educational Review, 59*(3), 297–324.

Goleman, D. (1995). *Emotional intelligence: Why it can matter more than IQ.* New York: Bantam.

Hochschild, A. R. (1983). *The managed heart.* Berkeley, CA: University of California Press.

Hume, D. (1964). *The philosophical works: A treatise of human nature and dialogues concerning natural religion, vol. 2.* London: Scientia Verlag Aalen.

Jaggar, A. (1989). Love and knowledge: Emotion in feminist epistemology. In A. Jaggar & S. Bordo (Eds.), *Gender/body/knowledge* (pp. 145–171). New Brunswick, NJ: Rutgers University Press.

James, W. (1890). *The principles of psychology, vol. 2.* New York: Dover.

Janks, H. (2002). Critical literacy: Beyond reason. *The Australian Educational Researcher, 29*(1), 7–26.

Kehret, P. (2004). *Abduction.* New York: Penguin.

Leander, K. & Boldt, G. (2013). Rereading 'A pedagogy of multiliteracies: Bodies, texts, and emergence.' *Journal of Literacy Research, 45,* 22–46.

Lewis, C. (2000). Limits of identification: The personal, pleasurable, and critical in reader response. *Journal of Literacy Research, 32,* 253–266.

Lewis, C. & Tierney, J. (2011). Mobilizing emotion in an urban English classroom. *Changing English: Studies in Culture & Education, 18*(3), 319–329.

Lindquist, J. (2004). Class affects, classroom affectations: Working through the paradoxes of strategic empathy. *College English, 67,* 187–209.

Massumi, B. (2002). *Parables for the virtual: Movement, affect, sensation.* Chapel Hill, NC: Duke University Press.

McLaughlin, M. & DeVoogd, G. (2004). Critical literacy as comprehension: Expanding reader response. *Journal of Adolescent & Adult Literacy, 48,* 52–62.

Nussbaum, M.C. (2001). *Upheavals of thought. Intelligence of emotions.* Cambridge: Cambridge University Press.

Ransom, J.C. (1937). Criticism, inc. *The Virginia Quarterly Review, 13*(4), 586–602.

Richards, I.A. (1929). *Practical criticism: A study of literary judgement.* New York: Routledge.

Rosenblatt, L. (1978). *The reader, the text, the poem.* Carbondale: Southern Illinois University Press.

Solomon, R. C. (1995). *A passion for justice: Emotions and the origins of the social contract.* Lanham, MD: Rowan and Littlefield.

Steinbeck, J. (1994). *Of mice and men.* New York: Penguin Books.

Thein, A.H. & Schmidt, R.R. (under review). Challenging, rewarding emotion work: Critical witnessing in an afterschool book club.

Thein, A.H., Guise, M., & Sloan, D.L. (2015). Examining emotional rules in the English classroom: A critical discourse analysis of one student's literary responses in two academic contexts. *Research in the Teaching of English, 49*(3), 200–223.

Tompkins, J. (1987). Me and my shadow. *New Literary History, 19*(1), 168–178.

Trainor, J.S. (2006). From identity to emotion: Frameworks for understanding, and teaching against, anticritical sentiments in the classroom. *Journal of Advanced Composition, 26*(3/4), 643–655.

Trainor, J. S. (2008). *Rethinking racism: Emotion, persuasion, and literacy education in an all-white high school.* Carbondale: Southern Illinois University Press.

Wimsatt, W. K. & Beardsley, M. (1949). The affective fallacy. *Sewanee Review, 57*(1), 31–55.

Winans, A. (2012). Cultivating critical emotional literacy: Cognitive and contemplative approaches to engaging difference. *College English, 75,* 150–170.

Zembylas, M. (2002). 'Structures of feeling' in curriculum and teaching: Theorizing the emotional rules. *Educational Theory, 52*(2), 187–208.

Zembylas, M. (2005). *Teaching with emotion: A postmodern enactment.* Greenwich, CT: Information Age Publishing.

Zembylas, M. (2014). Theorizing 'difficult knowledge' in the aftermath of the 'affective turn': Implications for curriculum and pedagogy in handling traumatic representation. *Curriculum Inquiry, 44*(3), 390–412.

6

ASSESSING RESPONSE TO LITERATURE AND THE SOLO TAXONOMY

David Baxter and Cal Durrant

Introduction

In the first volume of this series, Bethan Marshall (2014) made some important observations about the knowledge of—and assessment in—the subject of English. As she wrote then, one of the problematic aspects of English is its resistance to being defined, which makes it very difficult to categorically describe what it actually means to be 'good at English' (Marshall, 2014: 13). For example, to perform well in external exams in English requires some content-related knowledge about English, but 'the knowledge needed to produce a good essay goes beyond content' (Marshall, 2014: 14). Content knowledge is really only advantageous in that it helps the student to firstly make an interpretation—usually of 'the text'—and then form an argument in response to the exam question itself.

Further, researchers such as Newfield et al. (2003) and Johnson (2003) have drawn attention to the challenges faced by disadvantaged urban students when it comes to external examinations. Both suggest that success is only possible when they are permitted to use modes of expression in which they are fluent—modes for which there may be very few formal criteria. Broadfoot and Black (2004) also note that at the macro-level, such external examination contexts invariably fail to take into consideration the

> interface of question with student, where student anxiety, motivation, understanding of the process and of the language used, and the whole context of the encounter can all affect performance in ways for which users remote from that context cannot make allowances.
>
> *(Broadfoot and Black, 2004: 15)*

Yet national and international reliance on high-stakes testing in English/literacy continues to expand unabated. And just as the growing public status of the

Key Stage texts in the United Kingdom has helped drive a greater 'desire to make the criteria for assessment explicit to pupils' (Marshall, 2014: 13), here in Australia similar pressures have been exerted by NAPLAN (National Assessment Program – Literacy and Numeracy) testing regimes and the continued focus on Year Twelve public examination performances as a basis for gaining university entrance. But as Broadfoot and Black (2004) observe, even a focus on making examination criteria more specific and transparent does not mask the critical questions surrounding just 'who promulgates criteria and whose interests they serve, and so brings the argument round to the context of social control within which all assessment activity is framed' (Broadfoot and Black, 2004: 18).

In attempting to address some of these concerns, this chapter explores the appropriateness of the SOLO Taxonomy (Biggs and Collis, 1982) in providing nuanced descriptions of the various levels of student response to Literature both in English and literature specific courses and/or units. While responses to literature, especially in public examinations in Australia, have increasingly been assessed using criteria-based rubrics, such rubrics have tended to depend on adjectival or adverbial progressions to reflect different levels of achievement and on the consensus established within a community of practice or interpretive community (Fish, 1980, 1989) to achieve inter-rater reliability. We argue that the SOLO Taxonomy provides a better description of different levels of response to literature because it accounts for the different cognitive operations of students at each level rather than relying upon ineffable progressions from 'limited' to 'adequate' to 'competent' to 'effective' versions of the same sort of product (NSW BOSTES, 2015: 1). Instead, SOLO acknowledges that students at the extremes of quality in responding to literature create both different types of texts as well as different levels of textual interpretation and insight.

What types of responses to literature are most rewarded in the education system?

Hunter (1988, 1991) has maintained that school English, especially in relation to literature and literary analysis, has always rewarded responses in which the relationship between form and meaning is explicitly established rather than those which focus on one or the other independently. Viewed thus, the type of response that is most likely to be evaluated at the highest levels is one that demonstrates the inter-relationship between form and meaning, firstly at a conceptual macro-level as an overview of the literary text, which forms a thesis-like frame to the response, and then at a micro-level by close readings of specific sections of the text which serve to justify the thesis.

Another way of looking at response to literature represented by Iser (1978) is to see the reader as a sense-maker and consistency-builder, looking for patterns of meaning that relate the contextual details of the text to larger patterns of significance. Iser's phenomenological approach to the act of literary reading has been supported by Armstrong's work on the links between neuroscience and literary response in which he asserts that 'there is extensive neurological evidence about how the brain interprets shapes and words that is consistent with the phenomenological view of reading as a process of filling in textual indeterminacies and building consistent patterns' (Armstrong, 2013: 21). Again, this entails a capacity to identify relationships rather than to pursue textual elements separately.

Recent Australian school examination questions often explicitly seek to elicit identification and justification of relationships between form and meaning. In New South Wales (NSW), for instance, the 2015 Higher School Certificate (HSC) questions for the Standard English paper (the course studied by the majority of students) focused exclusively on how ideas were presented rather than inviting students to justify their own interpretations of the meaning of texts, which was the focus of literacy response questions for students in the Advanced course. In the latter examination, students were provided with a general statement about the text or author and asked to discuss how it aligned with their own understanding. In both cases, students were expected to marshal justification of their thematic interpretations by close reading of sections of the text, with the marking guidelines for the Advanced questions stipulating the demonstration of understanding of 'context, language, form and ideas' (BOSTES, 2016b: 3) while the Standard guidelines required 'relevant, detailed textual knowledge' (BOSTES, 2016a: 3).

Senior students in Victoria may elect to study a course entitled *Literature*. In the 2015 examination for this course, students were asked to use nominated extracts from each text as a basis for a discussion of the whole text. This style of question, while much more open-ended than those used in NSW, still required students to demonstrate their thesis by close reading of sections of the text; that is, by articulating the relationship between textual elements and the larger pattern that the elements illustrate when taken together. The Examination Report cited weaker responses as unable to demonstrate this sort of relationship, focusing on each passage 'in isolation rather than on engaging with the text as a whole construction' or presenting a formulaic interpretation that was unsupported by the rest of the essay (VCAA, 2016: 3). Even in the medium range of texts, the examiners reported a predominance of paraphrase and explanation rather than the sort of analysis that linked language features to thematic meaning (VCAA, 2016: 2). These failings were accompanied by an inability to convey a personal engagement with the text expressed in a way that united accurate and extensive use of appropriate literary metalanguage and a distinctive 'voice'. In phenomenological terms, such responses would seem to indicate a failure to grapple with individual textual elements in order to build them into a consistent pattern.

The comments made in the Victorian Literature Examination Report concerning the differences between good and inadequate responses can be found in most such publications dating back well into the previous century. It is our contention that the SOLO Taxonomy provides a useful tool in unlocking the cognitive processes and stages involved in the growth of the sort of conceptual understanding represented by response to literature because it pays attention to the phenomenological nature of the task and gives a more convincing description of the various levels of understanding exhibited in student responses than the typical marking guidelines currently used for assessment.

The SOLO Taxonomy

The SOLO Taxonomy devised by Biggs and Collis (1982) is based on Piagetian descriptions of learning and was constructed through detailed observations of the developmental pattern of student behaviors and responses in relation to assessment tasks in a wide variety of school subjects, including poetry appreciation and creative writing in English. It has been used as an effective instrument for assessing levels of conceptual understanding across a wide range of subject areas, including English Literature (Svensson et al., 2015).

In the SOLO Taxonomy, Biggs and Collis (1982: 24–25; 95–96) described five levels of the learner's movement from surface to deep conceptual understanding. They also identified transitional stages between each level in which a student may exhibit both an upper and lower level in the same assessment task. The descriptions of the levels below include the original descriptions supplemented by specific reference to the understanding of literary texts:

1 Prestructural: students cannot engage with or understand the concept or the literary text;
2 Unistructural: students' understanding of the concept or the literary text is focused on one element of it;
3 Multistructural: students understand a number of elements of the concept or the literary text but cannot see the pattern of relationships between those elements;
4 Relational: students identify the links between the elements of the concept or the literary text—pattern or thematic recognition;
5 Extended Abstract: students can relate the concept or the literary text to other concepts or literary texts at a generalised level of abstraction—critical evaluation.

Relational and Extended Abstract responses have been linked to the achievement of deep learning, while Unistructural and Multistructural responses reflect surface approaches (Ramsden, 2003: 57). The strength of SOLO has been identified in its capacity to measure and categorise different levels of conceptual understanding (Boulton-Lewis, 1998; Chan et al., 2002; Hattie and Brown, 2004) and it is particularly applicable to open-ended tasks (Smith and Colby, 2007), making it especially appropriate for response to literature tasks where students are required to provide and justify an interpretation of a text or texts.

Marking guidelines in English

Marking guidelines, sometimes called rubrics, differ from assessment criteria in that the former provide differentiated descriptions of levels of achievement while the latter list the essential elements of the task without reference to levels of achievement. Marking guidelines are used widely in schools and in public examinations and are often provided to students by teachers in advance of school-based assessment tasks. They are seen as necessary instruments for discrimination between answers and the awarding of marks by examination markers. In NSW, HSC marking guidelines are published in the year subsequent to the particular examination and supplement official examination reports. Marking guidelines have the advantage of creating transparency and equity in assessment.

In English, marking guidelines such as those used for the NSW HSC tend to discriminate among levels of achievement by an adjectival or adverbial progression from an inadequate response ('limited') to a mid-range response ('sound') to a high-level response ('effective') to the highest-level response ('thoughtful', 'skilful'). The marker is required to recognise the appropriate level in the absence of precise definitions of the differences between the adjectives or adverbs. Characteristically, in public examinations—prior to beginning the full assessment operation—sample responses at each level are provided to markers based on the work of senior, experienced markers in culling out such samples based on their capacity to recognise and distinguish between the levels of achievement. A moderation process then occurs in order for markers to internalise the distinctions between the levels based on the ability to recognise and remember. The marking then proceeds on the basis of the establishment of an interpretive community, with continual moderation processes to ensure that discrepancy from the standards implemented by the community is minimised, if not eliminated.

The weakness of adjectival/adverbial marking guidelines is simply that they depict levels of achievement in response to literature as no more than different versions of the same thing. However, it is apparent from the VCE Examination report that lower-rated responses are in fact doing something quite different from the main game of consistency building and justification. In SOLO terms, the main game in response to literature is reaching Relational level by identifying relationships between textual elements while lower-rated responses are operating at Unistructural or Multistructural levels because they are not able to play that game and hence fall back on cognitive operations that are a pre-condition for reaching Relational level.

In one way, this should not be surprising—while it is not that difficult to access standard interpretations of most of the sort of literary texts set for study for senior English examinations, it is another thing altogether to move from the act of memory to a personal literary response that, as defined by Iser or Armstrong, is the result of a busy internal process of continual detective work in relation to the text. To describe what is happening at the mid-range level as 'sound' and yet at the same time to acknowledge that medium-level responses are often not personalised or insightful about either stylistic devices or patterns of meaning, as the VCE examiners do, seems to us like a significant mismatch. It suggests that the vast majority of responders find the game of personal literary response too hard, too unfamiliar or too uninteresting and that rather than enter into it they fall back upon responses that are within their comfort zone of memory and comprehension. Such responses are seen as 'sound' because there are a lot of them and they are predominantly accurate, albeit superficial. This raises questions about the actual nature of the game being played. Is it about providing personal responses to literature or is it about something less, something more technical, ultimately less personal than learned but where discrimination between responses is still based on the personal response discourse?

Focusing on the nature of the questions may be helpful here. Contemporary senior English examination questions are rarely framed as if their main goal was to elicit a fully unrestrained personal response to literature, or at least one created by the cerebral, internalised struggles of the private reader as described in the phenomenological approaches to reading of Iser and Armstrong. Indeed, questions are framed precisely to avoid unfettered personal responses by providing specific contexts and limitations—that is they generally examine the whole by focusing on the part. The 2015 Victorian Literature examination previously cited is the best example of a seemingly open-ended question, where students were required to provide a 'discussion' of two literary texts but it needed to be based on a textual analysis of two excerpts from each text. The best answers according to the examiners worked closely with the language of the text and gave the impression they were enjoying doing so (VCAA, 2016: 1). In SOLO terms, these answers were at Relational level, with students behaving as if the rules required them to perform an integrating or matching exercise. For other students at 'sound' levels and below, they behaved as if the rules required them to conduct separate operations, to explain what was happening in the excerpts, to find and report textual features and also to show a knowledge of the text as a whole, with an uncontroversial generalisation, usually at either end of their response. In SOLO terms, responses were thus at the Multistructural level. Brown (2004) has shown that there is often a significant mismatch between the way teachers and students perceive what is required in assessment tasks, with teachers generally expressing their goal as setting questions that require deep understanding whereas students see teachers as most interested in factual accuracy and being able to demonstrate surface learning. It is unsurprising then to see such a mismatch at system of education level.

The 2015 NSW questions were even more directed. At Standard level, students were asked how various texts portrayed ideas about a nominated topic, like difference or acceptance or relationships while at Advanced, students were presented with a statement about the text as a portrayal of thematic content and asked about the extent to which it aligned with their own response. This is not the same thing as asking students for their responses to a literary text. Rather it positions literary response for examination and assessment purposes as a debating exercise in which the depth of an individual interpretation of a text is reducible to the capacity of the student to be able to react intelligently to any stimulus provided. In other words, the prior fully formed personal response to literature will enable students to discuss any part of a text or any other interpretation and any lower level of understanding will be evidence of a superficial or less than perfect understanding of the text. Also attached to this view is one associated with the need for assessment to discriminate between levels of student achievement by providing stimuli unseen prior to the examination and hence less likely to reward pre-planned and formulaic answers.

However, it is possible to look at the whole area of literary response and assessment in a different way by applying a SOLO lens to the process. If Biggs and Collis are right, then the preliminary stages for the assembly of a fully personal and coherent interpretation of a text will be a focus on the details, especially the story. Rather than indicative of a flawed soundness, responses that are preoccupied with what happens or with examples of textual devices and that cover one thing at a time (i.e., Unistructural and Multistructural) rather than integrate, represent necessary stages prior to the achievement of fully relational literary responses. SOLO accounts for the way in which learning moves from surface to deep without the deficit scales of contemporary marking guidelines. It is also consistent with the phenomenological approach to reading literary texts developed by Iser in the 1970s and updated and refreshed by Armstrong.

Conclusion

Just like many other nations, Australia has an extensive system of national-, system- and school-level student assessment. Such assessments form the basis for key performance indicators towards national goals, state and territory system evaluation and individual student progress (Santiago et al., 2011: 48). Yet opinion is still divided about the purpose, effectiveness and reliability of such assessments. As Masters suggests concerning assessment more broadly:

> The field has been divided into perceived 'multiple purposes' of assessment (for example, formative, summative, diagnostic, screening and large-scale surveys), which are often assumed to require entirely different approaches and are sometimes characterised as being in opposition (for example, formative versus summative assessments). The field has also been divided into varying assessment 'methods' (for example, school-based versus external, tests versus assessments, authentic versus devised). Individual methods have attracted their proponents, who often view a specific method as inherently superior to others. The consequence of this fragmentation is a field characterised by contrasting philosophies, methods and purposes, and an often unproductive discourse.
>
> *(Masters, 2013: 5)*

Masters goes on to say that a more recent view of educational assessment is to establish where learners are in their learning at the time of assessment.

> 'Assessment, rather than being simply a process of judging how well students have learnt what they have just been taught, is conceptualised as the process of establishing where students are in their long-term learning and what progress they are making over time, usually in terms of their developing knowledge, skills and understandings'.
>
> *(Masters, 2013: 6)*

We conclude that English Literature teachers face a rapidly expanding list of outcome and marking criteria in relation to preparing their students for public examination questions. As Neil Bechervaise put it, 'from a classroom teacher's viewpoint, the lists of outcomes are exhaustive and exhausting' (Bechervaise, 1998: 334). For us, the Biggs and Collis approach through SOLO Taxonomy represents one way of creating an assessment protocol that enables the teacher/examiner to assess the range of student responses to literature without resorting to fuzzily framed descriptors and approximations.

On the basis of the analysis presented above, we believe that some of the benefits from using SOLO in assessment in English literature include the following:

1   SOLO represents a rigorous theoretical framework based on cognition that accounts for the development of student learning.
2   SOLO explains and allows a richer and more detailed description of levels of student achievement than conventional criterion-referenced practices in English.
3   SOLO provides a rationale for setting and marking assessment questions in English that allows students to demonstrate all levels of achievement.
4   SOLO reinforces familiar practices in English assessment, notably those associated with senior English teaching and therefore demonstrates an overall affinity with the subject.

References

Armstrong, P. (2013) *How literature plays with the brain: The neuroscience of reading and art*, Baltimore: Johns Hopkins University Press.

Bechervaise, N. (1998) Assessment in English, in W. Sawyer, K. Watson and E. Gold (eds) *Re-viewing English*, Sydney: St Clair Press.

Biggs, J. and Collis, K. (1982) *Evaluating the Quality of Learning: The SOLO Taxonomy (Structure of the Observed Learning Outcome)*, New York: Academic Press.

Board of Studies, Teaching and Educational Standards (BOSTES) (NSW) (2016a) *2015 HSC English (Standard) Paper 2 Marking Guidelines*. Sydney: BOSTES. www.boardofstudies.nsw.edu.au/hsc_exams/2015/.

Board of Studies, Teaching and Educational Standards (BOSTES) (NSW) (2016b) *2015 HSC English (Advanced) Paper 2 Marking Guidelines*. Sydney: BOSTES. www.boardofstudies.nsw.edu.au/hsc_exams/2015/.

Boulton-Lewis, G. (1998) Applying the SOLO taxonomy to learning in higher education, in Dart, B. and Boulton-Lewis, G. (eds) *Teaching and Learning in Higher Education*,
201–221. Melbourne: ACER.

Broadfoot, P. and Black, P. (2004) Redefining assessment? The first ten years of Assessment in Education, *Assessment in Education: Principles, Policy & Practice*, 11(1), 7–27.

Brown, G. (2004) Teachers' conceptions of assessment: Implications for policy and professional development, *Assessment in Education: Principles, Policy & Practice*, 11(3), 301–318.

Chan, C., Tsui, M. and Chan, M. (2002) Applying the structure of the observed learning outcomes (SOLO) taxonomy on students' learning outcomes: an empirical study,
Assessment and Evaluation in Higher Education, 27(6), 511–527.

Fish, S. (1980) *Is There a Text in This Class?: The Authority of Interpretive Communities*,
Cambridge, MA: Harvard University Press.

Fish, S. (1989) *Doing What Comes Naturally: Change, Rhetoric, and the Practice of Theory in
Literary and Legal Studies*, Durham & London: Duke University Press.

Hattie, J. and Brown, G. (2004) Cognitive processes in asTTle: The SOLO Taxonomy,
in *asTTle Report #43*, University of Auckland/Ministry of Education, New Zealand.

Hunter, I. (1988) *Culture and Government: The Emergence of Literary Education*, London:
Macmillan Press.

Hunter, I. (1991) Learning the literature lesson: the limits of the aesthetic personality, in
C. Baker and A. Luke (eds) *Towards a Critical Sociology of Reading Pedagogy*, Amsterdam
and Philadelphia: Johns Benjamin Publishing Company.

Iser, W. (1978) *The Act of Reading: A Theory of Aesthetic Response*, Baltimore and London:
Johns Hopkins University Press.

Johnson, D. (2003) Activity theory, mediated action and literacy: Assessing how children
make meaning in multiple modes, *Assessment in Education: Principles, Policy & Practice*,
10(1), 103–129.

Marshall, B. (2014) What does it mean to 'know' in English? in A. Goodwyn, L. Reid
and C. Durrant (eds) *International Perspectives on Teaching English in a Globalised World*,
Oxford: Routledge.

Masters, G. (2013) *Reforming Educational Assessment: Imperatives, Principles and Challenges*,
Camberwell: Australian Council for Educational Research.

Newfield, D., Andrew, D., Stein, P. and Maungedzo, R. (2003) 'No number can describe
how good it was': Assessment issues in the multi-modal classroom, *Assessment in Education: Principles, Policy & Practice*, 10(1), 61–81.

Ramsden, P. (2003) *Learning to Teach in Higher Education*, London and New York:
Routledge Falmer.

Santiago, P., Donaldson, G., Herman, J. and Shewbridge, C. (2011) *OECD Reviews of
Evaluation and Assessment in Education: Australia*, OECD. www.oecd.org/edu/school/
48519807.pdf.

Smith, T. and Colby, S. (2007) Teaching for deep learning, *The Clearing House*, 80(5),
205–210.

Svensson, A., Manderstedt, L., and Palo, A. (2015) 'Think of it as a challenge': Problem-
atizing pedagogical strategies for progression when assessing web-based university
courses in literary studies, *Læring og Medier*, 8(13), 1–24.

Victorian Curriculum and Assessment Authority (VCAA) (2016) *2015 VCE Literature
Examination Report*, Melbourne: Victoria. www.vcaa.vic.edu.au/Pages/vce/studies/
literature/exams.aspx.

PART II

Readers, texts and contexts

7

DIALOGUING IDENTITIES AND TRANSNATIONALISING THE SPACE OF THE AUSTRALIAN LITERATURE CLASSROOM

Monika Wagner and Mary Purcell

Introduction

Our contention in this chapter is that the texts located within the Australian 'canon' have predominantly focussed on the struggle of the European settler to forge a place within a 'forbidding' landscape, have often wrestled with a barely repressed violence born of guilt, have been predominantly male-centred, rural centred and have theorised land (and women) as something to be possessed and conquered. Implicitly, these texts have been marked by the trace of the 'Other', by the dark knowledge of the founding exclusions of a country that persists in a defiant racism, that refuses to look beyond its repressed guilt and fear. It is very much a history of the western self in conflict with its context, language and customs. Our claim is that it is only by recognising the unspoken 'Other' implied in these narratives, by hearing the subjectivity of those hitherto undescribed, by training ourselves to be the implied readers of culturally different texts, that the Australian literature classroom can become a space of ethical engagement and transformation.

The three Australian texts we have chosen for analysis have been used to explore different dimensions of reading practices as the inevitably political aspects of texts are grappled with. By moving away from a conceptualisation of text as monologic to recognising the dialogic ('heteroglossic'/'polyphonic') nature of the novel, as argued by Bakhtin (1981), the reader is moved away from merely being a receiver of a single, authoritative textual discourse. David Malouf's *Remembering Babylon*, written in 1993, is valued as an Australian canonical text. It explores the experience and challenges to identity faced by the early British settlers exposed to a seemingly hostile yet inhabited land which resisted being reinscribed and 'worlded' (Spivak, 1990, p. 1). *The Shadow King* (2014) was a collaboration between actor Tom Lewis and theatre director Michael Kantor.

It adapts Shakespeare's *King Lear* to a contemporary Australian context, set on land 'legally owned' by First Peoples. *The Visitors* (2013) takes us further back in Australia's history. Written by acclaimed playwright Jane Harrison, *The Visitors* challenges official versions of the arrival of the British in 1788, reversing the gaze to those of an Aboriginal Council of Elders.

We are proposing that modelling a dialogic exploration of text within the literature classroom opens the possibility for reading as the 'ethical motor' (Spivak, 2013, p. 352) of our teaching. Thus, we problematize the concept of the Australian 'canon' and explore the nature of its implied reader. As we attempt this, we recognise our position as urban, Anglo-/European-Australian women who work within institutions that privilege Western structures of knowledge production. While we are clearly situated, by explicitly addressing the multiple voices in a text—including those which are (traditionally) silenced or overlooked—we hope to begin the process of 'unlearning our privilege' (Spivak, 2013, p. 72). Although we are here focused on Australian texts and reconceptualising the dialogue between Indigenous and non-Indigenous Australians, this clearly does have implications for how we conceptualise any 'Other' who sits outside 'mainstream', 'canonical' texts. Further, we believe that in addressing texts in this way, students will be able to understand 'how the world is now constituted by cross-border relationships ... and complex affiliations and social formations that span the world' (Rizvi, 2010, p. 160).

Locating Bakhtin and Spivak

'A philosophy of life,' Bakhtin wrote, 'can only be a moral philosophy' (1993, p. 56); in saying this, he proposes the concept of answerability to express the sense in which understanding the relationship of self to the 'Other' is at the heart of understanding human existence, and central to this is dialogue. By invoking the historical exploitation of the disempowered, Spivak constantly reminds us that any act of reading has important social and political consequences (Morton, 2003, p. 141). Together they affirm the necessarily ethical nature of the call of the 'Other'.

'Otherness' is a structural necessity in Bakhtin's dialogism, as 'I' can only exist in dialogue with an 'Other'. Further, Bakhtinian selfhood is based on a tripartite structure: how 'I' see myself, how 'others' see me, and how 'others' appear to 'me' (Morson and Emerson, 1990, p. 180). Bakhtin's dialogism, therefore, provides a way of understanding being human, offering a concrete ethical construct rather than merely an abstract ontology (Hicks, 2000). In very rudimentary terms, the dialogic assumes 'every utterance must be regarded primarily as a response to preceding utterances' (Bakhtin, 1986, p. 91); it is part of an ongoing and complex chain, which is always social and always 'situated'. Bakhtin insists we acknowledge that experience always occurs within cultural, historical, and material contexts; even individuated activity is part of a social collective. Because human existence is dialogic, and because being human means being 'answerable' to others, we have *no alibi in existence*, that is, we have no defensible excuse to avoid or evade this responsibility, and are thus ethically accountable. As both individuals and texts are dialogic, we are required to acknowledge the relational nature of all interactions, as well as understand that texts convey and generate new meaning. Another reason dialogism embodies a deeply ethical space is because we are always required to respond to an addressee, the subject only arises through dialogue in the interpersonal encounter; human *being* is, by its nature, intersubjective. Because the self is always already dialogic and heteroglossic, that is, containing simultaneous multiple social/textual discourses, Bakhtin is not essentialising the subject (self *or* 'Other'), or engaging in simplistic pluralism. That the self is always an ongoing event also means there is thus no possibility of a 'finalised' sense of a dialogic self, and we are all in part determined by 'the grip and grasp of the gaze of the Other' (Jefferson in Hirschkop & Shepherd, 1989, p. 153). The animating 'force' at this borderline is the fundamental alterity of the 'Other', which both sustains the dialogue and the 'self'. Thus the ethics inherent in dialogism is built not on our universal sameness, but on our radical alterity and the 'unfinalisability' (Bakhtin, 1984) of the I/'Other', which guards against universalism and idealism.

West-Pavlov (2005) links Spivak and Bakhtin through dialogism and hybridity, suggesting that the classroom dialogue is a hybrid process working both subserviently and subversively at once. His conception that dialogism be 'deliberately mobilised as a strategy against hegemonic monologism' (West-Pavlov, 2005, p. 39) unites Spivak and Bakhtin in a common commitment to hear the voice of the 'Other'. Salazar-Sutil (2008) suggests that for Spivak the 'I' in the dialogue is more divided against itself and that the gaze of the 'I' appropriate to the epistemological mode also belongs to a strategy of domination that pits the 'I' against the 'Other'. Thus, he problematizes the political nature of the dialogic more for Spivak than Bakhtin, who he says 'levels out the binary relationship' between I and 'Other' (Salazar-Sutil, 2008, p. 3). Letiche links the two thinkers through the practices of polyphony, diversity, and intertextuality, claiming that Spivak is not as sure as Bakhtin seems to be that another speaks at all in such practices (Letiche, 2010, p. 261). Spivak inflects 'answerability' with contemporary political power, fashioning an ethics to meet present-day injustices raised by a globalised economy dominated by corporate interests (Spivak, 1994, p. 63). She presents the study of literature as the exercise of suspending yourself in another's text, and thus as training for the ethical impulse. The implied reader is already constructed within a consolidated system of cultural representation (Spivak, 2013, p. 38) and predisposes readers to respond from their particular situatedness.

The implied reader of the text is in many ways the assumed audience, the reader enculturated to receive the text, one who does not question its values, conventions and assumptions. When exposed to culturally unfamiliar texts, the reader needs to train her or his imagination through attending to the particular imagery, language and conventions to learn to understand aspects of culture from which the text emerges. The text figures forth meanings in a clandestine way that is different from the argument or obvious story-line and it is in submitting to these literary features that the reader learns to become the text's implied reader. As a seeming paradox, however, Spivak wants us to submit and deconstruct simultaneously. Deconstructing hidden assumptions, hierarchies and power agendas requires being aware of the situatedness and concrete circumstances from which we perceive. As we unlearn our privilege, the 'Other' moves from the margins to take a position central to our awareness and our reading. Thus, as we submit to the figures and forms of the less familiar text, we gain imaginative access to new and unfamiliar ideas and subjectivities.

Spivak's postcolonial analyses question assumed distinctions between centre and periphery by looking at literature as the 'staged battle-ground of epistemes' (Spivak, 2013, p. 55), and she never forgets that she is situated within the western tradition. She critiques western academic writing as inevitably colonizing as it theorises the 'Other' as a construct of western knowledge. According to Letiche, the challenge of Spivak's work is to try to keep all the conflicting voices alive in the text, without 'collapsing into a single truth, principle or totalisation' (Letiche, 2010, p. 263). To have agency, Spivak maintains you reverse, displace and seize the apparatus of value-coding (Spivak, 2013, p. 70). This strategic approach is grounded in economic and social realities. As with Bakhtin, Spivak shows answerability is part of material existence by employing concrete examples of political and social silencing, such as the collection of hydrological data by the World Bank as if, despite the intimate learning born of 'an ongoing response to the weave of land and river' (Spivak, 2008, p. 89), the Bangladeshi peasant had known nothing at all.

Our interest is to explore the ethical implications of sustained textual study through applying a Bakhtinian and Spivakian reading to texts. We are opening up the possibility of relationality, working at the level of 'I' and 'you' rather than 'we'. As Mulcahy (2006) says, using 'betweenness' helps us move away from such normative, singular models which embrace essentialist accounts. As changing the nature of the dialogical space will problematize the way in which we engage with and explore text, our aim is to render visible the clash of epistemes implicit in the transnational spaces of our classrooms. Both Bakhtin and Spivak lead us to the possibility that a literary pedagogy, through judicious selection of texts, can and should prepare another space that reveals limitations of a western-centred view and allows discursive space for the 'Other' within literary education in countries such as Australia.

The texts

As we have articulated, the theories of both Bakhtin and Spivak are concerned with ethical practice which insists on concrete action. The translation into classroom practice through grappling with meaning between multiple social/textual discourses does afford such 'material action'. The call to answerability is addressable through work with students in textual study in part because recognising the heteroglossic nature of texts invites the posing of unresolved questions with which readers can actively engage. Building on this, as we learn to become the implied reader of texts produced outside dominant discourses, we are drawn into patterns of cultural value that are challenging and that invite ideological transformation.

In contemporary Australia, negative 'Othering' is frequently the norm—in the broader community, in politics and in education. Such alienation is often portrayed in literary texts as being due to fear of the 'Other', as it is by Malouf in *Remembering Babylon*. As a result of this fear, the subordination and estrangement of the 'Other' also leads to an impoverishment of broader society through increased insistence on normative homogeneity of ideas.

It could be argued that *Remembering Babylon* attempts to address this. The Aboriginal Elders who come to visit the hybridised character Gemmy, when he is living with the settlers, are voiceless to the readers. We only get a sense of what they embody through the narrator's explanation of how they mystically impart memory of land and culture to him. By rendering mute the First Peoples he represents in this novel, Malouf does 'Other' the indigenous characters. The aboriginal people in this novel are still clearly 'Other' to the European-Australian—in the sense of dialectical opposition—and seem to have no standing within the western mind other than as a source of fear.

Hence the focus remains both within and on the western consciousness and its limits and changes. Malouf, therefore, inadvertently highlights the one-sidedness and blindness of the canonical conversation. Through images of impenetrable dark, he renders the fear of the colonisers as a palpable force; a fear which is in many ways the strongest narrative presence in the novel. It dominates the violent minds of Jock's erstwhile 'mates', it interrupts Ellen's gentler perceptions and it is caricatured in Lachlan's initial encounters with Gemmy. Malouf reveals that, while the assumption of terra nullius might suggest emptiness, none of the inhabitants see the land as empty. The British-Australian 'colonisers' see the land as threateningly filled, haunted by the trace of the remote 'Other' that they hope can be silenced from history with determination and group will.

In *The Shadow King*, Lewis and Kantor intertwine voices, languages and cultural symbols to provoke a clash of epistemes within a dialogic process. The ironic opening stage direction, 'the community is celebrating their recent win in a native title claim, and Lear has done a deal with the mining company', immediately foregrounds the capitalist master narrative which is only implicit, and remains unquestioned, in *King Lear*. Just as the nation-state of Shakespeare's play is a space established and constituted by violence and dispossession, so too, in this adaptation, the land is co-opted into a western consumerist frame and viewed by some as merely a source of profit and of power. Lear's conferring of his lands upon his daughters also represents *them* in terms of physical space and thus as emblems of property. As they are destined to be the bearers of Lear's legacy and his lineage, this scene, in both plays, situates the female body as a site of male inscription regarding the transmission of property. Lewis and Kantor's

Edmund, whose use of English betokens his internalisation of western values, is characterised as both a rapist and a grasper of land. Thus, he lays claim to both sites of capitalist possession. In so doing he is doubly betraying his heritage within Australian Indigenous culture, because the land, as the Fool says at the end of *The Shadow King*, 'imm noma blong la you/It is you who blong na this land'. Cordelia, in her refusal to proclaim her love for Lear, denies her father's property rights to her, indicating her strength of character and principle. In *The Shadow King,* her proclamation that 'you can't gibbit me what you don't own' is an expression of her respect for land and its sacredness as well as an expression of her right as a woman to be a subject not an object within this society. Her refusal to use the language of political sycophancy is expressed in Kriol, not the language of the colonisers: 'They noma lub their children … lub their land? I'm not lookin round bla big fortune, specially not from this blood money'. This is a central speech in the play as Cordelia dissociates herself from the western capitalist notion of land, and the contempt in 'blood money' suggests her stance is at least part political protest.

In *The Shadow King* we start with the Fool's appropriation of 'one of <u>your</u> dreamtime storie'. The elegant simplicity of appropriating such a canonical English text as *King Lear* really does change the dialogue. When the Fool clarifies in his opening monologue that what we are about to witness is in fact 'bad business this mili mili, a sad business: / a tragedy this mili mili, *our* tragedy', the audience is led to understand that the tragedy experienced by Australia's First Peoples is and is not the same as what is meant by 'western tragedy'. In *The Shadow King* the audience is going to observe loss of land, of culture, of language, of family, of the source of the sense of self. But this play is not a romanticisation or mysticalisation of the indigenous 'ways of seeing'—in *The Shadow King*, just as is true in *King Lear*, it is 'all about money, jealousing allabut, greed'.

Whereas Lear's vacillation in *King Lear* between poetry and prose enacts his disintegrating hold on his constructed identity, the disintegration dramatized in *The Shadow King* is as much between cultural values as within the protagonist's psyche. This is demonstrated in the various language uses of the characters. Cordelia uses Kriol as she claims her own political power. In both *The Shadow King* and *The Visitors*, Kriol and language are used as equal to English; through context and the audience's intertextual awareness, meaning is understood even when individual words are not known. With both the Cantor/Lewis and Harrison plays, the audience is invited to move beyond simple/simplistic othering; 'we' are simultaneously in and out of the text. Gloucester, recast as a woman who speaks equally in language and in English, asserts the power of the feminine in *The Shadow King*, as her 'dilly bag holds all the lores'. But she is manipulated and exploited by the disenfranchised and westernised Edmund. The vulnerability of both land and the feminine is underscored even as questions about what is 'legitimate', raised by Edmund's character, take on extra depths within the indigenous context. Thus, *The Shadow King* intertextually invites us to be the implied readers of culturally diverse texts, to become comfortable in not always being on the 'inside' of language and in submitting to this text, to imbibe the dialogic values it enacts.

While 'difference' used to mark separateness or the declaration of 'a stranger among us' provides 'justification' for the 'othering' of cultures, if we develop a social space which facilitates a rich dialogue of voices rather than a fight for recognition and domination, then 'otherness is no longer considered foreign or threatening' (Gardiner, 1996, p. 140). Dialoguing itself can actively be employed 'against the privileging of one over the Other' (Gurevitch, 2000, p. 244). In Australia, texts such as *The Shadow King* invite interrogation of the status quo which emphasises 'European' sensibility as defining Australians and Australian culture. Harrison's play, *The Visitors*, opens another dialogue; she successfully inverts the expectations of the 'Other' so that there is no sense of threat, no sense of the foreign in this conception. The Elders come onto stage in suits— an immediately recognisable symbol of western 'ready-for-business'. The men talk according to custom—of the board room as well as of more ancient rituals. The nature of the negotiations, both the content and the approach to conflict, are also fully recognisable for the audience. It thus opens the way for being able to embrace—not just recognise—the point of view which was traditionally 'othered' by dominant western discourse.

Through the eyes of the seven Aboriginal Elders, Harrison challenges the assumption of moral and intellectual superiority of western culture, by which the British were able to 'justify' the invasion of Australia as a civilising mission. Harrison bases her story on events in eighteenth century Australian history but ironically plays between different subjectivities and points in history to render visible the structures of prejudice and injustice. In the deliberations of the Council of Elders she provides an allegory of the postcolonial struggle within the shifting historical moment and provides an important counterpoint to the silencing of Australian First Peoples in the British colonial archives and official historical writing in Australia. The competing epistemologies which Harrison's play addresses challenge Euro-centred assumptions about land, capitalism and the colonial legacy.

It could be argued that Harrison has achieved a truly heteroglossic text here; a 'special type of double-voiced discourse' (Bakhtin, 1981, p. 324). The two voices—of the First Peoples and of the invaders—are simultaneously expressing meaning through the ironic inversion of the application of language. When, for example, the Burramattagal elder Walter (the academic) says that 'they might die … of hunger or illness or simple stupidity', when the Elder of the Gadigal people, 'general' Gordon, suggests dismissively that these travellers/visitors/invaders cannot follow required protocols because they 'don't understand our language', when Albert's, the Bidjigal Elder and engineer muses, 'Maybe they're not very intelligent', there are always two meanings in all of these exchanges—nearly always comic as well as deadly serious—for the audience as well as for the author.

Literary texts can provide an alternative rhetorical site for articulating the histories of those without social position or power. They can expose the epistemic violence implicit in the ways western knowledge has been used to justify the exercise of political, economic and military force over other cultures. Such exposure can shake the foundations of the externally validated cultural norms, and it is this which makes possible for us, as individuals, teachers and students, a change in approach to normativity. What we are doing by making this part of a formalised, institutionalised discourse, is to make this moving, this breaking through, explicit and recognisable.

In the classroom

An ethical classroom is facilitated by acknowledging the fundamental centrality of the dialogic to developing understandings of the self and 'Other' (for example, Ryan & Johnson, 2009). When teaching text, we argue, it is this dialogic process which supports student knowledge of themselves through their exposure to the 'Other' in literature.

Within the context of globalisation and new forms of colonisation, Spivak maintains, echoing Bakhtin, that to 'be human is to be intended toward the Other' (Spivak, 2013, p. 338); however, she places this within the frame of a world without binaries and borders, 'daring to take dialogics to its logical consequence … to control globalisation interruptively' (Spivak, 2013, pp. 347–348). The implications for the classroom are profound. As Parr asserts, her arguments can legitimately 'be translocated into a framework for describing and understanding literature teaching and learning in Australian secondary schools' (Parr, 2011, p. 78). To only select and teach texts from within a canonical perspective, particularly if it is done without adopting a deeply critical lens, is to be complicit with the 'isolationist expansionism of mere nationalism' (Spivak, 2013, p. 285). Using texts from outside the canon, or at least reading such texts alongside canonical texts, the strategic ruses by which hegemonic groups exclude others can be unmasked, rendering visible the trace of the 'Other' as part of the classroom and cultural dialogue. To produce a deeper engagement with the 'Other' we need to interrogate the hidden assumptions and philosophical commitments by which they operate and through which they form desires.

If, as Spivak suggests, literature 'buys your assent in an almost clandestine way and therefore it is an excellent instrument for a slow transformation of the mind' (Spivak, 2013, p. 38), then our task is to make visible what is usually clandestine. With this in mind, we are showing how the English-language 'canon', usually represented as the stable centre of knowledge in Australian literature classrooms, can be disrupted. This is not done merely to disrupt first language privilege, but because these texts privilege a narrow view which has limited applicability in the contemporary Australian space. Euro-centred Australian texts fail to give adequate epistemic access to the complexity of Australian dialogues. Engaging the imagination of our students for ethical encounters with those traditionally 'othered' within this context is both our goal and challenge.

References

Bakhtin, M. M. (1981). Emerson, C., and Holquist, M. (Eds.). *The Dialogic Imagination: Four Essays by M. M. Bakhtin* (Michael Holquist, Trans.). Austin: University of Texas Press.

———— (1984). *Problems of Dostoyevsky's Poetics* (C. Emerson, Ed. & Trans.). Minneapolis: University of Minnesota Press.

———— (1986). Emerson, C. & Holquist, M. (Eds.). *Speech Genres and Other Late Essays* (Y. McGee, Trans.). Austin: University of Texas Press.

———— (1993). *Towards a Philosophy of the Act* (Vadim Liapunov, Trans.). Austin: University of Texas Press.

Gurevitch, Z. (2000). Plurality in dialogue: a comment on Bakhtin. *Sociology, 34*(2), 243–263.

Harrison, J. (2013). *The Visitors*. Unpublished manuscript, Melbourne, Australia.

Hicks, D. (2000). Self and other in Bakhtin's early philosophical essays: prelude to a theory of prose consciousness. *Mind, Culture and Activity, 7*(3), 227–242.

Hirschkop, K. & Shepherd, D. (Eds). (1989). *Bakhtin and Cultural Theory*. Manchester and New York: Manchester University Press.

Kantor, M. & Lewis, T. E. (2014). *The Shadow King*. Unpublished manuscript, Melbourne, Australia.

Letiche, H. (2010). Polyphony and its other. *Organisational Studies, 31*(3), 261–277.

Malouf, D. (2009). *Remembering Babylon*. North Sydney, Australia: Random House.

Morson, G. & Emerson, C. (1990). *Mikhail Bakhtin: Creation of a Prosaics*. Stanford: Stanford University Press.

Morton, S. (2003). *Gayatri Chakravorty Spivak*. London: Routledge.

Mulcahy, D. (2006). The salience of space for pedagogy and identity in teacher education: Problem-based learning as a case in point. *Pedagogy, Culture & Society, 14*(1), 55–69.

Parr, G. (2011). Toward an understanding of literature teaching in Australia: hanging on and letting go. In van de Ven, P. and Doecke, B. (Eds.), *Literary Praxis: A Conversational Inquiry into the Teaching of Literature* (pp. 69–87). Rotterdam, The Netherlands: Sense Publishers.

Rizvi, F. (2010). International students and doctoral studies in transnational spaces, The Routledge Doctoral Supervisor's Companion. *Supporting Effective Research in Education and the Social Sciences, 1*, 158–170.

Ryan, M. & Johnson, G. (2009). Negotiating multiple identities between school and the outside world: a critical discourse analysis. *Critical Studies in Education, 50*(3), 247–260.

Salazar-Sutil, N. (2008). Carnival post-phenomenology: mind the hump. *Anthropology Matters Journal, 10*(2), 1–11.

Sempere, J. P. (2014). *The Influence of Mikhail Bakhtin on the Formation and Development of the Yale School of Deconstruction*. Newcastle upon Tyne: Cambridge Scholars Publishing.

Spivak, G. (1990). Harasym, S. (Ed.). *The Post-colonial Critic: Interviews, Strategies, Dialogues*. New York: Routledge.

———— (1994). Responsibility. *Boundary, 21*(3), 19–64.

———— (2009). *Outside in the Teaching Machine*. New York: Routledge.

———— (2013). *An Aesthetic Education in the Era of Globalisation*. Cambridge, MA: Harvard University Press.

West-Pavlov, R. (2005). *Transcultural Graffiti: Diasporic Writing and the Teaching of Literary Studies*. Amsterdam: Editions Rodopi.

8

EARLY-CAREER ENGLISH TEACHERS' PERSPECTIVES ON TEACHING LITERATURE IN SECONDARY SCHOOLS

Don Carter and Jacqueline Manuel

Introduction

Together with the deeply held desire to influence the quality of young people's lives, a 'love of literature' is consistently invoked as one of the principal motivations for choosing to become a teacher of English (cf. Goodwyn, 2012; Heinz, 2015; Manuel and Brindley, 2005). When prospective secondary English teachers speak of their aspirations, they do so with conviction about the transformative power of education in shaping the lives of individuals and society more broadly, and the centrality of teaching literature to realising their goals. Their imagined professional identity and expectations are often intricately bound up with their idealised beliefs about the affordances of literary experience and its anticipated impact on the selfhood and life chances of the students they will teach (Goodwyn, 2012: 222). Less well documented, however, are early-career English teachers' views of teaching literature once they enter the classroom as accredited professionals and the extent to which their initial motivations and goals have been sustained, modified or disrupted by the experience of the first years of teaching.

Our purpose in this chapter is to report on the findings of one component of our research with pre-service and early-career teachers: a small-scale study with 22 secondary English teachers in New South Wales (NSW) who have been teaching for between one and four years. Since empirical studies in the field have identified a causal relationship between initial motivations and expectations, the quality of the early-career experience, levels of career satisfaction and trends in teacher retention and attrition (cf. Buchanan et al., 2013; Heinz, 2015; Manuel, 2003), our research has sought to explore these dynamics in the particular context of secondary English teaching. Because early-career English teachers' perspectives are generally under-represented in the corpus of research in the field, paralleling their often marginalised and even isolated status as novice teachers in schools (Buchanan et al., 2013; Schaefer, 2013), an additional aim of this chapter is to foreground their views.

The modest sample size of this study, along with the recognised limitations of an instrument such as a questionnaire, means that the findings reported here are not generalisable. The findings do, however, offer provisional interpretations that chime with those evinced from analogous national and international research in the fields of English teacher motivation (cf. Goodwyn, 2012; Manuel and Brindley, 2005); early-career teacher development (cf. Britzman, 1992; Bullough, 1997; Lortie, 1975/2002); and teacher recruitment, retention and attrition (cf. Ewing and Manuel, 2005). The findings from the present study therefore contribute additional empirical evidence of worth to the larger discourses around the future of English in schools; the place and significance of literature and the teaching of literature; and the factors influencing the retention or attrition of early-career teachers of English.

Background and context for the research study

A rich stream of scholarship in English curriculum history has yielded considerable insights into the origins of an enduring commitment to literature as the subject's centre of gravity: a commitment just as, if not more evident in versions of English in NSW curriculum documents over the course of more than a century as it has been in other Australian and international jurisdictions (cf. Ball, 2003; Ball, Kenny and Gardiner, 1990; Brock, 1984, 1996; Green and Beavis, 1996; Manuel and Brock, 2003; Manuel and Carter, 2016). Thus, when they come to Initial Teacher Education (ITE) programs, many prospective English teachers have already internalised a set of 'epistemic assumptions' (Reid, 1996: 32) about the subject, shaped by their own schooling and their more personal engagements with literature (cf. Davies, 1996; Mathieson, 1975).

For those attracted to teaching English, there is a marked consistency in their motivations despite heterogeneous contexts, backgrounds and biographies. In Goodwyn's longer-term studies with pre-service English teachers in England, for example, the recurring motivations to teach were identified as a 'love of/ enthusiasm for/passion for the subject; working with young people; a love of literature/reading; and being good at the subject' (Goodwyn, 2012: 219). Similarly, Manuel and Brindley's research with pre-service English teachers at the University of Sydney and the University of Cambridge found that the top-ranked reasons for choosing to teach were: 'personal fulfilment /fulfilment of a dream; enjoyment/ love of/passion for English/literature; working with young people; and a desire to contribute to society' (Manuel and Brindley, 2005: 42). Indeed, aspiring teachers of English typically invoke the qualities of 'passion', 'love' and 'desire', along with allusions to 'dreams', to describe their goals and give form to their ideations of teaching, reflecting the degree to which the decision to teach is inseparable from an individual's subjectivities, ideals and envisioned future.

Each year in NSW an average of five hundred people are accepted into NSW university ITE programs to become English teachers.[1] As the largest educational jurisdiction in the Southern Hemisphere, NSW schools are responsible for the education of more than one million students in any one year. There is a steady demand for secondary English teachers across the State (NSW DoE, 2015). In the face of consistent negative media and dissuasive public attitudes towards teachers and their work, coupled with the burgeoning administrative workload, political interventionist agendas and constraining accountability regimes operating in schools, ITE programs in many universities in NSW continue to attract healthy numbers of aspirant English teachers.

The present study

Participants and method

At the end of 2015 and the beginning of 2016, data were gathered via a questionnaire from 22 English teachers who have been teaching for between 1 and 4 years. Each participant had successfully completed a two-year graduate-entry Master of Teaching (Secondary) degree in the year immediately prior to taking up employment. Each entered the ITE program having attained a degree with either a double major, major, minor or Honours in English, with a minimum of four semesters of undergraduate study in literature-based courses.[2] Each specialised in teaching secondary English and one other school subject. 80 percent of the sample is currently teaching English in full-time positions in mainstream secondary schools in NSW, with 20 percent teaching casually, part-time or in extended temporary blocks.

The questionnaire comprised 24 items with a series of multiple choice questions and short-answer items. Collated responses to all multiple choice items were initially analysed to identify general trends. Questions requiring a written comment were thematically coded. Each participant's full set of responses was then individually analysed.

The findings: questionnaire responses

For the remainder of this chapter we concentrate on presenting the key findings of the study. The limitations of space preclude a detailed analysis of all questionnaire items. We report here on the findings that are directly pertinent to our focus on early-career English teachers' perspectives on teaching literature in secondary schools.

Profile of the participants

In the research sample of 22 early-career teachers, 20 were female and 2 were male. The average age of this sample was 31 years. The slightly higher than expected average age of the sample can be attributed to the inclusion of participants who were mature-age entrants into teaching. There was an over-representation of female teachers in this sample, reflecting to some extent the national data on female to male ratios in secondary teaching of 3:1 (Weldon, 2015).

Motivational factors that influenced the initial decision to teach

Participants were asked to rank the motivational factors that influenced their initial decision to become a teacher. Responses were on a scale from 'very important', 'important', 'somewhat important', 'not sure' and 'not important'. The motivational factors rated as 'very important' are shown in descending order in Table 8.1 below.

The highest ranked 7 out of 12 factors listed in Table 8.1 are altruistic (factors 1, 5 and 7) and intrinsic (factors 2, 3, 4 and 6). The intrinsic motivations—emerging from the individual's values and subjectivities and therefore 'rooted in personality and experience' (Kagan, 1992: 163)—are invested with a socially-oriented purpose through the altruistic, 'service theme' (Lortie, 1975/2002) motivations: 'making a difference in people's lives' and 'making a difference to social and other types of disadvantage'. Tacit in these motivations is the importance of inter-relational and social justice dimensions of teaching. Taken together, the altruistic and intrinsic motivations 'represent[s] a distinctive and deep service ethic' (Bullough and Hall-Kenyon, 2011: 128) continuous with an optimistic belief in the transformative potential of individual and collective agency.

Significant in Table 8.1 is the third most highly ranked factor of a 'love of a wide range of texts'. This finding is idiosyncratic to the present study. For teachers who completed their secondary schooling in NSW the term 'texts' is normative. For at least two decades, NSW English syllabus documents have referred to

TABLE 8.1 Motivational factors influencing the decision to teach

Rank	Factor influencing the initial decision to teach
1	Making a difference in people's lives
2	Love of literature
3	Love of a wide range of texts
4	Love of English as a subject
5	Making a difference to social and other types of disadvantage
6	Personal goal/dream
7	Working with young people
8	Looking for a career change
9	Quality of professional life
10	Further career opportunities in the teaching profession
11	Salary and working conditions
12	Portability of degree and skills for other kinds of work

'texts' rather than 'literature', with recurring attention to the need for students to experience a 'wide range of texts' (Board of Studies NSW, 1999). 'Texts' are understood to include a wide range of print, visual, film, media, multimedia and digital materials of which the traditional category of literature (that is, print literature considered to be of high cultural value and merit) forms a part. A wide range of texts is prescribed for study in secondary English. A 'love of literature' (ranked second) and a 'love of English as a subject' (ranked fourth) can therefore be seen to be co-extensive with a 'love of a wide range of texts' (ranked third).

The status and relevance of initial motivations to teach in the light of early-career teaching experience

We sought to draw out the extent to which the participants' original motivations to teach have retained their currency and cogency after one, two, three or four years of teaching. Research in the field of work motivation theory has found that 'salient motivations trigger, sustain, and concentrate behavior. They are, thus, closely linked to and impact on individuals' work commitment (retention, concentration)' (Heinz, 2015: 259).

Three-quarters of the participants in the present study stated that their initial motivations to teach have been generally affirmed in their daily working lives. Interestingly, of the three-quarters who responded positively to this question, a majority were teachers in their first one, two and three years of teaching. Those who were more equivocal about the durability of their initial motivations were in their third or fourth years of teaching. This suggests the potential for teachers' original motivations to modulate according to the length of time teaching, with implications for teacher retention and attrition. Bullough and Hall-Kenyon's research, for example, found that 'teachers who have 6–10 years of experience reported having a lower sense of calling compared to any of the other groups' (2011: 134), supporting Yee's conclusion that altruistic and intrinsic motivations to teach may diminish over time (1990).

Greatest challenges as a teacher and impediments to the realisation of a teacher's goals

Participants were asked to identify their greatest challenges as a teacher and to then nominate the aspects of teaching that have hindered the realisation of their goals. The most consistent themes in response to the question were: time management (professional and personal); teacher wellbeing; concerns about the tension between the ideals of generating a love of literature and the subject and the constraints imposed by a content-heavy and assessment-driven curriculum; and challenges around differentiation in teaching, student engagement, motivation and behaviour. The stated challenges can be seen to be interdependent. Taken together, they foreground the intensity and often all-consuming nature of teachers' work, reinforcing the impact of this on their personal lives and professional goals, especially for the fledgling teacher (Buchanan et al., 2013).

Early-career teachers' initial altruism and hopefulness, particularly in relation to their 'love of literature', were disturbed by the exigencies of real classrooms and school systems. On this point, some research has warned that 'a growing awareness of the[se] less exciting realities of teaching [that] can be followed by feelings of ineffectiveness, loneliness, and alienation from the profession' (Schlichte, Yssel and Merbler, 2005: 38), leading to teacher attrition, especially in the early-career phase (Clandinin et al., 2015) and teacher burnout which has been theorised in relation to new teacher motivation and teacher goals (Mansfield, Wosnitza and Beltman, 2012: 24).

For English teachers in the present study, one of the greatest challenges involved 'reconciling the wonder and passion for exploring literature for pure enjoyment whilst balancing the need for rigorous assessment in the classroom'. When asked to list the aspects of their work that they regarded as the most troubling threats or impediments to the realisation of their goals, the responses echoed those identified as the 'greatest challenges':

1   Dealing with constraints on time due to syllabus content.
2   Preparing students for the Higher School Certificate (HSC) exams.[3]
3   Classroom management.
4   Relationships with colleagues.

Of these major concerns, the first and second were named by more than 90 percent of participants, suggesting the extent to which the prescriptive demands of syllabus content and the omnipresence of external, high-stakes examinations have had a constraining effect on their daily work as teachers, inhibiting their pursuit of the more holistic goals of generating a love of literature and texts. Goodwyn's (2012) research with English teachers in England reported comparable major concerns and 'extreme frustrations (220) about the distorting impact of instrumentalist testing regimes on the teaching of literature, student engagement and students' attitudes to literary study.' For participants in the present study, the gap between their beliefs about the purpose of teaching literature and the immediate need to prepare their students for tests and matriculation examinations was particularly striking.

Teaching literature in the senior years and early-career teachers' sense of agency

In these questions, we sought to ascertain the degree of symmetry—or the mismatch—between teachers' beliefs, values, goals and sense of agency, and their experiences of teaching literature in the 'outcomes' intensive crucible of the NSW Higher School Certificate.

100 percent of participants 'strongly agreed' and 'agreed' that 'the external HSC examination drives the way teaching occurs in HSC English'. More than

90 percent believed that their 'approach to teaching literature is determined by the need to prepare students for the examination', with more than 80 percent agreeing that 'if there were not an HSC exam, I would approach the teaching of literature differently'. Fewer than half of the respondents agreed that they 'participate in decision-making that impacts on [their] teaching'. Embedded in these responses are cogent indicators of the extent to which extrinsic forces—in this case, the HSC examinations, external regulatory demands and marginalisation from curricular and other decision-making processes—can erode a teacher's sense of professional agency when it comes to the teaching of literature and senior English more generally.

Collectively, participants' responses to these questions exposed a telling disjunction between the 'subject paradigm' and pedagogy they are obliged to enact in senior English and their stated motivations and beliefs about the purpose and value of teaching literature. These early-career teachers' individually constructed narratives about the self-as-teacher and the transformative potentialities of teaching literature were manifestly interrupted by the externally imposed requirement to 'teach to the test'. As a result, their sense of professional agency—their 'active contribution to shaping their work and its conditions' (Biesta, Priestley and Robinson, 2015: 624)—was diminished by the performative expectations that accompany teaching the senior secondary English syllabus.

Participants' current views of and levels of satisfaction with teaching English

The culminating questions in this study were designed to synthesise key aspects of the previous questions and to invite a more holistic consideration of the overall quality of the early-career teacher's experience: have the participants' motivations, values, beliefs and goals shifted, remained stable, been affirmed or challenged; do they believe they are 'making a difference'; have they maintained their ideals; is teaching rewarding; and have they felt supported by colleagues and the 'system'?

While a majority of participants responded positively to statements related to their professional agency; self-efficacy; ability to maintain their values, ideals and beliefs; collegial support and the rewards and satisfactions of teaching, a considerable proportion of the responses evinced ambivalent and adverse views about the overall quality of their teaching experience. Of specific concern was the number of participants who reported that they do not feel they are making a difference as a teacher (18 percent); that their beliefs about themselves as a teacher have not been affirmed (25 percent); that they have not been able to maintain their ideals as a teacher (33 percent); and that their values have been challenged by colleagues or the 'system' (50 percent).

Of the range of motivations that influenced the participants' initial decisions to enter teaching, 'making a difference in people's lives' was the top ranked factor for more than 90 percent of this sample. Around one in four to five teachers in this study—after one or more years of teaching—felt that they were not fulfilling this highly significant aspiration to make a difference. Of these, a majority indicated that they were 'unsure' about or could not see themselves teaching five years from now. This finding underscores the vital relationship between the durability of initial motivations, the quality of early-career teaching experiences and future career intentions.

Notably, 50 percent of this sample reported that their values had been challenged by colleagues or the 'system' in which they were working. The implication here is that for half of the early-career teachers in this study there was friction between their 'subject paradigm' and 'subject pedagogy' and that perceived to be promoted, authorised or assumed by some colleagues, systems and official curriculum documents. This may in part be attributable to what the participants earlier reported as the constraining impact of the senior secondary English syllabus and examinations. Antithetical responses to statements in this question serve to reinforce the potentially disruptive effect of a number of institutionalised practices and discourses on the early-career teacher's values, beliefs, ideals and level of satisfaction with teaching. This, in turn, may trigger a reconsideration of the motivations to teach and a re-evaluation of a teacher's career trajectory (Clandinin et al., 2015; Manuel, 2003; Schaefer, 2013). Research has found that when 'teaching motivations cannot be realised, it is likely that professional satisfaction and fulfilment will deteriorate and that teachers will experience burnout or leave the profession' (Heinz, 2015: 271).

In the light of these understandings from research in the fields of teacher motivation, retention and attrition the responses to the question of 'professional satisfaction' disclosed a troubling degree of discontent. 17 percent were 'very satisfied' with teaching English; one third were 'satisfied'; and the remaining 50 percent were 'unsure'. If levels of professional satisfaction can be taken as one of the predictors of teacher burnout and potential attrition (cf. Clandinin et al., 2015; Gold, 1996; Heinz, 2015; Mansfield, Wosnitza and Beltman, 2012; Schaefer, 2013) then the responses from the present study are cause for alarm.

Concluding reflections

The findings in this study corroborate those from other similar empirical studies nationally and internationally. Foremost amongst these are the consistencies in the altruistic and intrinsic motivational factors influencing the decision to teach: 'making a difference in people's lives'; a 'love of literature'; and a 'love of English as a subject'.

While a proportion of teachers in this study believed that their initial motivations, beliefs, values and ideals had been affirmed in their work, an equally significant proportion (50 percent) identified a dissonance between their 'subject paradigm' and 'subject pedagogy' and that apparent in the syllabus documents and assessment programs they were obliged to implement. These teachers' initial motivations proved vulnerable to the challenges posed by an intense workload, time-management and divergent views of the purpose of the subject in the senior years. Those who indicated that their beliefs about the subject and the role of literature did not cohere with the conceptualisations evident in official curriculum documents were those who also expressed:

- greater levels of dissatisfaction with their work;
- concerns about the constraining impact of syllabus requirements and examinations;
- uncertain or equivocal views about their efficacy and professional agency; and
- strong reservations about their career futures.

Of note in the data was the correlation between the length of time teaching, a decline in the potency of initial motivations and a waning of a sense of professional agency.

These findings have a number of implications. Firstly, it is necessary to conduct larger-scale inquiries to collect more substantial and representative data about early-career English teachers' experiences. Research in the field of teacher retention and attrition more generally has stressed the need to further understand the factors and conditions that contribute to new teachers' work satisfaction, wellbeing and continued motivation to teach (cf. Buchanan et al., 2013; Heinz, 2015). Conversely, it is equally vital to identify the factors and conditions that may imperil a new teacher's longevity in the profession (cf. Bullough and Hall-Kenyon, 2011; Ewing and Manuel, 2005; Goodwyn, 2011).

Secondly, the findings prompt a reconsideration of the ways pre-service English teachers are initiated into the profession. Explicit attention in the ITE phase to an ongoing process of self-reflection, problematising beliefs, values, ideals, goals and expectations, is a crucial means of building 'capacities for resilience and empowerment' (Johnson et al. 2010 cited in Buchanan et al., 2013: 126). As new teachers journey through the liminal phase of ITE, they can be supported more effectively to cross the threshold from imagined teacher to fully-fledged professional, equipped with 'badges of the faithful' and 'truths' (Brooks, 1983: 72) that are no longer taken as 'self-evident' but have been tested and validated by reflection and practical teaching experience.

Thirdly, this study has reinforced the finding from previous research that early-career English teachers encounter significant workload pressures, particularly in relation to teaching senior secondary English. Mentoring programs along with schemes that provide for a reduced teaching load in the first years of teaching (which do operate at the local level in some jurisdictions in NSW) can potentially ameliorate the commonly identified adverse conditions and experiences of early-career teachers.

The participants in this study entered teaching to maintain their engagement with the cognate discipline of English and were stirred by motivations that encompassed deeply-felt personal, intellectual and social aspirations. School systems and cultures that do not acknowledge and create cultural and intellectual spaces for new teachers to pursue these altruistic and intrinsic aspirations put at risk the 'long-term resilience and commitment' (Manuel and Hughes, 2006: 21) of the early-career professional.

Fourthly, and closely connected with these issues of teacher retention and attrition, it is incumbent upon those who work with early-career teachers to more consciously orchestrate their greater participation in decision-making processes that inevitably impact upon their classroom practice, beliefs and values, their levels of satisfaction and their professional agency.

Finally, the evidence gathered in this study has underlined the extent to which new teachers' ideals are at once robust but at the same time susceptible to being shaken by situational forces that they cannot readily or simply alter or overcome. The perspectives presented here have offered a window into the aspirations and lived experiences of one group of early-career English teachers. Their love of literature, their passion for influencing young people's lives and their profound investment in the subject of English are values that are not only worth celebrating, they bespeak the integrity of their vocation and forecast the future quality of the English teaching profession. For these reasons alone, research must continue to address the processes of their identity formation as teachers and the impact of contextual forces and conditions that may ultimately jeopardise their altruistic commitment to 'making a difference'.

Notes

1 The model of ITE in Australia is typically 70 percent university-based, with in-school professional experience or practicum comprising around 30 percent of the program (in both undergraduate double degrees and graduate-entry degrees).
2 The teacher accreditation authority, the Board of Studies, Teaching and Educational Standards (BoSTES), requires entrants to English ITE programs to have a minimum number of 'literature-based' undergraduate units as pre-requisites for study.
3 The Higher School Certificate is undertaken in the final year of senior secondary schooling. It is the exit credential and matriculation requirement for a majority of students in NSW.

References

Ball, S. J. (2003) The teacher's soul and the terrors of performativity. *Journal of Education Policy*, 18 (2): 215–228.

Ball, S. J., Kenny, A., and Gardiner, D. (1990) Literacy, politics and the teaching of English. In I. Goodson and P. Medway (eds) *Bringing English to Order: The History and Politics of a School Subject* (47–86), London: The Falmer Press.

Biesta, G., Priestley, M., and Robinson, S. (2015) The role of beliefs in teacher agency. *Teachers and Teaching*, 21 (6): 624–640.

Britzman, D. (1992) *Practice Makes Practice: A Critical Study of Learning to Teach*. Albany, NY: SUNY Press.

Brock, P. (1984) *A History of the Development of English Syllabuses in New South Wales Secondary Education, 1953–1976: A 'Continuum' or a 'Series of New Beginnings'?* Unpublished PhD Thesis, Armidale: University of New England.

Brock, P. (1996) Telling the story of the NSW Secondary English curriculum: 1950–1965. In B. Green and C. Beavis (eds) *Teaching the English Subjects: Essays on English Curriculum and History in Australian Schooling* (40–70), Geelong: Deakin University Press.

Brooks, C. St. John (1983) English: A curriculum for personal development. In M. H. A. Hargreaves (ed) *Curriculum Practice* (37–59), Lewes: The Falmer Press.

Buchanan, J., Prescott, A., Schuck, S., Aubusson, P., Burke, P., and Louviere, J. (2013) Teacher retention and attrition: Views of early career teachers. *Australian Journal of Teacher Education*, 38 (3): 112–128.

Bullough, R. V. (1997) Becoming a teacher: Self and the social location of teacher education. In B. J. Biddle, T. L. Good, and I. F. Goodson (eds) *International Handbook of Teachers and Teaching* (79–134), Dordrecht/Boston/London: Kluwer Academic Publishers.

Bullough, R. V. and Hall-Kenyon, K. M. (2011) The call to teach and teacher hopefulness. *Teacher Development*, 15 (2): 127–140.

Clandinin, D. J., Long, J., Schaefer, L., Downey, C. A., Steeves, P., Pinnegar, E., McKenzie Robblee, S., and Wnuk, S. (2015) Early career teacher attrition: Intentions of teachers beginning. *Teaching Education*, 26 (1): 1–16.

Davies, C. (1996) *What is English Teaching?* Buckingham: Open University Press.

Ewing, R. and Manuel, J. (2005) Retaining quality early career teachers in the profession: New teacher narratives. *Change: Transformations in Education*, 7 (1): 4–18.

Gold, Y. (1996) Beginning teacher support: Attrition, mentoring, and induction. In J. Sikula (ed) *Handbook of Research on Teacher Education* (548–592), New York: Simon and Schuster Macmillan.

Goodwyn, A. (2004) The professional identity of English teachers. *English in Australia*, 139: 122–130.

Goodwyn, A. (2011) The impact of the framework for English: Teachers' struggle against 'informed prescription'. A. Goodwyn and C. Fuller (eds) *The Great Literacy Debate*, London: RoutledgeFalmer.

Goodwyn, A. (2012) The status of literature: English teaching and the condition of literature teaching in schools. *English in Education*, 46 (3): 212–227.

Green, B. and Beavis, C. (eds) (1996) *Teaching the English Subjects: Essays on English Curriculum History and Australian Schooling.* Geelong: Deakin University Press.

Heinz, M. (2015) Why choose teaching? An international review of empirical studies exploring student teachers' career motivations and levels of commitment to teaching. *Educational Research and Evaluation*, 21 (3): 258–297.

Kagan, D. M. (1992) Professional growth among preservice and beginning teachers. *Review of Educational Research*, 62: 129–169.

Lortie, D. (1975/2002) *Schoolteacher: A Sociological Study.* Chicago, IL: University of Chicago Press.

Mansfield, C. F., Wosnitza, M., and Beltman, S. (2012) Goals for teaching: Towards a framework for examining motivation of graduating teachers. *Australian Journal of Educational and Developmental Psychology*, 12: 21–34.

Manuel, J. (2003) Such are the ambitions of youth: Exploring issues of retention and attrition of early career teachers in New South Wales. *Asia-Pacific Journal of Teacher Education*, 31 (2): 139–151.

Manuel, J. and Brindley, S. (2005) The call to teach: Identifying pre-service teachers' motivations, expectations and key experiences during initial teacher education in Australia and the United Kingdom. *English in Australia*, 144: 38–49.

Manuel, J. and Brock, P. (2003) W(h)ither the Place of Literature?: Two Momentous Reforms in the NSW Senior Secondary English Curriculum. *English in Australia*, 136: 1–18.

Manuel, J. and Carter, D. (2016) Continuities of Influence: A critical analysis of subject English in the New South Wales' secondary school curriculum of 1911. *History of Education Review* (in press).

Manuel, J. and Hughes, J. (2006) 'It has always been my dream': Exploring pre-service teachers' motivations for choosing to teach. *Teacher Development*, 10: 5–24.

Mathieson, M. (1975) *The Preachers of Culture: A Study of English and Its Teachers*. London: George Allen and Unwin.

New South Wales Department of Education (2015) *2015 Teaching Workforce Supply and Demand*. Sydney: Author.

Reid, I. (1996) Romantic ideologies, educational practices, and institutional formations of English. *Journal of Educational Administration and History*, 28 (1): 22–41.

Schaefer, L. (2013) Beginning teacher attrition: A question of identity making and identity shifting. *Teachers and Teaching*, 19 (3): 260–274.

Schlichte, J., Yssel, N., and Merbler, J. (2005) Pathways to burnout: Case studies in teacher isolation and alienation. *Preventing School Failure*, 50: 35–41.

Weldon, P. R. (2015) The teacher workforce in Australia: Supply, demand and data issues. *Policy Insights*, Issue 2. Melbourne: ACER.

Yee, S. M. (1990) *Careers in the Classroom: When Teaching is More Than a Job*. New York: Teachers College Press.

9

RETHINKING LITERATURE 'INSTRUCTION'

An experiment with student-controlled pedagogy and *Animal Farm*

Lisa Scherff

Classroom conversations have long been a topic of research, with findings highlighting intrinsic patterns in this type of institutional talk (e.g., Cazden, 1988; Mehan, 1985; Nystrand & Gamoran, 1991): the prevalence of monologic talk and a heavy emphasis on the initiation-response-evaluation (IRE) pattern, both of which can be used to establish control and/or position students in ways that set up a cultural model of learning that privileges the teacher (Lester, Scherff, & Paulus, 2015).

While the IRE sequence may help students learn what they are supposed to know, it can also inhibit students' participation in both teacher-student and student-student interactions, which can result in missed opportunities for students to construct their own knowledge and understandings (Bloome, 1994; Nystrand, Gamoran, Kachur, & Prendergast, 1997). Blau (2011) notes that in order to actually learn ideas, students must have them first, and that means reaching an understanding of ideas through their own reading and experience. When teachers impart textual meanings, students do not really know the material.

Breaking away from monologic (and IRE) patterns can be difficult. Most teachers 'suffer from ... 'the anxiety of the right reading,' (Blau, 2003) and take great pains to give their students the reading they regard as standard or authoritative' (Blau, 2011, p. 6). As such, students can attain success in their English classes without having to earn it through work, as Hinchman and Zalewski (1996) found. Complicating the issue, because students have been exposed to the IRE pattern so often during their schooling, they come to expect that this is how classroom discussions should be run (Johannessen & Kahn, 2005). Moreover, many students are also unwilling to do the interpretive work required for class discussions and activities. Thus, without stamina and practice they do not know how to answer the questions posed by the teacher (Blau, 2011).

As a high school English teacher I am often disappointed in the quality of classroom discussions around text. The same few students who read the text and are prepared for class answer most of the questions I pose. The rest sit passively and wait to hear the answers so they can write them down. Or, as my colleagues and I have seen, with the prevalence of smart phones, students take pictures of their peers' work, copy the answers, and turn in 'their' work. Both of these result in the same thing: most students do not actually learn the material, which then results in them doing poorly on formative and summative class assignments and—worse—not passing high-stakes tests required for graduation.

In an attempt to make students more responsible for their learning, I designed a unit of instruction around the novel *Animal Farm* where students were given the work ordinarily completed by the teacher: present background knowledge, create discussion questions, and lead class discussions. This chapter reports on action research undertaken in the fall of 2015 in a tenth grade honors English classroom to answer the question: *how can I transfer control of teaching and learning of* Animal Farm *to students in a way that promotes authentic learning?* A secondary, related question is: *when, and how, do I step in when needed and still honor the students' autonomy?*

Theoretical foundations

Theoretically, this research is based broadly on sociocultural theories, which posit that teaching and learning are interactive processes where students and the teacher play important roles (Maloch, 2002), and 'our ways of understanding the world … are sustained through daily interactions … especially those that involve language' (Burr, 2003, cited in Unrau & Alvermann, 2013, p. 61). Literature discussions are an important sociocultural activity because through language students respond to others' interpretations and use this information to generate new understandings or verify what they already believe (Hall, Burns, & Edwards, 2011). In this way, literature discussions also foster critical thinking: 'a process whereby a person reflects upon his/her own thinking process so as to create clear, well-reasoned ideas for the benefit of him/herself and others' (Mulcahy, 2008, p. 17). Also influencing the research is constructivism, in particular Vygotsky's (1978) research on the role of talk between individuals in collaboratively building knowledge (Unrau & Alvermann, 2013).

Integral to both of these theories is the role of instructional scaffolding (Bruner, 1973). Langer and Applebee (1986) define instructional scaffolding as

> simplifying the situation, clarifying the structure, helping the student accomplish tasks that would otherwise be too difficult, and providing the framework and rules of procedure that the student will gradually learn, so that the instructional support will no longer be necessary.
>
> *(p. 181)*

The study

As stated earlier, I undertook action research to answer the question: *how can I transfer control of teaching and learning of Animal Farm to students in a way that promotes authentic learning?* Action research is a systematic process of inquiry conducted by and for those taking the action. The primary goal is to help the researcher improve and/or refine his or her actions (Sagor, 2000). Action research uses a cyclical, action-reflection model to investigate and attempt to make change in a setting (Noffke & Somekh, 2009).

Setting

I teach at a public high school (grades 9 through 12) with roughly 1,700 students in Southwest Florida. In tenth grade, students are assigned to either a regular (on level) or honors (advanced) English class. Honors-level classes typically include more essay writing and novel study than the regular classes. With our mandated textbook comes two novels for classroom use: *Animal Farm* and *Farewell to Manzanar*. I chose to use *Animal Farm* as I thought it would be more challenging for the students. *Animal Farm* is a 'classic' novel that is taught all over the world and in a range of schools. Moreover—and more even more timely in our current political climate(s)—it 'is a fable that offers simple, valuable political lessons … power corrupts; revolutions tend to come full circle and devour their peoples; and even good, decent people not only hunger for power, but also worship powerful leaders' (Rodden, 2003, p. 75). At the time of this research, I taught 5 sections of tenth grade honors English, each class ranging from 29 to 32 students. 75% of the students were white, and 25% were students of color.

The *Animal Farm* unit came in the second quarter of the school year. Our school district uses a quarter system; each quarter lasts nine weeks and two quarters make up a semester. Prior to this unit, students had been reintroduced to literary elements (plot, theme, symbol, etc.) through the study of short stories. They had also briefly studied rhetorical devices and written argumentative essays.

Procedures

Before teaching the novel, I read it twice through and, looking through a range of teaching resources (e.g., EdSitement, literary criticism guides), I determined the end goals I hoped to accomplish: to have students take more ownership of their learning, an understanding of the author's intent in writing the novel; the novel as an allegory; the novel's connection to the present; the role of propaganda in the novel and society; and, foundational to English classes, literary elements in the novel (satire, plot, characterization, themes, etc.). However, beyond these goals, an overarching objective was to make novel study more fun and engaging than what traditional instruction often entails (vocabulary words to learn by chapter, chapter-based, teacher-made discussion questions, chapter quizzes, reading chapter-by-chapter in class out loud, or listening to the book on tape).

Before beginning the novel, students ($n = 162$) in all five classes were given: (1) a brief PowerPoint overview of the novel unit, including themes, key ideas and background, their tasks, and how they would be assessed; (2) a handout explaining the goals for the unit and their responsibilities (see Figure 9.1); and (3) options for a final project. For each class I created a Google Classroom to house all materials for the unit and as a place for students to upload and share their work with each other. Students were told that we would read and discuss the first chapter together, with me presenting sample discussion questions. After that, students would read Chapters 2 through 4 on their own and prepare discussion questions for the group based. We would repeat that process after they read the remaining chapters. Students would be assessed on their contributions not only in their self-created discussion groups but also through participation in the whole class discussions. Instead of a test at the end of the novel, students would have an in-class essay and choice among three project options (see Appendix).

The first task for students was to get into groups of two to five students of their choosing and select and research one of the background area/terms (fable, satire, irony, Communism, Marxism, propaganda techniques, Russian history and revolution, Orwell's life and influences) to research and present it to their peers in a 4 to 6 minute presentation involving some type of multimedia or handout. Students were given 90 minutes of class time to work in the computer lab and prepare their presentations, two days at home (if they chose), and 15 minutes in class to finalize their work.

Guidelines for students

After the group presentations were completed, I read chapter one aloud to them, stopping to talk about parts that connected to their work on the background terms and ideas. I then posed sample discussion questions and provided students with a handout that offered a range of question stems. I showed how these could be used to help students as they read on their own and prepared for their class discussions. Students were given three weeks to read Chapters 2 through 4 and prepare for their discussions; they were given two additional weeks to read the remaining chapters and prepare for discussion.

I collected several forms of data including audiotapes of two whole class discussions (the remaining recordings were inaudible), teacher-made materials (PowerPoints, handouts, etc.), student-generated materials (discussion questions, handouts, PowerPoints, etc.), communication and posts on Google Classroom, student end-of-unit surveys, and field notes/reflections. In the section that follows, I present findings and discussion related to two forms of data I collected: student-generated discussion questions and student surveys. Unfortunately, the audiotapes from the classroom discussions were corrupted and could not be used. However, the student-generated questions served as the base for these, so I felt I had enough data to proceed with analysis.

Findings and discussion

In this action research study I wanted to know if I could transfer control of teaching and learning to students in a way that promoted authentic learning and if and when I would need to step in and still honor the students' autonomy. Although on the surface these seem like modest questions, they are, in fact, rather complex when it comes to answering them. As such, in this section I weave the findings and discussion together in order to convey the analysis best.

Animal Farm group guidelines

This year we will be trying something different with reading and discussing novels. Gone are teacher-made packets of vocabulary and questions chapter-by-chapter. Instead, you will be in charge of what we re-read, discuss, and examine more closely. As mentioned on the PowerPoint, you will be responsible for nearly all that we do (I will fill in if critical points are missing).

Both times that we meet to discuss the novel, each group will be expected to have ready: (a) two to three discussion questions; (b) one to two important quotes to discuss; (c) a passage (at least one paragraph) for close reading and analysis (for literary elements, characterization, etc.); and (d) themes to talk about. In addition, each group should also consider tough/key vocabulary and other important literary elements (irony, symbolism, characterization, etc.) as they come up.

You will have plenty of time to read and collaborate together in order to lead classroom discussions.

Steps:

1   Select one to four other classmates to work with (groups of two to five students)
2   Access the Google Classroom site with the code provided
3   READ the assigned chapters
4   Communicate with each other via google docs and face-to-face (all documents that you create must be uploaded to the Google Classroom or emailed to me)
5   Collaborate during class meeting times to have your 'instructional plans' ready (items 1 through 4 above)
6   Groups will audio record their discussions and upload to the Google classroom site

Prepare instructional materials (passages to close read, handouts for peers, etc.) and get them to me at least 24 hours before class (so I can copy).

I first turn to results from the student survey. Figure 9.1 presents results from the eight-question survey I gave to students at the end of the *Animal Farm* unit. The questions were written to gain insight into the extent to which students preferred the unit design as opposed to traditional teacher-centered teaching and learning.

Most students (73%) agreed and strongly agreed that their past experiences with reading novels was the traditional chapter-by-chapter method with vocabulary to define and discussion questions to answer. This finding supports the idea that teachers, for the most part, control the teaching and learning, with students relying on them for the direction of study and, most likely, the 'correct' answers. Students, however, were split in terms of how they felt about this traditional instruction: 38% reported liking this type of instruction, while 32% said they did not. This finding is not surprising as students' need for more teacher-centered instruction, and support, can change from text to text depending on that text's complexity in terms of language difficulty, and need for

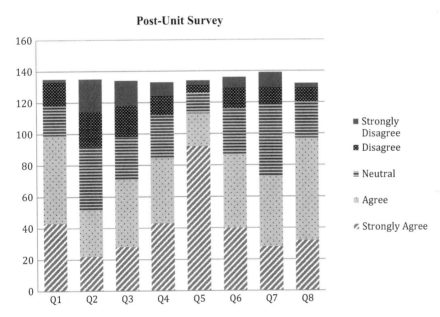

Post-Unit Survey

- Strongly Disagree
- Disagree
- Neutral
- Agree
- Strongly Agree

FIGURE 9.1 Post unit survey. Q1-In past English classes I read novels chapter-by-chapter with questions, vocabulary, reading checks, etc.; Q2-I like reading novels chapter-by-chapter with discussion questions, vocabulary, and reading quizzes; Q3-I liked reading *Animal Farm* in chunks; Q4-I liked coming up with questions rather than being assigned questions; Q5-I like not having a big test at the end of the novel; Q6-I like doing projects associated with novels; Q7-I learned a lot from reading this novel; Q8-I will remember what I read (at least elements or important points from the novel) next year or the year after.

background knowledge, among other items. As one student commented, 'It's [an] interesting way, but I don't like how lost I was in this reading. All of the papers you get for the book I think should be given in a packet.' However, this perspective was the minority. Many students wrote that they preferred this way of reading and discussing.

When asked specifically about reading *Animal Farm* in chunks (Question 3), rather than chapter-by-chapter, 53% indicated they liked this method. And, 63% responded (Question 4) that they liked coming up with the discussion questions themselves rather than me assigning them questions to answer. Many students remarked that they enjoyed this way of reading a novel. A student noted, 'I think reading *Animal Farm* this way was nice. Preferably I like to read the book on my own where I don't have to rely on everyone else and on the people who take their time reading.' For students like this, the chapter-by-chapter method in class is limiting. However, others needed (or wanted) more time in class for reading as vocalized by another student. 'I prefer to read novels in class. I can ask questions when I have them. If you continue the at-home reading, it would be nice to have more reading in class, to make sure everyone is understanding it.' One individual suggested that in the future we continue to do this but that I have more discussions in class so that they can, 'see [my] thoughts on the interpretation of the book,' which echoes back to Blau's (2011) notion of one standard interpretation of a work to impart on students.

As the findings show, for the most part, students liked coming up with their own questions; however, I learned from their comments that a few lacked self-confidence regarding their ability to create questions on their own or in groups. For such students, teacher-assigned questions are easier and perhaps build confidence in students' ability to answer them. Another set of students was frustrated with what they perceived as not enough accountability for them and their peers, which comes in the traditional teacher-led model of novel study. In my November 5th field notes, for example, I wrote, 'Some students/classes are not ready for this type of work (immature, lack of foundational knowledge). Does our system/pacing guide[1] not prepare them?'

Several commented that they liked coming up with discussion questions, but they knew some of their peers went to online sources (like Shmoop, an online study site) and copied questions down. Another issue was the number and type of questions I asked groups to come up with (see Figure 9.1). Upon reflection, this amount of work is too much to ask students to do at once, especially with a short novel. For example, while nearly all students were able to come up with discussion questions and/or quotes to discuss, many had difficulty with the close reading passages. Looking back, close reading passages and quotes are very similar, so I would eliminate one of them.

Another issue that has been presented is students' request for more time in class for discussion. Here, the issue is the novel itself. *Animal Farm* is rather short in comparison to other full-length works the students read. Because it is short, chunking the reading did not work as well as it would have with another novel. As one student aptly noted,

> I didn't like the idea of reading *Animal Farm* in chunks, which is why I ended up reading ahead and finishing it early. This didn't really work well considering some of the students have said that they did not even start the book, but that's their own fault.

With a longer novel, not only might there have been a better balance between in-class and out-of-class reading but also students' ability to come up with discussion topics and questions would have been increased.

The final question (#8) served as the bigger picture question: would students remember concepts and important points in the long term? Seventy-three percent noted that what they learned would be remembered in the future. This finding, for me, is powerful in terms of how well the unit went, overall. One student's open-ended response supports the survey findings and is a segue to the lessons I learned from this action research.

> I absolutely loved reading the novel this way! It actually made it easier to understand and more enjoyable. In past English classes the chapter-by-chapter and random quizzes almost made it dreadful. Plus I like when we come up with the discussion questions because that makes us have to know the question and the answer rather than the teacher give us the question all we have to do is find the answer rather than actually know it. I think we should definitely do it again. The only thing I'd changed is a better way to make sure we are reading, like maybe more frequent discussions. I really like the discussion.

The first lesson I learned is that if I do this type of unit again, I need to provide much more scaffolding for students. Reading one chapter and going through the process with students is not enough. I need to more explicitly and slowly implement instructional scaffolding (e.g., Bruner, 1973; Langer & Applebee, 1986), where I simplify the situation, clarify the structure, help students complete tasks that might be too hard, and provide the framework and rules for instruction. I found that coming up with quotes worked better than selecting close reading passages; so I need to provide direct instruction on how to do this. In addition, asking students to find a range of literary elements was not needed for what I hoped to accomplish. In the future, I will ask students to complete some tasks and I will complete the others.

Another lesson learned is that students generally liked chunks of reading over chapter-by-chapter reading; however, quite a few said they wanted more guidance and leading from me. Again, part of the issue was the novel being short; another was my lack of planning and time management. Based on student feedback, I think there are benefits of both methods—chunking and chapter-by-chapter—so in the future I will implement a combination of both methods.

More demanding chapters in a novel could be read and discussed in class, ensuring that more students understand the material, and other chapters could be read at home in chunks with students responsible for coming up with topics for the class to discuss.

When looking across the data, it seems that students who read the novel on their own and completed the work appreciated this type of novel study and even asked for more accountability (quizzes, reading checks) so that they could be validated for their efforts. However, those students who were not self-motivated needed more structure to ensure that they not only completed the reading but also participated in their discussion groups more fully and fairly.

Conclusion

One of the saddest ironies of conventional practice ... is that English teachers are endlessly worried about teaching their students the skills and processes of critical thinking and seem constantly to be lamenting the failure of their students to think critically about ... texts ... Yet, in trying to protect their students from the sense of failure that accompanies the confusions and problems that students inevitably experience in their encounters with difficult texts, teachers deprive students of the richest and most authentic opportunities that are likely to be found in an English class to engage deeply and productively in the kind of critical thinking that would allow them to recognize how and when they can exercise their own capacity for such thinking (Blau, 2011, p. 11).

The extended quote above from Sheridan Blau captures fittingly the tension I feel as a literature teacher: I want my students to think critically about texts—question them, react to them, respond back to them—yet I also need for them to understand the texts so that they perform well on the high-stakes tests, and in response to this tension I have often resorted to imparting knowledge rather than having students generate knowledge.

This action research project was a bold step in moving from telling to generating, and perhaps it was a little too bold for many of my students. As I approach designing the unit for this year, I will still incorporate aspects from my instructional plan, such as the students presenting background elements of the novel. And, I still hope to have more student-generated questions and discussions. However, I will have to provide more scaffolds and more in-class reading to confirm that more students are completing the work necessary to foster more critical thinking and engagement.

Appendix

Animal Farm final project options

Choose one of the following options. You can work alone, in pairs, or with the group you worked with throughout this novel unit. Please note that if you work with a group, you will be expected to produce A+ work, and no matter who does what everyone will receive the same grade. Choose group members carefully.

Option 1: propaganda posters

Create four propaganda posters of your own based on *Animal Farm*. Keep in mind the eight common propaganda techniques. Possible ideas:

- a poster that Old Major could have accompanied his speech with to convince the animals of the evils of man
- a poster that Napoleon could have created to motivate the animals to rebuild the windmill
- a poster that Squealer could have used to persuade other farms that *Animal Farm* is a wonderful place to live
- a poster Mr. Jones could have used to influence the animals to return control of the farm to him
- a poster that Boxer could have made to express his devotion to hard work
- a poster that any character, animal or human, might have used

Each poster must be at least 8.5 × 11 in. in size. None can be pencil drawings on notebook paper! Be professional!
Reference: https://sites.google.com/a/aveson.org/mr-tom/Home/johnny-tremaine/unit-5-persuasion-and-propoganda/propaganda-posters---animal-farm.

Option 2: theme triangle (Kelly Gallagher)

Identify what you believe is the central theme in the novel and write it in a complete sentence. Once you have decided on your theme, do the following:

- Analyze how the theme is developed in the novel (chapter-by-chapter)
- Choose a film to watch that addresses the same theme (you cannot use the film *Animal Farm*). Choose an appropriate film; obtain parent/guardian permission prior to watching the film. Everyone (if a group) is responsible for watching the film on his/her own time, with special attention paid to the theme.
- Find the theme in one example of some other medium or genre (song lyrics, art, photography, sculpture, speeches, books, etc.) in the modern world.
- Present your findings/theme triangle in a 5 to 10 minute presentation to the class in which you discuss the importance of your theme and how it relates to the other two points of the triangle—get as creative as you want!

Option 3: your own thug notes

Modeled after Thug Notes, create a video summary and analysis of *Animal Farm* from a particular 'perspective' (Southern, snobby, movie/TV character, etc.). Whatever perspective you choose, the language, dress, background, media examples, etc. must fit that perspective. Get creative!! You cannot do Thug Notes!

- Your video must be 4 to 7 minutes in length
- The entire video must fit the perspective chosen
- Even if not on camera all group members must have an active role (script writing, filming/editing, background/set design, costumes, etc.)
- Please use school-appropriate language (no four letter words).

Note

1 At the time of this research our school district had a mandated pacing guide that all teachers had to follow. It dictated which texts from the literature book were to be taught and when. The district linked these to quarterly online assessments that the students took.

References

Athanases, S. (1988). Developing a classroom community of interpreters. *English Journal, 77*(1), 45–48.

Blau, S. (2003). *The literature workshop: Teaching texts and their readers.* Portsmouth, NH: Heinemann.

Blau, S. (2011). Fostering authentic learning in the literature classroom. In J. O. Milner & C. Pope (Eds.), *Engaging American novels: Lessons from the classroom* (pp. 3–17). Urbana, IL: NCTE.

Bloome, D. (1994). Response to McCarthey: On the nature of language in classroom literacy research. *Reading Research Quarterly, 29*, 232–240.

Burr, V. (2003). *Social constructionism* (2nd ed.). New York: Routledge.

Bruner, J. S. (1973). *The relevance of education* (2nd ed.). New York: Norton.

Cazden, C. B. (1988). *Classroom discourse: The language of teaching and learning.* Portsmouth, NH: Heinemann.

Hall, L. A., Burns, L. D., & Edwards, E. C. (2011). *Empowering struggling readers: Practices for the middle grades.* New York: Guilford.

Hinchman, K. A., & Zalewski, P. (1996). Reading for success in a tenth-grade global-studies class: A qualitative study. *Journal of Literacy Research, 28*(1), 91–106.

Johannessen, L. R., & Kahn, E. (2005). Engaging students in authentic discussions of literature. In T. R. McCann, L. R. Johannessen, E. Kahn, P. Smagorinsky, & M. Smith (Eds.), *Reflective teaching, reflective learning: How to develop critically engaged readers, writers, and speakers* (pp. 99–116). Portsmouth, ME: Heinemann.

Keefer, M. W., Zeitz, C. M., & Resnick, L. B. (2000). Judging the quality of peer-led student dialogues. *Cognition and Instruction, 18*(1), 53–81.

Langer, J. A., & Applebee, A. N. (1986). Reading and writing instruction: Toward a theory of teaching and learning. *Review of Research in Education, 13,* 171–194.

Lester, J. N., Scherff, L., & Paulus, T. M. (2015). The ideological dilemmas inherent in informal learning spaces: A discourse analysis of preservice teacher talk. *The Qualitative Report, 20*(6), 830–846.

Maloch, B. (2002). Scaffolding student talk: One teacher's role in literature discussion groups. *Reading Research Quarterly, 37*(1), 94–112.

Marshall, J. D. (1989). *Patterns of discourse in classroom discussion of literature* (Rep. Series 2.9). Albany, NY: Center for the Learning and Teaching of Literature.

Mehan, H. (1985). The structure of classroom discourse. In T. A. van Dijk (Ed.), *Handbook of discourse analysis, Vol. 3. Discourse and dialogue* (pp. 119–131). Malden, MA: Blackwell.

Mulcahy, C. (2008). The tangled web we weave: Critical literacy and critical thinking. In L. Wallowitz (Ed.), *Critical literacy as resistance* (pp. 15–27). New York: Peter Lang.

Noffke, S. E., & Somekh, B. (Eds.) (2009). *The SAGE handbook of educational action research.* Thousand Oaks, CA: SAGE.

Nystrand, M. (2006). Research on the role of classroom discourse as it affects reading comprehension. *Research in the Teaching of English, 40,* 392–412.

Nystrand, M., & Gamoran, A. (1991). Instructional discourse, student engagement, and literature achievement. *Research in the Teaching of English, 25,* 261–290.

Nystrand, M., Gamoran, A., Kachur, R., & Prendergast, C. (1997). *Opening dialogue: Understanding the dynamics of language and learning in the English classroom.* New York: Teachers College Press.

Rodden, J. (2003). Appreciating *Animal Farm* in the new millennium. *Modern Age, 45*(1), 67–76.

Sagor, R. (2000). *Guiding school improvement with action research.* Alexandria, VA: ASCD.

Unrau, N. J., & Alvermann, D. E. (2013). Literacies and their investigation through theories and models. In D. E. Alvermann, N. J. Unrau, & R. B. Ruddell (Eds.), *Theoretical models and processes of reading* (6th ed., pp. 47–90). Newark, DE: International Reading Association.

Vygotsky, L. (1978). *Mind in society: The development of higher psychological processes.* In M. Cole, V. John-Steiner, S. Scribner, & E. Souberman (Eds.), Cambridge, MA: Harvard University Press.

10

'WHOSE ENGLISH IS THIS, ANYWAY?' MOTHER TONGUES AND LITERATURES OF THE BORDERLANDS

Rodrigo Joseph Rodríguez

Rivers of languages
los ríos de idiomas
flow here
past deltas and borders and boundaries into towns and cities
rise in homes and libraries and schools,
voices rising like poetry and bread.
Languages remind us where we begin.

—R. Joseph Rodríguez (2017)

English language arts and literacy education can be contested subjects, especially in the preparation of educators who will teach in secondary-level schools with students whose first language may be Arabic, Chinese, Hindi, Kachiquel, Spanish, and Vietnamese, among additional world languages spoken by families in the United States. For some U.S. teachers and students alike, English may be perceived as the language of domination and imperialism, while others may practice English as a language of access and opportunity with the elements of literacy in action—both in and out of school: knowing, listening, memorizing, noticing, observing, performing, questioning, reading, speaking, thinking (metacognition), understanding/you (literati), viewing, and writing. In an essay on community language learning and maintenance, Fránquiz (2011) acknowledges, 'Not knowing the individual stories behind our efforts to retain our bilingualism and biliteracy makes us vulnerable to divisions. Our diverse stories provide the foundation for coalition building and achieving solidarity' (p. 132).

Teachers interested in the inclusion of diverse literary and linguistic traditions have re-examined their attitudes and perceptions about the role of reading, writing, authorship, and representation in the classroom and in our global society.

The act of literacy is neither a solitary nor political act, but one that calls for awareness, positionality, and advocacy in the act of becoming literate in our participatory democracy. In fact, Carol D. Lee and Anika Spratley (2010) note, '[A]ttitudes about language and assumptions about ability have served as a lens through which curriculum, assessment, and teacher training have been filtered' (p. 253). The filtering can influence how students are introduced to diverse literatures and its connection to their lived lives.

World languages are native to the continental United States and challenge the perception of English as the sole language of imperialism and domination. The result of domination is language loss and even indifference toward the civic and cultural communities a world language represents. In particular, Stephen May (2012) observes,

> Language loss is not only, perhaps not even primarily, a linguistic issue— it has much more to do with power, prejudice, (unequal) competition and, in many cases, overt discrimination and subordination. […] The loss of a minority language almost always forms part of a wider process of social, cultural and political displacement.
>
> *(p. 4)*

In response to the growing losses and indifferences, the sense of belonging is essential for language learners in English language arts classrooms. In fact, their cultural origin and contributions for dual language learning further affirms their identity formation.

In the presence of English and in recognition of the vast human cultures and world literatures that encounter English as the academic standard, however, students in secondary-level schools and higher education are adapting to diverse world languages that co-exist with English as the media of communications in everyday literacies and for literary studies. Moreover, the expansion of the redefined and reformed literary canon now includes diverse storytellers, narratives, and multiliteracies across multigenres. In the guideline titled *Professional Knowledge for the Teaching of Writing* (2016) and issued by the National Council of Teachers of English, teachers are informed about the linguistic and cultural wealth students possess alongside English: 'Knowledge of students' cultural and linguistic background and the way that background intersects or differs from English language conventions helps ensure that students are receiving instruction appropriate for their current stage of language learning.'

Prior to reaching a period of valuing multiculturalism and the rich literary traditions of peoples native to the formation and growth of the United States, colonial practices and oppressive regimes against world language education reigned among many legislators and curriculum leaders. For instance, in the book *The Strange Career of Bilingual Education in Texas, 1836–1981* (2007), Carlos Kevin Blanton notes the linguistic and cultural wealth of native, migrant, and immigrant communities in Texas and the making of public education. He writes:

> The bilingual tradition in Texas during the nineteenth century was rich and vibrant, involving several different ethnic and immigrant groups such as Tejanos [native Texas Mexicans], German Americans, and Czech Americans. Policymakers and ethnic communities saw bilingual education's greatest potential as that of Americanizing children. [...] Mexican Americans found Americanization during the next decades to be synonymous with racial segregation; its curricular adjunct, English-Only pedagogy, became the pedagogical tool to ensure the legality of such segregation.
>
> *(p. 153)*

The segregation of children and adolescents in schools further alienated them from equal access to resources and equitable treatment in their schooling with limited access to postsecondary studies. In fact, Blanton argues, 'English-Only proponents regarded bilingual education as educationally backward, ineffective, and un-American, and required teachers to instruct language minorities in English, without any reference to or use of native languages' (p. 153).

In the twenty-first century, English remains a significant language in the study of American and adolescent literatures in U.S. secondary-level schools. To further interrogate the uses of English and the presence of additional native and world languages, this chapter documents the ways to navigate a prominent English-language presence in coexistence with additional world languages on the printed and electronic page as well as in both private and public spaces. The following two questions are addressed in the chapter: (1) How are mother tongues (indigenous languages, Spanish, and a few others) introduced and negotiated through the study of American and adolescent literatures in secondary-level schools? (2) What can teachers do through the vision of an expanded and revisionist American literary canon to define English language arts and literacy education as the medium for students in a diverse U.S. and global society?

Accordingly, language arts and literacy education must coexist with world languages interconnected to English with the following two goals: (a) to advance a literate, socially responsible and caring citizenry; and (b) to increase the sum of knowledge across mother tongues and literatures in the borderlands and global corridors on planet Earth.

Naming the world for understanding

To name the world often begins in one's first language, or mother tongue, which is a critical language for literacy that informs the learning of additional world languages as well as sociocultural identity formation. Bharati Mukherjee (2004) acknowledges,

There is a reason why the language we inherit at birth is called our mother tongue. It is our mother, forgiving, embracing, naming the world and all its emotions. Though I have lived for the last forty years in cities where English or French is the language of the majority, it's Bangla that exercises motherly restraint over my provisional, immigrant identity.

(p. 11)

With this declaration, Mukherjee establishes the origin of world languages in her life and what informs her meaning-making through Bangla, or Bengali, a language spoken by more than 300 million people in Bangladesh with speakers around the world. She adds,

To be born displaced *Bangal* was to inherit loss of, and longing for, one's true home. Identity had to do with mother tongue, but home was the piece of land that our forefathers had owned, the soil that they had slept and walked on.

(p. 13)

Mukherjee's perspectives are instructive for our reading and understanding of English language arts and literacy education in the United States, even across geographies. She notes the British colonial presence that partitioned a continent and even international relief workers who perceive Bangla as the 'mother tongue of esurient poverty' (p. 11). Mukherjee describes the literary traditions that include drama, epic poetry, ghost stories, and orature. Overall, borderlands, economies, homelands, identities, lands, origins, and ownership reveal the interconnectedness of world languages and literatures and how these unfold in hierarchies and the valuing of human creativity, imagination, and intellect.

Efforts for the inclusion of diverse American letters challenge the traditional study and compartmentalization of English language arts and American, British, and world literatures as is the case in borderlands regions around the world. English and literary study need not possess solely an exclusive European lens for reading, interpretation, and value-added measures. The canon must be expanded in both representation and interrogation across time to the present and representative of diverse peoples' contribution to the narratology. Aranda (2003) explains,

Despite the multiple, non-Anglo Saxon, colonial enterprises that also laid claim on the North American continent from the 1500s on, the field of Early American literature has been consistently constructed to promote a singular cultural vision of United States history and literature.

(p. xvii)

To challenge such an enterprise, researchers and teachers of literature cannot overlook the encounter of various languages and literatures, which deliver meaning that becomes transnational and transcultural and thus reveal human interconnectedness across nation-states and human cultures for understanding. The construction of what constitutes valid and classical literature, even as a contemporary classic text, must be questioned for positionality as well as disregard for an inclusive canon that represents diverse voices and ethnicities for the study of literature.

For instance, in the poem '*Tu que sabes de amor*' ('You Who Speaks of Love') by Sandra Cisneros (1994b), borderlands law enforcement and binational citizenship meet nature and humanity with telling humor in harsh, competing circumstances. In two poignant lines, the speaker comments on the free, unrestricted movement of clouds across the Río Grande and between two countries (p. 73). For the natural movement of clouds, legal documentation is not a requirement. Further, in juxtaposing imagery, the poem reveals the geographies of the borderlands that apprehend, control, and disrupt humans daily: their languages, lives, and psyches. Additional lines from the poem capture a splitting of both selfhood and space with angst that rises daily in binational citizens' everyday lives. The speaker in the poem acknowledges the encounters and disruptions that unfold through biculturalism, bilingualism, biliteracy, and difference, and are faced by citizens across geographies. The poem is further demarcated by the presence of a named defect with deficit-based repercussions in language, literature, and migration that appear as a crack or fissure for many bodies and migrants who must possess documentation and non-alien identities.

In the book *Indian Given: Racial Geographies across Mexico and the United States* (2016), Saldaña-Portillo explains,

> Geography is not only a discipline for mapping the world to be seen: it is also a way of disciplining what we see, of disciplining us into seeing (and knowing) mapped space as racialized space. [...] Colonialisms produced not only large reservoirs of cultural meaning attached to race but also new spaces and modes of apprehending landscapes.
>
> *(p. 18)*

The geographies that Saldaña-Portillo acknowledges extend beyond the hemispheric Américas and apply to countries such as Bangladesh, Belgium, Czechoslovakia, France, Germany, Greece, Israel, Italy, Iran, Kenya, Pakistan, Spain, Syria, and Turkey, among others, and the mother tongues that provide communications and access for human deliberations and transactions. Also, the act of seeing and experiencing literature is also a 'discipline for mapping the world,' which is influenced by the literatures teachers select to teach in English language arts and literacy education. As a result, teachers can bring the realities, struggles, and turmoil of the world to the literature classroom, so students can enact multiliteracies as socially responsible citizens across nations and cultures.

As a majority language in the presence of cultural confluence and linguistic diversity, English poses questions about language hierarchies and colonization, yet communicates the need for rethinking terms and perspectives about non-majorities who choose English and inclusive world languages for literary production and communications. For educators, the teaching of English and its diverse literatures becomes a fluid act in constant movement and change. Literary narratives adopt and redefine various Englishes, indigenous languages, and community and heritage languages, ranging from sanctioned erasure to current language maintenance approaches alongside the English language as a channel or vessel for communications.

Gorter, Zenotz, and Cenoz (2013) insist,

> Whereas in the past relative isolation in a peripheral area worked as protection for the survival of minority languages, globalization enters the life of minority speakers. Advances in telecommunications and international transport make it impossible to remain isolated from the influences of ideas and products of other cultures.
>
> *(p. 2)*

As a result, in the borderlands of the United States and global corridors around the world, teachers and students explore the crossroads, meeting points, and divergences of mother tongues and diverse literacies to becoming educated and learned in English. The languages of communications via technologies and social media provide more interactive modes of enacting literacies for communications and progress, albeit in varied measures of participation that can still isolate global communities. World communications also introduce approaches relevant to the study of literature and ways of introducing students to characters who face dilemmas, struggle with identities, and thrive while gaining a sense of belonging.

Finding American literatures

To define culture in a classroom and society and to see and experience it in practice in the English language arts classroom across geographies and narratives calls for introspection by students and rethinking by teachers who are ultimately responsible for what they select and sanction as possessing literary merit for study and inclusion. Teachers with decision-making authority from text selection to literary valuing communicate which stories matter and must maintain readership in their classrooms. Consider the following reflection from a younger reader about finding literature in a secondary-level school.

The boy at the window is thumbing through a high school reader of American literature. He is in the second-floor bookroom of his high school on Dickson Street in Houston, Texas. The books are lined neatly in the wall cases, and only the sun lights the room's solitude. As he sits on a desk before the large pair of bright window panes, the boy makes use of the light and seclusion to read at leisure. The bookroom has a leathery scent with bound texts everywhere, everywhere, everywhere! The wooden floorboards creak with each step the boy makes through the aisles. He hears the hum of the air-conditioner unit. The boy moves cautiously between the aisles, so as not to be heard or get caught. He is not in his assigned classroom as he should be; he fears detention, boredom; he wants victory through books. Today he has chosen the bookroom as his classroom to discover the literary readings he is not assigned.

The boy in the high school bookroom was me when I was searching for narratives and poetics about families, languages, cultures, and worlds that resembled that of my own and my global neighbors. Although I was getting groomed in the classics and for standardized exams (mostly criterion-referenced assessments), I had contemporary and everyday interests about growing up that I yearned to find, read, and discuss in my English language arts classes. While a few teachers were interested in a democratic process for text selection, the majority followed and supported the scripted, rote model of instruction and learning. This was in 1989; I was fourteen and, like any ninth grader, full of lofty ideas and haphazardly driven by popular and diverse cultural knowledge.

Our high school library holdings hardly reflected our school reader population and equity standards, and the local neighborhood library was still in its infancy regarding diverse collections. Municipal libraries, although growing with books and periodicals, needed more diverse volumes and multimedia in its holdings to reflect its residents. Fortunately, my home library was growing steadily with the extra money I earned from after-school employment and candy sales.

In retrospect, I must have seemed like an outcast because of the ideas I shared with my peers and teachers and because of the limited inspiration I found in the textbooks the state adopted for our student use. Yes, I was living in my native Texas in the late 1980s, and the age of high-stakes testing was taking shape. The high-stakes testing approach, founded upon scripted instruction in the name of accountability, was born and has led, in part, to government programs such as Race to the Top and other performance pay and incentive systems that dictate teacher quality and education across the country.

Although I believed I was on a college-bound path, I became aware of how tests were driving what I learned and unlearned. Because of them, I could neither express myself with creative freedom on the blank page nor question what I read and reread in the classroom. Instead, testing dictated the conditions for learning for both adolescent students and teaching professionals in public schools. For instance, I was trained to read disassembled passages and mimic a formulaic persuasive essay exercise for scorers to grade and later to determine my graduation eligibility. The competitive scoring approach hardly reflected learning and research to increase the sum of knowledge.

By contrast, during the school hours, the bookroom was my haven and offered my introduction to diverse U.S. literatures. Rules were absent as I read out of interest and conviction and unbound from state standards and punitive regulations. To my surprise, I found a high school reader that braided many of our national voices and advanced literacy education. Literature was not exclusionary, but held an intentional inclusion approach by those who assembled the textbook. The

1979 *United States in Literature* (Miller et al.) began with the poems 'It Bids Pretty Fair' by Robert Frost and 'My Mother Pieced Quilts' by Teresa Palomo Acosta. The poems complemented each other for biliteracy across various traditions from New England to the Southwestern United States and captured my attention as a young reader.

The series editors, affiliated with the professional organization National Council of Teachers of English (NCTE), modeled and advanced an independent approach through literary inclusion, defining 'American' through pluralism and diverse viewpoints. The editors' approach redefined canonical literature at the secondary-school level. Though ten years later the book was no longer in use, I had found it on a bottom shelf of the bookroom and read from it as much as I could on a day spent outside of the classroom. I was motivated by what I had discovered as a young, voracious reader in adolescence.

I read with a mixture of awe and fear. Why did I feel like Esperanza Cordero, the protagonist in Sandra Cisneros's *The House on Mango Street* (1994a), who feels both alone, lonesome, and valiant? Why did I resemble the middle-grade character in Jeff Anderson's series named *Zack Delacruz: Me and My Big Mouth* (2015)? Although later hailed as a hero with convictions, Zack initially goes out of his way in avoiding the world before him and the early adolescents among him in middle school. Besides, this was my first civil disobedience in the name of literacy. Perhaps I felt this way because, as an active reader, I became power- and text-literate; I challenged the schooling norms and scripted reading tasks. I wanted the unwritten, hidden curricula to be revealed and taught, and through my search I found the readings that led to my self-actualization.

The irony of Frost's poem rang true for this emerging thinker, especially the last line about the lighting not changing or, even worse, going out in the room. The high school reader I had found was modeled on an American, quilt-like mosaic described in Acosta's poem, braiding and 'cementing' a diverse canon of voices relevant to our nation's formation, thought, and identity through the centuries (Acosta 7). The textbook series editors explained that their vision and approach were not driven by a formula, but by a sense of wholeness and optimism (Miller et al., p. 4). In addition, the series resembled an initiation for the next generation of readers, writers, teachers, and scholars into the language arts profession. The irony would be that ten years later the book was no longer in use, yet a newly adopted series from the publisher Harcourt Brace Jovanovich, Pegasus edition, favored the practice of literary inclusion with more authors of cultural and linguistic backgrounds.

NCTE and high literacy standards

The visionary approach for a high school reader was enlightening and resembled the high standards of teaching reading, writing, language, and literature I later came to associate with NCTE. In the process of expanding my interests in English and cultural studies, I began regular correspondence with authors, educators, and editors such as Toni Cade Bambara, Gwendolyn Brooks, Carlota Cárdenas de Dwyer, Denise Chávez, Sandra Cisneros, Roseann Dueñas González, Pat Mora, Naomi Shihab Nye, Américo Paredes, Richard Rodriguez, Gary Soto, Tino Villanueva, and Alice Walker. These thinkers encouraged me in my literary pursuits toward higher education.

While pursuing my undergraduate studies at Kenyon College, I examined my own interests in the advancement of diverse U.S. letters and how I could cultivate a readership among my future students in the teaching profession. I read Toni Cade Bambara's (1996) essay on language, form, and societal change and understood then that I had a responsibility as a global reader and apprentice teacher for cultural preservation and orature:

> There is no American literature; there are American literatures. There are those who have their roots in the most ancient civilizations—African, Asian, or Mexican—and there are those that have the most ancient roots in this place, that mouth-to-ear tradition of the indigenous peoples that were here thousands and thousands of years before it was called America, thousands of years before it was even called Turtle Island. And there is too the literature of the European settlement regime that calls itself American literature.
>
> *(p. 140)*

Bambara's concept of American literatures informed my graduate teaching apprenticeship, dissertation research, and later the literature, language, and culture courses I taught in secondary-level schools and at the university level.

What makes a language, a language for literary study? The poet and scholar Ofelia Zepeda (1995) explains about the orature and language of the Tohono O'odham indigenous people of southern Arizona,

> 'Throwing words into the air'—this is what O'odham say about talking, storytelling, praying, singing—all of which make up the genre of oral tradition. The words are thrown into the air in the form of spoken word, song, oration or invocation. Words, like things that can be carried by the air, are at the mercy of the winds. The listener who happens to be on the receiving end of these words is also at the mercy of the winds.
>
> *(p. 5)*

Zepeda promotes what she calls the 'continuum of literacy' in which students 'mesh the oral and written tradition into one' (p. 10). In her studies of student thinking and writing, Zepeda found narratives grounded in 'the common series of events where the hero or the heroine of the story must go through some magnificent metamorphosis if they are to succeed in some adventure, dilemma, or journey' (p. 15). In a similar vein today, teachers work closely with students in secondary schools as they co-lead author studies, literature circles, digital narratives, and reading groups. Working alongside other teachers and our own students, we learn that students seek literary characters and favor reading and writing experiences that reflect their life choices and questions in both public and private spaces. These choices and questions can be explored through both classics and contemporary classics in English language arts and additional world languages.

The literary readings that sustain our students have authentic interest, build trust, and may even transport them to other times, problems, and spaces and back again. Over the years and through the support of NCTE colleagues and mentors, I engage in conversations about teaching, scholarship, leadership, and service. Since joining NCTE in 1997, I have worked with members who include preservice, beginning, and experienced educators and scholars; we have formed committees and founded groups for professional inclusion, learning, and growth. Overall, we are committed to social change, justice, action, and reflection that can bring literacy opportunities to the lives of our students—of all ages, abilities, backgrounds, colors, and interests—and their diverse communities.

Revisit and rethink our actions

Critical reflection and deeper thinking on schooling habits and practices are essential to maintain an interactive and reciprocal relationship for teaching and learning between teacher and student and among students. To take a case in point, Vasquez, Tate, and Harste (2013) propose a practice of critical literacies for social change. They argue,

> Education, like literacy, is never innocent. Even further, it is always about change, and even more specifically, cultural change. While one can argue that education should preserve culture, in reality education has always been about changing culture. The trick, we suppose, is to continually re-visit and re-think what we are doing.
>
> *(p. 6)*

Thus, English language arts and literacy education teachers must remain cognizant of their practices as they relate to human cultures, world languages, and literary study in support of literacies that are representative of diverse people, perspectives, and narratives.

To whom does English language arts belong? In fact, whose English is this, anyway? Literacy in action is synonymous with advocacy work and belongs to us all. Both teachers and teacher educators can advocate for language arts education that involves our everyday society and engages students, families, and community members across all ages, backgrounds, colors, interests, and needs in the practice of literacy for learning and understanding. Oftentimes, this means experiencing literacy as a social transaction as advanced by Rosenblatt (1995) to Morrell's (2015) most recent 'four challenges around which the practice of powerful English teaching in the twenty-first century can be conceptualized' (p. 5). Essentially, the language arts and literacy classroom is about collaborating, connecting, and creating among thinkers and learners with diverse mother tongues. Morrell emphasizes, 'No matter what technological innovations arise, the core classroom transactions are between teachers and students, students and students, and students and the texts that they consume and create' (p. 5). More specifically, the four challenges advocated by Morrell are as follows:

1   Develop powerful readers of multicultural texts.
2   Develop powerful authors of multimodal texts.
3   Connect classroom production to social action.
4   Build the discipline around the student.

Public support for language arts and literacy education requires both advocates and advocacy from the home, school, and civic communities.

Burke (2013) acknowledges, 'An excellent education should not be an accident; it should be a right, though nowhere in the United States Constitution or any of our other founding documents do we find that right listed' (p. xv). Further, he states, 'The word "education" stems from the Latin word *educare*, meaning to draw out that which is within, to lead' (p. xxi). As educators continue to 'draw out' language learning and multiliteracies in action across borderlands and global corridors, we must be prepared to provide language arts and literacy education that is culturally sustaining, engaging, learner-driven, socially responsible, text-rich, and powerful.

Languages and literacies for seeing and imagining

In a volume of letters titled *Zing! Seven Creativity Practices for Educators and Students* (2010), Pat Mora guides teachers in the development of their personal and professional creativity. Mora reminds teachers to reflect on their work, influence, and persistence to rethink their creative and language arts practices for student learning, understanding, and achievement in a changing world.

Today's students need not spend their reading time in a bookroom like I did years ago, seeking new discoveries; new digital media and social networks allow an alternate, yet holistic and integrated transaction among reader, text, media, and society. The connections across media also mean that students have the opportunity to adopt socially responsible and responsive literacies as they engage with texts and in a world in need of more equality and equity for all citizens.

Further, students need not read and live in isolation from the worlds they study and respond to as readers, thinkers, writers, and editors. By extension, Carol Jago (2010) reminds us: 'Reading literature helps students see the world both as it is and as it might be. It helps prevent political blindness' (p. 11). Among colleagues, we must ask ourselves: do we build classrooms that foster dialogue in mother tongues for our students to discover and hear inclusive literary voices, so they can read and interpret their past and to write and imagine their future in a changing, dynamic world? As educators, we must guide students to see the world and pay attention. We must examine and re-examine our reading and languaging lives as we learn from a global society that is interconnected to language arts and literacy education.

Acknowledgements

Grateful acknowledgement is made to the National Council of Teachers of English for permission to reprint an earlier version of the article 'The Literary Changes: From the Book Room to the Discovery of American Literatures and NCTE,' which appeared in the centennial issue of *English Journal* (Volume 101, Number 1, September 2011), pages 53–55, edited by Leila Christenbury (guest editor) and Kenneth Lindblom (editor). Copyright © 2011 by the National Council of Teachers of English (Urbana, IL).

References

Acosta, T. P. (1994). My mother pieced quilts. In R. Fernández (Ed.), *In others words: Literature by Latinas of the United States* (pp. 6–7). Houston, TX: Arte Público Press.

Anderson, J. (2015). *Zack Delacruz: Me and my big mouth.* New York: Sterling Children's Books.

Aranda, J. F. (2003). *When we arrive: A new literary history of Mexican America.* Tucson, AZ: The University of Arizona Press.

Bambara, T. C. (1996). Language and the writer. In T. Morrison (Ed.), *Deep sightings and rescue missions: Fiction, essays, and conversations* (pp. 139–145). New York: Pantheon.

Blanton, C. K. (2007). *The strange career of bilingual education in Texas, 1836–1981.* College Station: Texas A&M University Press.

Burke, J. (2013). *The common core companion: The standards decoded, grades 9–12.* Thousand Oaks, CA: Corwin Press.

Cisneros, S. (1994a). *The house on Mango Street.* New York: Alfred A. Knopf. (Original work published 1984.)

Cisneros, S. (1994b). *Loose woman: Poems.* New York: Vintage Contemporaries.

Fránquiz, M. E. (2011). *Borinquen Querido*: Growing up bilingual in a military family. In M. de la Luz Reyes (Ed.), *Words were all we had: Becoming biliterate against the odds* (pp. 121–132). New York: Teachers College Press.

Frost, R., & Lathem, E. C. (Ed.). (1979). *The poetry of Robert Frost: The collected poems, complete and unabridged.* New York: Henry Holt.

Gorter, D., Zenotz, V., & Cenoz, J. (Eds.). (2013). *Minority languages and multilingual education: Bridging the local and the global.* New York: Springer.

Jago, C. (2010). A literacy education—priceless. *Council Chronicle, National Council of Teachers of English, 20*(1), 10–11.

Lee, C. D., & Spratley, A. (2010). Working toward social justice in the classroom, school, and community. In E. Lindemann (Ed.), *Reading the past, writing the future: A century of American literacy education and the National Council of Teachers of English* (pp. 253–280). Urbana, IL: National Council of Teachers of English.

May, S. (2012). *Language and minority rights: Ethnicity, nationalism and the politics of language* (2nd ed.). New York: Routledge.

Miller, J. E., Jr. (Ed.), et al. (1979a). *Teacher's resource book to accompany United States in literature, America reads* (Medallion ed.). Glenview, IL: Scott, Foresman and Company.

Miller, J. E., Jr. (Ed.), et al. (1979b). *United States in literature, America reads* (Medallion ed.). Glenview, IL: Scott, Foresman and Company.

Mora, P. (2010). *Zing! Seven creativity practices for educators and students.* Thousand Oaks, CA: Corwin Press.

Morrell, E. (2015). Teaching English POWERFULLY: Four challenges. *English in Texas: A Journal of the Texas Council of Teachers of English Language Arts, 45*(1), 5–7.

Mukherjee, B. (2004). Bangla: The way back. In W. Lesser (Ed.), *The genius of language: Fifteen writers reflect on their mother tongue* (pp. 11–24). New York: Anchor Books.

National Council of Teachers of English [NCTE]. (2016). *NCTE guideline: Professional knowledge for the teaching of writing.* Urbana, IL: Author.

Rodríguez, R. J. (2011). The literary changes: From the book room to the discovery of American literatures and NCTE. *English Journal, 101*(1), 53–55.

Rodríguez, R. J. (2017). Rivers of languages (unpublished poem).

Rosenblatt, L. M. (1995). *Literature as exploration* (5th ed.). New York: The Modern Language Association of America. (Original work published 1938)

Saldaña-Portillo, M. J. (2016). *Indian given: Racial geographies across Mexico and the United States.* Durham, NC: Duke University Press.

Vasquez, V., Tate, S. L., & Harste, J. C. (2013). *Negotiating critical literacies with teachers: Theoretical foundations and pedagogical resources for pre-service and in-service contexts.* New York: Routledge.

Zepeda, O. (1995). The continuum of literacy in American Indian communities. *The Bilingual Research Journal, 19*(1), 5–15.

11

IN PRAISE OF SLOW LEARNING IN LITERARY STUDIES

Thomas Day

Problems of education are very often problems of time or, more precisely, of timing. This is Milton's angle of entry into the topic in his 1644 treatise 'Of Education'. There, Milton deplores 'the plucking of untimely fruit' by means of the Latin and Greek composition demanded of callow youth and he proceeds to interrogate the overhasty pedagogical practices that would have Arts (or Humanities) students run before they can walk:

> And for the usual method of teaching Arts, I deem it to be an old errour of Universities not yet well recover'd from the Scholastick grossness of barbarous ages, that in stead of beginning with Arts most easie, and those be such as are most obvious to the sence, they present their young unmatriculated Novices at first comming with the most intellective abstractions of Logick and Metapysicks: so that they having but newly left those Grammatick flats and shallows where they stuck unreasonably to learn a few words with lamentable construction, and now on the sudden transported under another climate to be tost and turmoil'd with their unballasted wits in fadomless and unquiet deeps of controversie, do for the most part grow into hatred and contempt of Learning, mockt and deluded all this while with ragged Notions and Babblements, while they expected worthy and delightful knowledge.[1]

It is the contention of this chapter that in certain crucial respects we are not fully recovered from the old errors of universities that Milton diagnoses, and that the contemporary pressures to quantify and commodify teaching and research identified threaten to lead us further into such errors. My concomitant claim is that matters of timing, of the pacing, of education are, or ought to be, of especial concern to students and teachers of English. To read and write and think in English is, I want to suggest, to cultivate a relationship with time that has its own delicate integrity, which cannot and should not be artificially accelerated, as Milton recognises. Ripeness is all.

The first of these contentions isn't original. Indeed, the Milton passage came to my attention in a 2009 prose piece by Geoffrey Hill entitled 'Confessio Amantis', his contribution to the 'Old Members at Work' section of *The Record*,[2] the alumni magazine of Keble College, Oxford (Hill's alma mater). In it Hill reflects, not altogether happily, on half a century spent teaching in British and American universities. He recalls his entry into the profession, at Leeds University, as a 'gauchely ill-prepared twenty-two-year-old' (p. 45) with a First from Oxford but without a doctorate, having to learn the intellectual requirements of the job on the job, chiefly through the mentorship of the Coleridge scholar, J P Mann. And yet Hill insists that this was 'a more testing apprenticeship than would have been provided by working on a doctorate, its topic creamed from the shallows [Milton's word] of my twenty-one-year-young ignorance and vanity' (p. 47). The article variously censures 'the deadening effects of doctoral work' and the 'tunnel vision' (p. 46) it can induce. Hill argues, moreover, that 'many people [...] are not suited intellectually or temperamentally to pursue [research] with the necessary breath as well as rigorous attention at so early an age' (p. 46), and he includes himself among the many, saying that he was 'well into [his] forties' (p. 47) before he felt properly equipped for scholarly and critical work. He notes that he was six years in post before he published his first academic paper, 'a length of time that would not [...] be tolerated' (p. 47) in the 'publish or perish' culture of today. Hill's diffidence is, as he implies, now something of an endangered species in institutions of learning, but isn't it in the long run the more reliable means of raising standards and expanding horizons? For the feeling that 'I am not (yet) worthy' often goes together with a highly refined sense of what is worthy; and perhaps it also goes together with an unshowy confidence, a belief, a self-belief, that given time and effort things will fall into place. As a poet, Hill has sought to create a body of work that requires a necessarily slow assimilation, albeit with a simultaneous awareness of the pressures of time that are incumbent upon the reader and upon reading—one of which, for the critic trying desperately to keep up and/or keep the REF wolves from the door, is the astonishingly quick rate at which Hill has been publishing poetry since the mid-nineties, in marked contrast to the painfully slow gestation of his earlier collections. He alludes to this in his 2012 collection *Odi Barbare*, playfully suggesting that both he and we ought to spend longer working on his poetry: 'Nine months more might better equip this labour / Strange to our bodies'.[3] Similarly in *Scenes From Comus* (2005) he bids the reader to 'Take it slowly', which, he goes on to say, is 'like walking / through convalescence, the load / bearing not yet adjusted' (*Broken Hierarchies*, p. 431): it is the Milton of 'Of Education' rather than *Comus* who comes to mind, who deplores how students just starting out are 'now on the sudden transported under another climate to be tost and turmoil'd with their *unballasted* wits'.

The argument I am making about time and the need to take it, I ought to say, doesn't underestimate the degree to which the spectre of Casaubon haunts these matters: budding researchers need to be as alert as Will Ladislaw (and George Eliot) to 'the pitiable instances of long incubation producing no chick'.[4] I also ought to recognise that some of my points may be perceived as pitiable instances of what Ben Knights, in an astute article, calls 'The Implied Aesthetic of English Teaching', citing in this connection 'a powerful consensus within the subject [which] values struggle in writing, and student writing which bears the traces of that struggle'.[5] Such values, Knights asserts, bear relation to a set of 'tacit rules' which teachers of English Literature 'expect students to internal-ise [...] but, generally speaking, without explaining the necessity of doing so, or even suggesting that the rules exist', and perhaps my quasi-mystical recourse to 'belief' and 'things falling into place' looks vulnerable in this regard—an at best unhelpful, at worst deliberately exclusionary, obfuscation of the actual processes through which students learn to read and write well. But I would suggest that the balance of power is not, as things stand, in the favour of those who value struggle; it is, in my experience, weighted very much in the fa-vour of the management culture whose idiom—in its jargonesque guises far more obfuscating—Gary Day has incisively brought to account, pointing up 'its stress on accountability, its ceaseless innovation [...] its highly instrumen-tal character'[6]—its implacable desire to render the implied aesthetic of English teaching and learning wholly explicit. And I would agree with Day that the nature of the subject is such that its aims and outcomes can't be rendered wholly explicit in this way: English very often deals with the ineffable and the un-knowable, and, as Day puts it, adducing D. H. Lawrence, 'Not being able to explicate the "value of the saying" awakens a sense of humility that makes us more receptive to the unknown that surrounds us' (p. 216). Knights puts his finger on the same phenomenon when he avers that 'Implicit is an existential position: tolerance for ambiguity and cognitive delay—a refusal to give way quickly to the simplistic desire for interpretative closure'—indeed, 'cognitive delay' and the 'refusal to give way quickly' to interpretative closure might serve very well as synonyms for the slow learning my paper speaks in praise of. (Al-though Knights, if I understand him rightly, remains somewhat distrustful of the implicit, calling for a greater awareness of the ways tacit rules and expecta-tions govern teaching and learning practices.)

My sympathies, as should be clear, are with those who speak up for a salutary reticence and restraint that knows just when to unfurl what it has been working up to, that allows the thought time to mull, to harden into adequate expression; those who value not only the struggle but the patient accomplishment of the writer. And it is testimony such as Hill's admissions of not feeling ready, which strikes me as candid not tacit, that has inspired me to aspire. I might also mention Jonathan Smith, an English teacher (in secondary schools), novelist, and writer for radio and television, who writes in his wonderful memoir *The Learning Game*: 'I'm glad I did not rush into writing because I was and still am a slow learner'.[7] Nevertheless Smith is beautifully attuned to different speeds of learning, or at least to the semblance of precociousness, in his follow-up, *The Following Game* (2011), where he remembers reading an essay appraising Aufidius's famous speech in Act Four, Scene Three of *Coriolanus* crafted by the young Vikram Seth, a former Sixth Form student of his:

> And, when you are reading something *that* good you slowly put the essay down, your hands fall to your side, and you stand up and you walk around your room and you pick the essay up again and you read it through once more just to be quite sure that you haven't allowed yourself to be carried away and overrated it (and you haven't) and you notice for the second time the sharp but light touch, the penetrating point, [...] the quickness of mind, [...] the sense of a hidden armoury, the timing and feel of the sentences, the ease of the comparisons, the sense that really hard work has been done but that somehow it has all been made to look easy, the art that hides art.[8]

The timing and feel of Smith's sentences, or this fragment of a very long one, say a great deal, I feel, about the kind of learning that went on under his direction: the momentum, which mustn't mean getting carried away, is gleaned from a preparedness to pause, to stop and think and rethink and rephrase, in a way that takes you deeper into your material: 'the quickness of mind' partly derives from slowness, 'you slowly put the essay down'. In a university I taught at, postgraduates were put through compulsory generic training courses in 'speed reading'; what they most need are courses in slow reading, which cultivate the 'rigorous attention' that Hill sets alongside the breadth necessary for advanced research. And it is worth pausing over the fact that 'to attend' means both to 'pay heed to' and 'to wait'.

My own slow learning in literary studies was significantly steered by the teacher, poet, and critic, Michael Edwards. Edwards's 1990 book *Of Making Many Books: Essays on the Endlessness of Writing* points in various ways to a slow learning underlying the plethora it addresses, not least by means of its biblical title, which leaves silent—the art that hides art—the attendant sense of scholarly struggle which completes the verse from the final chapter of Ecclesiastes: 'of making many books there is no end; and much study is a weariness of the flesh' (Ecclesiastes 12.12), says the Preacher, admonishing prolixity. Edwards's book is centrally concerned with the anxieties of writing in a world already far too full of the stuff: 'the sense', as he puts it in the 'Preface', 'that whenever one writes it is late'.[9] The opening chapter considers Montaigne's *Essays* to be a book oppressed by its own compulsion towards linguistic excess. He gives particular consideration to the essay 'On Vanity', vanity being, as Edwards notes, the watchword of Ecclesiastes. In that essay Montaigne bemoans the contemporary preponderance of 'scribblers', which seems to him a 'sign of a disordered and licentious age'. This surfeit of self-important scribbling, Montaigne says, is a betrayal of 'That which divinity has so divinely expressed to us [which] ought to be carefully and continually meditated by understanding men'. But immediately he turns the proscription on himself: 'Who cannot see that I have taken a path along which, without cease and without labour, I shall continue for as long as there are ink and paper in the world?' Edwards asks us to hear the 'underlying pain' (*Of Making Many Books*, p. 8) of that sentence, salutary reticence and restraint succumbing to a malaise of incessant utterance: thus, he tells us, 'Montaigne chose the only form which seemed adequate to the vision of writing as having no end [...] a stream of chimerical essays, a fantastical proliferation of "attempts"' (ibid.). Montaigne's exemplariness for Edwards further consists in 'the manner in which he lived the relationship between his essays and his life', which he says is 'close to [that] of a poet': he cites a manuscript edition of the *Essays* in which Montaigne notes 'I have no more made my book than my book has made me' and claims that his book is 'consubstantial with its author' (quoted, p. 6). What I admire about Edwards's writing is his effort to make books which are in some way consubstantial with their author, and his implicit conviction that that is what the critic, as well as the poet, does. In a later chapter entitled 'Not I', which mainly deals with Christian perspectives on the self, he makes parenthetical mention of the writer to whom 'Not I' alludes, noting that Beckett 'might have been central to this chapter, but for the fact that I realise I am not ready for him' (p. 104). That strikes me as a fine thing for a literary critic to say, and just the sort of thing that a lesser critic might have wanted to conceal. It affirms that readers have to grow into, and up to, a great writer. And it lives up to one of Derek Attridge's criteria of perspicacious criticism: 'The best criticism', Attridge has argued, 'is personal, written by a critic willing to acknowledge the particular, unique history that has formed him or her, and the specific situation from which he or she writes';[10] judging by the number of English students who think it is a heinous offence to use 'I' in an essay, that is something not often enough acknowledged.

I might have chosen to work towards a conclusion by considering one or two literary late starters—Edward Thomas and Amy Clampitt spring to mind. But instead, I want to synthesise some of my reflections by thinking about an early finisher, Eliot in *Four Quartets*.

I've long been interested in the ways that poem seeks to bring the growth of the poet's mind into contact with the capacities of its readers for living and learning. Lines like 'I sometimes wonder if that is what Krishna meant' from 'The Dry Salvages'[11] speak to Montaigne's conviction that 'That which divinity has so divinely expressed to us ought to be carefully and continually meditated by understanding men', and the *Quartets* also need to be read in this way, to be wondered over, over time, their meaning evolving in the light of experience, experience which can preserve within it the innocence of wonder. Yet that 'that'—'I sometimes wonder if *that* is what Krishna meant'—also admits a hint of intolerance for ambiguity and cognitive delay, which the *Quartets* simultaneously recognise as a readerly perspective. And as a writerly perspective too: 'the intolerable wrestle / With words and meanings' (p. 179) spoken of in 'East Coker' comprises a desire to pin meaning down, predicating a kind of fixity that is the inverse of the spiritual stillness invoked in the following section, in which the speaker more readily embraces cognitive delay: 'I said to my soul be still [...] Wait without thought, for you are not ready for thought' (p. 180). But that is not an easy thing to do; like Hill's poetry, Eliot's poem cannot seal itself off from pressures of time, and accordingly slow, patient learning is constantly endangered, as it is by the deceitful bird at the beginning of 'Burnt Norton' who commands us to be 'Quick' (p. 171).

Teaching and learning are integral to the *Quartets*: masters are to be heard addressing novices, with Eliot sitting on both sides of the desk, passing through different stages of his age and youth. The best criticism of the poem that I've read in recent times comes from an unlikely source, the journal *Studies in Continuing Education*: an article by a Canadian academic, Jane Dawson, uses the poem to interrogate 'the sanitised certainties of managerialism which [...] dominate the discourse about lifelong learning at the policy level', and to conceptualise the transformative and radical aspects of lifelong learning that the discourse overlooks or suppresses.[12] What Dawson's article lacks in Empsonian finesse it makes up for in its unabashed conviction—a thoroughly Eliotic one—in the uses of literature for life, as distinct from the 'instrumental rationality' that constructs the dominant discursive paradigm. Dawson discusses how the poem bears out 'the balky recalcitrance of the learning process' (p. 119), moments of insight having to be wrested from the messiness of experience. In alluding to 'mess' she has in mind the final section of 'East Coker', where Eliot speaks as one half-way through a life, 'in the middle way' (*The Complete Poems and Plays*, p. 182), and I want to amplify Dawson's reading of the poem as providing the grounds for a critique of the market-orientated discourse surrounding lifelong learning through a little further attention to this passage. The concern with learning is made explicit here: Eliot says he is 'Trying to *learn* to use words' (I would also wish to emphasize his use of the word 'use'), but again the learning process is felt to be frustratingly slow, giving rise to the sense that whenever one writes it is late: 'Because one has only learned to get the better of words, / For the thing one no longer has to say, or the way in which / One is no longer disposed to say it' (p. 182). But the poem recovers a sense of purpose from that, which I think has a bearing on Dawson's critique; indeed the management culture's language of 'ceaseless innovation' (Day) is just what Eliot finds unavailable to him in articulating how language outpaces the learner. Earlier in 'East Coker' management types ('merchant bankers', 'Distinguished civil servants', 'chairmen of many committees') had been sent 'into the dark' (p. 180), and the passage works up to a conclusion which perhaps punningly shuns the business imperatives, the 'sanitised certainties of managerialism', that impinge on learning: 'For us, there is only the trying. The rest is not our business' (p. 182). Eliot's philosophy of learning might be summed up in that line. He values the struggle in writing, a struggle which stems from the unavoidable feeling that one is not good enough, not worthy; and yet the mode of teaching is lovingly encouraging, at once implicit ('The rest is not our business') and inclusive ('For *us* [...] *our* business'). Thus, the poem takes on the twin temporal perspectives of Ecclesiastes: the trying necessarily entails the pain of failing, but at another level failure is neither here nor there, 'publish or perish' ceasing to be a dichotomy.

Such is the moving cessation of John Williams's 1965 novel *Stoner*. Seeing out his time, William Stoner rakes over an academic career that has failed to fulfil its early promise, producing a solitary, inconspicuous monograph, yet as he draws his last breaths all utilitarian imperatives melt away and the intrinsic value of literary studies, which has been Stoner's touchstone from the first, is finally reaffirmed:

> It hardly seemed to matter to him that the book was forgotten and that it served no use; and the question of its worth at any time seemed almost trivial. He did not have the illusion that he would find himself there, in the fading print; and yet, he knew, a small part of him that he could not deny *was* there, and would be there.[13]

It wouldn't cut it on a funding application, but it's as convincing a case for the importance of research in English Literature as I know.

Notes

1 John Milton, *Complete Prose Works*, ed. by Don M Wolfe (New Haven: Yale University Press, 1953–1982), vol. 2, p. 375.

2 Geoffrey Hill, 'Confessio Amantis', *The Record* (Oxford: Keble College, 2009), pp. 45–54.

3 Geoffrey Hill, *Broken Hierarchies: Poems 1952–2012* (Oxford: Oxford University Press, 2013), p. 851.

4 George Eliot, *Middlemarch* (London: Wordsworth Editions, 1994), p. 68.

5 Ben Knights, 'The Implied Aesthetic of English Teaching', *Wordplay: The English Subject Centre Newsletter* (April 2010). www.english.heacademy.ac.uk/explore/publications/magazine/wordplay3/knights.htm.

6 Gary Day, 'Beyond Management Culture: The Experience of English', *The Cambridge Quarterly*, 34.3 (2005), 213–220 (p. 215).

7 Jonathan Smith, *The Learning Game* (London: Abacus, 2000), p. 81.

8 Jonathan Smith, *The Following Game* (Woodbridge, Suffolk: Peridot, 2011), p. 56.

9 Michael Edwards, *Of Making Many Books: Essays on the Endlessness of Writing* (Houndmills: Macmillan, 1990), p. vii.
10 Derek Attridge, 'Can We Do Justice to Literature?', *PN Review* 186, 34.6 (July–August 2008).
11 Thomas Stearns Eliot, *The Complete Poems and Plays* (London: Faber and Faber, 1969), p. 187.
12 Jane Dawson, 'Lifelong Learning and T. S. Eliot's *Four Quartets*', *Studies in Continuing Education*, 25.1 (2003), 113–124 (p. 120).
13 John Williams, *Stoner: A Novel* (London: Vintage, 2003), p. 288.

12

POETRY TEACHING IN MALTA

The interplay between teachers' beliefs and practices

Daniel Xerri

Introduction

Most research on poetry education identifies curricular and assessment constraints as the main factor for a lack of engagement with poetry on behalf of teachers and students (Benton, 2000; Dymoke, 2001, 2002, 2012; O'Neill, 2006). While it is undeniable that assessment plays a significant role in shaping classroom practices, to point an accusatory finger solely at assessment is to ignore its collusion with the shared beliefs held by teachers and students (Xerri, 2013a). Rather than on its own, it is in combination with these beliefs that assessment plays a pivotal role in moulding engagement with poetry.

As shown by comparative research (Peel, Patterson, & Gerlach, 2000), beliefs about English have played an important role in the formation of the subject due to how they determine classroom practices. Hence, it is helpful to start by defining these constructs and identifying the possible links between them. Borg (2001) defines a belief as 'a proposition which may be consciously or unconsciously held, is evaluative in that it is accepted as true by the individual, and is therefore imbued with emotive commitment; further, it serves as a guide to thought and behaviour' (p. 186). According to the American Psychological Association (2009), a belief is 'acceptance of the truth, reality, or validity of something … particularly in the absence of substantiation' (p. 54). Beliefs help to form practices. For example, a review commissioned by the Sutton Trust, an educational think tank in the UK, found that one of the six components of effective teaching consists of teacher beliefs due to some evidence of impact on student outcomes (Coe, Aloisi, Higgins, & Elliot Major, 2014, p. 3). Practice is defined as 'doing, performance, action' but it 'can also take the form of habitualized and institutionalized ways of doing something. This applies to all professional activities (e.g. teaching)' (Collins & O'Brien, 2011, pp. 362–363).

Research indicates that in many international contexts the interplay between beliefs and practices seems quite significant (OECD, 2009). This chapter seeks to explore how teachers' beliefs are related to their practices within the context of poetry education.

While poetry education lacks substantial research in this area (Wilson, 2010; Xerri, 2015), teachers' beliefs and practices and the relationship between them have been scrutinized by a wide range of studies in the field of language learning and teaching (e.g. Uysal & Bardakci, 2014). Given that such research is to a large extent missing from the field of poetry education, this chapter seeks to shed some light on teachers' beliefs about poetry and how these affect their practices.

Maltese post-16 educational context

The discussion presented in this chapter is largely based on research that took place in the post-16 educational context in Malta (Xerri, 2015). The country gained independence from the British Empire in 1964 after having been a colony since 1800. It joined the European Union in 2004. Maltese and English are the country's two official languages, with the latter being the second language for the majority of the population (Sciriha & Vassallo, 2006).

In Malta, education is compulsory up to the age of 16. In a country with a population of less than half a million, in 2011–2012, 5,960 students were enrolled in post-16 institutions (National Statistics Office, 2014), which typically prepare students for the Matriculation Certificate examination. Students hoping to be awarded the Matriculation Certificate and thus continue their studies at university need to obtain a pass in two Advanced level subjects and in four Intermediate level subjects.

Matriculation Certificate examinations are designed and administered by the Matriculation and Secondary Education Certificate (MATSEC) Examinations Board, which is affiliated to the University of Malta. Up to 1997, Maltese students sat for GCE Advanced level examinations offered by examination boards in the UK. Despite the fact that MATSEC decided that Malta should have its own homegrown Advanced level examinations, the educational system remains closely modelled on the one in the UK. For example, just as in the UK, in Malta A-levels are usually studied over a two-year period at a sixth form college that in most cases is independent of secondary education institutions.

Various post-16 institutions in Malta offer their students the opportunity of studying English at Advanced level and all these courses gravitate towards one examination. The Matriculation Certificate English examination measures candidates' success in their two-year course of study and enables them to gain admission to university; therefore its nature is that of a selective test. As an examination, its content is heavily biased in favour of literature components. Partly due to its colonial heritage, the study of English in Malta has for many decades valued the importance of a literary education, which is largely centred on the Anglo-American literary tradition. This means that literature is for the most part taught in the same way that it is taught to native speakers of English and for similar purposes.

The Matriculation Certificate English examination is a 9-hour examination made up of 3 papers and a 15-minute speaking examination. Candidates' knowledge of poetry is assessed in Paper 1, in which they are expected to answer an essay question on a set collection of poems (e.g. Wilfred Owen's war poems), and a question based on an unseen poem. In the latter component, candidates write an essay about a poem they would not have studied at school.

The study

This chapter synthesizes the discussion of some of the findings of a mixed methods study conducted at a post-16 institution in Malta (Xerri, 2015). Its participants consisted of eight poetry teachers, who were each observed teaching one 60-minute literary criticism seminar based on an unseen poem. The instrument used for this purpose consisted of an observation scheme that combined quantitative and qualitative components. An events checklist with time sampling was used to form a clear picture of the occurrence of a specific set of lesson events across the different observed sessions and to be able to make comparisons. A rating scale was completed at the end of each observed lesson in order to help determine the presence or absence of certain general events and behaviours. Observation notes were also taken in order to record any thoughts and questions evoked by what was observed in each session. After every observed lesson, the teacher in question participated in a semi-structured interview held in a one-to-one manner that lasted around 40 minutes. The data analysis process employed a balance of deductive and inductive coding.

Conceptions of poetry

The teachers in the study seemed to share conceptions of poetry that were seemingly influenced by Romantic notions of the genre. Their difficulty in defining poetry was motivated by their understanding of poetry as something that eluded conceptualization. They deemed poetry to be an inspired use of language that facilitated the expression of something deeply buried and which granted the reader access to emotional and cognitive insights.

The teachers shared the belief that poetry was an important genre that needed to be studied at school. This was mostly related to its capacity for personal growth and the development of 'insights' on life and the self. In this they seemed convinced of 'the effect that poetry can have on our perceptions, that is, on the way we see the world' (Jollimore, 2009, p. 132). Moreover, the teachers expressed the belief that the study of poetry provided access to some kind of durable set of values that transcended transitory and frivolous concerns. They seemed to consider the poet to be in a privileged position and the reader's task to be that of gleaning the wisdom within poetry. The fact that most of the teachers were opposed to poetry writing in class seemed to confirm that for them poetic expression was the preserve of a privileged few due to the belief that 'a poet is born not made' and that poetry was a product of talent and inspiration, not training. Sloan (2003) suggests that such conceptions are deep-rooted and pernicious. They go counter to the idea that creative writing is best fostered by teachers who are willing to engage in it themselves and who see themselves as writers (NAWE, 2010). The teachers' beliefs implied that the only poetry activity worthy of a classroom context was the analytical search for whatever truths the poet had hidden in the text. Dymoke (2009) suggests that such conceptions of poetry have helped to underscore its supremacy over other genres and, in the process, damage teachers' and students' relationship with it. The teachers' mystification of poetry stopped it from being seen as something accessible and enjoyable.

One of the reasons for which the teachers enjoyed teaching poetry was its challenging nature, this also being the reason for which they claimed not to read it for pleasure. Nemerov (1972) affirms that 'There is a sort of reader who finds everything difficult if it happens to be written in verse ... Such readers really have a very simple problem: they don't like poetry, even though some of them feel they ought to' (p. 24). The fact that the teachers were aware that students found poetry difficult made them prize the analytical skills developed via literary criticism seminars, skills seemingly employed to discover meaning in a poem. In fact, during half of the observed lessons teachers were noted encouraging students to look for a specific meaning in the text by means of an analytical approach. Their belief that poetry was intrinsically opaque was consonant with Reddy's (2010) admission that 'As a teacher of poetry, I try to encourage my students to cultivate a fascination with what's difficult about this art ... I tell them, poetry isn't for wimps' (pp. 7–8). However, Reddy (2010) also admits that 'the difficulty inherent to poetic expression is what makes this form of writing so marginal in our culture today' (p. 8).

The teachers' preference for reading a poem rather than listening to it was because of their belief that poetry required intense concentration in order for its meaning to become apparent. They seemed to be aware that students conceived of poetry as made up of riddles to be solved (Dymoke, 2003) and they claimed to discourage students from adopting such a stance. However, the observed lessons demonstrated that the opposite tended to happen. In a sense these poetry lessons were restrictive by not enabling students to achieve what Lamarque (2009a) considers the mark of a poetically sensitive reader: 'To read poetry (of any kind) *as poetry* is to adopt a certain attitude of mind, a receptiveness, among other things, to finegrained expression, the salience of perspective, and the play of images' (pp. 51–52). The almost exclusive attention given to poetry's meaning encouraged a reductive view of the genre, one in which hidden meaning is conceived of as some kind of message intentionally buried in the poem by its creator. The prominence given to poetry's meaning seemed to almost eclipse anything else associated with poetry, leading to an approach that could potentially dampen students' engagement (Fleming & Stevens, 2015).

Poetry classroom practices

The study's observation sessions showed that the main poetry lesson event consisted of the teacher explaining the poem from the front of the classroom. The level of initiation on the part of students was minimal, their participation being mostly limited to responding to teachers' open and closed questions, the latter being more common. The students' participation did not seem to be carefully planned and almost all the observed teachers failed to encourage students to work autonomously. Moreover, most of the teachers did not encourage students to come up with their own personal response to the poem and instead provided them with one specific reading of it. Cumming (2007) criticizes such pedagogy for failing to consider students' own contribution to a poetry lesson: 'if there is no opportunity to link a child's love of playing with language with what they are expected to learn about poetry in class, then that which they have could become irrelevant and devalued in school' (p. 99).

The way they engaged with poetry in class seemed to lead to ambivalent reactions on the part of the teachers in the study. They claimed to enjoy the experience of teaching poetry but at the same time they considered it onerous. Despite the fact that they affirmed that in teaching poetry they gave importance to a poem's use of language and its potential for personal enrichment, in the observed lessons the emphasis was mainly on providing students with a line-by-line explanation of what a poem meant. In fact, the teachers confirmed that the main lesson gain for students was the ability to analyse poetry, so much so that the term 'poetry lesson' was considered synonymous with 'analysis'.

Some teachers relished the analysis of poetry and most of them implied that in class this was the only acceptable approach to poetry. As suggested above, this was partly due to their conception of poetry as a difficult genre that carried hidden meanings, which could only be unravelled via analysis. While the teachers protested against this conception of poetry when interviewed, they also seemed to share the belief that students' enjoyment of poetry was bound to a teacher's ability to make students understand it through explanation. In this, the participants seemingly subscribed to Kivy's (2011) idea that 'poetry is paraphrasable, which is to say, can be interpreted as to meaning, if meaning it has' (pp. 376–377). Such a thesis is refuted by Lamarque's (2009b) claim that 'Reading a poem *as poetry* demands the assumption of form-content unity' (p. 411).

The teachers' belief that, in reading poetry, content could be explained apart from form was probably what led them to identify with the approach to poetry described in the interview stimulus material, Billy Collins's (1988) 'Introduction to Poetry'. The teachers indicated that while they wanted to make students enjoy poetry they could not avoid being party to its 'torture'. Some of them blamed examination demands for this while a few admitted that their poetry lessons were too teacher-centred. With respect to the latter, the fact that they admitted this after reading Collins's poem might suggest that it made them reflect on their classroom practices or else that, while always conscious of their practices, they felt unwilling or helpless to effect change (Xerri, in press).

The emphasis placed on reading a poem for a specific meaning seemed to be also linked to the teachers' scepticism about the place of literary theory in the A-level poetry classroom, which they claimed to be motivated by their concerns about students' cognitive maturity as well as by some unease about their own ability to use literary theory for the purpose of teaching poetry (Xerri, 2013b). It was most likely that the teachers' avoidance of theory at A-level would lead their students to shrink away from theory once they were expected to engage with it as undergraduates.

Teachers as gatekeepers to poetry

The study helps to show that the interplay between the teachers' beliefs and practices led them to consolidate their role as gatekeepers to poetry. One of the ways by which they positioned themselves as such was by controlling the choice of poems to be read in class. This was especially so in the case of literary criticism seminars given that choice was not determined by the syllabus or departmental procedures. For Connolly and Smith (2003), despite the fact that teachers cannot dispense with their authority due to their experience as readers, they can mitigate the effects of this authority by discovering a poem for the first time together with their students. This is in line with the idea that student engagement is more likely to occur if they are provided with an element of choice with respect to the texts read in class (Beach, Appleman, Hynds, & Wilhelm, 2006; Xerri, 2014). By being empowered to choose what they would like to read in class, students will be encouraged to stop seeing themselves as passive recipients of knowledge. The teachers in the study confirmed that they practically always chose the poems that were discussed in the seminars. In the observed lessons, teachers focused on poems that besides being highly canonical were also popular with syllabus and examination panels. These poems also happened to be written by some of the poets the teachers listed as their favourites, despite the admission on the part of most teachers that they did not read poetry for pleasure given its 'academic' connotations. Their failure to act as role models of enthusiastic readers in the poetry classroom probably helped to entrench the idea that poetry was solely an academic genre. Moreover, by controlling what kind of poetry students read in class, the teachers were positioning themselves as authoritative figures in relation to what poetry was worthy of lesson activities.

If a lesson's emphasis is primarily on helping students to understand a poem via explanation, teachers are enacting the role of gatekeepers to the text's meaning. This is even more so if teachers are reluctant to enable students to adopt a variety of critical lenses when reading a poem. Classroom observation confirmed that both the classroom layout and main lesson event helped to emphasise the power dynamic between teacher and students vis-à-vis the text's meaning. In most of the observed sessions, the line-by-line analysis of a poem was conducted exclusively by the teachers, who seemed to indicate that theirs was the only possible reading of the text. This contradicted the teachers' claim that during their poetry lessons they sought to cultivate students' personal enrichment and that they encouraged students to share their personal response.

The teachers' belief that poetry possessed an element of difficulty made them value the act of explaining a poem to students in order for them to understand it. In the study, the way poetry was approached in class helped to galvanise the idea that every poem had a meaning and that students were meant to imitate teachers' way of 'torturing' out that meaning, especially because students were expected to do this in the examination (Xerri, 2013a). By adopting the stance of gate-keepers to poetry, some teachers probably helped to consolidate students' belief that a poem would remain inscrutable as long as a teacher was not present to help them unravel its meaning by means of a highly analytical approach.

Conclusion

The effects of assessment on classroom practices in relation to poetry are still fundamental in the twenty-first century (Dymoke, 2003; Xerri, 2016b). However, as shown above, an equally significant factor is the contribution that teachers' beliefs about poetry have on the way they approach a poem in class. For this reason, teacher education and development should serve the purpose of enhancing teachers' beliefs and practices in relation to poetry, enabling them to see it as a multimodal genre that can be read in multiple ways and not solely in order to extract hidden meaning from a canonical poem for examination purposes. In this way they can influence their own students, who most often share their beliefs about poetry. Considering the nature and possible definitions of poetry is useful for both teachers and students (Stevens, 2001) given that it can lead to enhanced engagement in class (Pike, 2000). In fact, Fleming and Stevens (2015) consider it 'useful to examine the concept of "poetry", which may be a source of bewilderment or difficulty for pupils unless the term itself is subject to some discussion' (p. 182). The definition of what counts as poetry needs to be adequately ample so as to take into account as many different forms of poetry as possible and not just those typical of syllabi and examinations.

Moreover, teachers' beliefs should be revised in such a way that they come to see poetry as a democratic and inclusive genre, not just something produced by talented individuals who are 'born' poets. Teachers should be encouraged to see poetry as something that besides being read critically in class can also be read for pleasure. In fact, Borges (2000) believes that an exaggerated preoccupation with a poem's meaning diverts attention from the aesthetic qualities of poetry: 'I know for a fact that we *feel* the beauty of a poem before we even begin to think of a meaning' (p. 84). Teachers should not consider poetry to be the preserve of published poets but should conceive of it as something capable of being written by teachers and young people. In thinking and talking about poetry, teachers should emphasise its accessibility rather than its difficulty. They should be encouraged to challenge notions that help to mystify poetry and burden it with too much cachet (Xerri, 2016a). In this way they can allay students' anxiety in relation to poetry and help them to view it as enjoyable. Most importantly, this would enable teachers to become aware of the powerful influence exerted by their beliefs on the way they approach poetry in class.

References

American Psychological Association. (2009). *APA concise dictionary of psychology.* Washington, DC: American Psychological Association.

Beach, R., Appleman, D., Hynds, S., & Wilhelm, J. (2006). *Teaching literature to adolescents.* Mahwah, NJ: Lawrence Erlbaum Associates.

Benton, P. (2000). The conveyor belt curriculum? Poetry teaching in the secondary school II. *Oxford Review of Education, 26*(1), 81–93.

Borg, M. (2001). Teachers' beliefs. *ELT Journal, 55*(2), 186–188.

Borges, J. L. (2000). The Metaphor. In C. A. Mihailescu (Ed.) *This craft of verse* (pp. 21–41). Cambridge, MA: Harvard University Press.

Coe, R., Aloisi, C., Higgins, S., & Elliot Major, L. (2014, October). *What makes great teaching? Review of the underpinning research.* London: The Sutton Trust.

Collins, B. (1988). Introduction to poetry. *The apple that astonished Paris,* 58. Fayetteville: University of Arkansas Press.

Collins, J. W., & O'Brien, N. P. (Eds.) (2011). *The Greenwood dictionary of education* (2nd ed.). Santa Barbara, CA: Greenwood.

Connolly, B., & Smith, M. W. (2003). Dropping in a mouse: Reading poetry with our students. *The Clearing House: A Journal of Educational Strategies, Issues and Ideas, 76*(5), 235–239.

Cumming, R. (2007). Language play in the classroom: Encouraging children's intuitive creativity with words through poetry. *Literacy, 41*(2), 93–101.

Dymoke, S. (2001). Taking poetry off its pedestal: The place of poetry writing in an assessment-driven curriculum. *English in Education, 35*(3), 32–41.

Dymoke, S. (2002). The dead hand of the exam: The impact of the NEAB anthology on poetry teaching at GCSE. *Changing English: Studies in Culture and Education, 9*(1), 85–93.

Dymoke, S. (2003). *Drafting and assessing poetry: A guide for teachers.* London: Paul Chapman Publishing.

Dymoke, S. (2009). *Teaching English texts 11–18.* London: Continuum.

Dymoke, S. (2012). Poetry is an unfamiliar text: Locating poetry in secondary English classrooms in New Zealand and England during a period of curriculum change. *Changing English: Studies in Culture and Education, 19*(4), 395–410.

Fleming, M., & Stevens, D. (2015). *English teaching in the secondary school: Linking theory and practice* (4th ed.). Abingdon and New York: Routledge.

Jollimore, T. (2009). 'Like a picture or a bump on the head': Vision, cognition, and the language of poetry. *Midwest Studies in Philosophy, 33*(1), 131–158.

Kivy, P. (2011). Paraphrasing poetry (for profit and pleasure). *The Journal of Aesthetics and Art Criticism, 69*(4), 367–377.

Lamarque, P. (2009a). Poetry and abstract thought. *Midwest Studies in Philosophy, 33*(1), 37–52.

Lamarque, P. (2009b). The elusiveness of poetic meaning. *Ratio, 22*(4), 398–420.

National Statistics Office. (2014). *Malta in figures: 2014.* Valletta: National Statistics Office.

NAWE. (2010). Teachers as writers. Retrieved from www.nawe.co.uk/writing-in-education/writers-in-schools/teachers-as-writers.html.

Nemerov, H. (1972). *Reflexions on poetry and poetics.* New Brunswick, NJ: Rutgers University Press.

OECD. (2009). *Creating effective teaching and learning environments: First results from TALIS: Executive summary.* Retrieved from www.oecd.org/edu/school/43044074.pdf.

O'Neill, H. J. (2006). Once preferred, now peripheral: Poetry and the national assessment for year 11 students in New Zealand post-primary schools. *English Teaching: Practice and Critique, 5*(3), 93–126.

Peel, R., Patterson, A., & Gerlach, J. (2000). *Questions of English: Ethics, aesthetics, rhetoric and the formation of the subject in England, Australia and the United States.* London and New York: Routledge.

Pike, M. (2000). Pupils' poetics. *Changing English: Studies in Culture and Education, 7*(1), 45–54.

Reddy, S. (2010). What's difficult? In J. M. Wilkinson (Ed.), *Poets on teaching: A sourcebook* (pp. 7–8). Iowa City: University of Iowa Press.

Sciriha, L., & Vassallo, M. (2006). *Living languages in Malta.* Malta: Print It Printing Services.

Sloan, G. (2003). *Give them poetry!* New York: Teachers College.

Stevens, D. (2001). What do we mean by teaching literature in secondary English? In J. Williamson, M. Fleming, F. Hardman & D. Stevens (Eds.), *Meeting the standards in secondary English* (pp. 96–124). London: RoutledgeFalmer.

Uysal, H. H., & Bardakci, M. (2014). Teacher beliefs and practices of grammar teaching: Focusing on meaning, form, or forms? *South African Journal of Education, 34*(1), 1–16.

Wilson, A. (2010). Teachers' conceptualisations of the intuitive and the intentional in poetry composition. *English Teaching: Practice and Critique, 9*(3), 53–74.

Xerri, D. (2013a). Colluding in the 'torture' of poetry: Shared beliefs and assessment. *English in Education, 47*(2), 134–146.

Xerri, D. (2013b). 'Dissecting butterflies': Literary theory and poetry teaching in post-16 education. *International Journal of Adolescence and Youth, 18*(4), 205–214.

Xerri, D. (2014). Critical reading and student engagement with poetry. In S. Dymoke, M. Barrs, A. Lambirth, & A. Wilson (Eds.), *Making poetry happen: Transforming the poetry classroom* (pp. 29–35). London and New York: Bloomsbury Academic.

Xerri, D. (2015). *Attitudes, beliefs and practices in poetry education at a post-secondary school in Malta* (Unpublished doctoral thesis). University of York, United Kingdom.

Xerri, D. (2016a). 'Living in a house without mirrors': Poetry's cachet and student engagement. *Anglica: An International Journal of English Studies, 25*(1), 271–286.

Xerri, D. (2016b). 'Poems look like a mathematical equation': Assessment in poetry education. *International Journal of English Studies, 16*(1), 1–7.

Xerri, D. (in press). Poetry education research as an anchorage of thought: Using poetry as interview stimulus material. *International Journal of Research & Method in Education.*

13

THE SOCIAL CONSTRUCTION OF MEANING

Reading *Animal Farm* in the classroom

John Yandell

In what follows, I want to consider one kind of narrative, the class novel, partly by providing another kind of narrative, an account of a single English lesson. The place of the class novel within the secondary English curriculum has been threatened within the last decade or so by the increased emphasis on objective-led teaching and the attendant attitude to texts as little more than vehicles for the transmission of isolable skills. Even before the advent of the National Literacy Strategy (DfEE 2001), however, the class novel's position in accounts of reading and reading development was an uncertain one. If the shared reading of a book-length text has always posed practical difficulties—questions of how to organise the reading and how to get through it all in the time available—these were (and are) compounded by underlying theoretical uncertainties, stemming from the assumption that the novel is a literary form to be consumed by silent, solitary readers.

This view informs, for example, Early and Erikson's essay, 'The Act of Reading'. For all its openness to reader-response theories and to notions of a community of readers, the conclusion to which the essay drives is that, 'For all students, the ultimate goal must be: 'I can read it myself-and I will!'" (Early and Erikson 1998: 42). On this basis, the reading that is accomplished in the classroom becomes merely preparation for something else—the stabilisers, as it were, that can be removed once the tyro reader is sufficiently competent and confident to go it alone. Or, to take a second, more recent instance, Chris Richards' *Young People, Popular Culture and Education* (2011), a subtle, reflective account of work in and around cultural studies over the past four decades, paying careful attention to the complexities of culture and pedagogy, and provides sympathetic, properly theorised vignettes of situated textual practice. Richards' discussion of Melvin Burgess's *Doing It* (2003), however, reveals an acceptance of one reading practice as the default:

> Reading, and perhaps especially reading novels, has a history strongly anchored in individual privacy (Watt, 1957/1979). The reception of a novel

has not been primarily a social act, conducted in the presence of others. Reading a novel is mostly something done alone or, if in the presence of others, at least silently.

Transposed to a school classroom, the reading (aloud) of a novel is further entangled with the social relations of that site. Relations between students, but also between the student and the teacher, become the context of reception, a context absent when the novel is read alone and, most often, in silence.

(Richards 2011: 127, 128)

For Richards, one context for, and way of, reading (a novel) has assumed a normative status: this is the familiar image of the solitary, silent reader. Thus, the collective (noisy) reading of the classroom is represented in Richards as abnormal, as, in effect, interference, the interposition of a context that gets in the way of the normal, direct relationship of text and individual reader. Here, then, the class novel appears, at best, as a substitute for the authentic experience of private reading.

I want to contest this view of the class novel as merely preparation for, or an ersatz version of, the authentic experience of the solitary reader. To begin with, I want to suggest that the history of the novel is more complex than Richards, following Ian Watt, allows. Martyn Lyons (1999) has pointed to the continuing prevalence of 'oral reading' in the nineteenth century, even in the heyday of the classic novel: evidence from Mayhew and Kilvert, a contemporary journalist and diarist respectively, suggests that such reading practices were common across classes, in the cities as well as in rural areas (though Lyons does also argue that the increasing frequency of paintings in which women are represented reading alone is an indication of gendered differences in reading). In the same period, the modes of production and distribution were such as must complicate our picture of reading. Novels such as *Jane Eyre* were first published in the standard three-volume set favoured by the powerful circulating libraries:

The separate volumes made for convenience of fireside reading, and for sharing among members of a family; though it would be exasperating to finish volume I, which ends at the point where Jane rescues Mr. Rochester from his blazing bed, when one's elder sister had not quite finished volume II. For the three-volume form matched a formal literary design: in many novels the structural divisions are as clear as the three acts of a play.

(Tillotson 1954: 23)

If this is not Lyons' 'oral reading', neither is it quite the same as the isolation in which Jane Eyre herself takes pleasure in Bewick's *History of British Birds* (Brontë 1847/1948). Tillotson's image of shared—sequential—reading is an intriguing one, in which the line between the private and the social might have been somewhat blurred, to say the least. On the other hand, Dickens' favoured form, the serial publication which competed with, and largely re-placed, the three-volume sets of the circulating libraries, also cannot readily be accommodated within the paradigm of private reading. The fact that the first parts of novels such as *The Old Curiosity Shop* (1840–1841) and *Dombey and Son* (1846–1848) were being read while Dickens was still writing the later sections meant that the development of plot and the fate of individual characters became matters of public debate, among readers and in correspondence between readers and the author. Dickens, it would appear, was acutely sensitive to such dialogue, prepared to shape his narrative in response to indications of readers' interests (Tillotson 1954; Tomalin 2011). Such evidence disrupts assumptions about the reader's role, since readers were less the passive consumers of already-finished texts than active—often demanding—correspondents, keen to offer views on and contribute to the shaping of the novel as it was being produced. Such condi-tions of production and reception might make us want to question whether the history of the novel was ever quite so securely anchored in individual privacy as Richards believes.

An adequate account of reading, then, even in relation to the novel, might involve attending more carefully to the social dimension, historically located and culturally specific, of those practices. That said, the reading of the class novel involves, necessarily, a different kind of practice. It is distinct from other reading practices by the mere fact that it is accomplished, at least in part, in the classroom, a place largely inhabited by people who have not chosen to be there; and it is a text read by a group of people all but one of whom, generally speaking, have not chosen to read it. Even the teacher may only have exercised choice in a very limited sense: the text may have been selected by someone else (a head of depart-ment or an exam board) or it may have been the only text available in sufficient numbers for a shared reading to be practicable (Sarland 1991). These constraints are real—though not entirely unprecedented: it's perfectly possible that the elder sister in Tillotson's imagined family might have preferred to be reading Fanny Burney rather than Charlotte Brontë. But the existence of such constraints does not mean that we should view the practice itself as a series of deficits. I want to suggest that reading the class novel is a practice that should be taken seriously in its own right, as neither a substitute nor a preparation for private reading. And I want to suggest that it is precisely the fact that the reading of the class novel is, as Richards observes, entangled with the social relations of the classroom that offers the most rewarding perspective on this practice.

Support for this claim comes from a somewhat unexpected quarter. *Mixed Ability Work in Comprehensive Schools* (DES 1978) is a discussion paper produced by Her Majesty's Inspectorate. Its brief chapter on English contains the passing observation that 'English is not a linear or sequential subject in the way that a modern language or mathematics is' (DES 1978: 95)—an acknowledgement that was submerged, a decade later, by the unstoppable tide of national curric-ulum levels and assessment frameworks. HMI also provide a rationale for the class novel:

Moreover, in English, a shared experience and the development of a wide range of individual responses are perfectly compatible, and the very width of the response which mixed ability grouping facilitates can be turned to the advantage of those involved. As for the experience to be shared, happily it is often the finest literature, that which has the strongest human appeal, which will make the deepest impression on pupils of all abilities and allow them to meet on common ground.

(DES 1978: 95)

The argument that the inspectors were making—an argument for placing whole texts and rich, rewarding literature at the centre of work in English—was directed against the poor, thin diet of decontextualised comprehension exercises. For the inspectorate, it is the quality of the text that matters: the right kind of text has the effect on individual sensibilities, and hence produces the common experience that is the basis for a sociability that transcends differences in individual abilities.[1]

What does not feature in the inspectors' argument is the question of pedagogy: what do teachers and student do with these texts, what are the social relations of the classroom and how are these managed in the process of reading? These are questions that I want to address as I turn now to my second narrative, the story of a lesson, as a way of exploring what can be involved in, and produced by, the shared reading of the class novel. I would want to locate this account within a narrative-based tradition of inquiry into practice, a tradition of research that, in contrast to the dominant discourses of standards and testing, attempts to inquire closely into the specificity of classrooms, into the lived experiences of teachers and their students (Doecke and McClenaghan 2011; Parr 2010; van de Ven and Doecke 2011).

The lesson is one that was taught by Heather Wood, at the time a student on an initial teacher education course. It was observed by me as her university tutor.[2] Before telling this story, though, I should make it clear that I am not making large claims for the representativeness of the lesson. There are many ways of 'doing' the class novel, and many class novels. Reading *Holes* (Sachar 2000) is not the same experience as reading *The Curious Incident of the Dog in the Night-time* (Haddon 2003), and neither is the same as reading *Animal Farm* (Orwell 1945/1989). My decision to focus on one lesson is motivated, then, by a methodological commitment to the particular, to finding out what particular teachers and particular groups of students do in reading a particular text together (Freebody 2003).[3] Equally, my decision to focus on this lesson in particular is a motivated one: my claim is that this pedagogic practice is worth attending to.

It's an English lesson in a north London comprehensive, Heather's first practicum school: mixed ability eleven-and twelve-year-olds on a blustery January morning. The class is in the middle of *Animal Farm*. The classroom is organised cafe style, with six tables. Before the students arrive, Heather places a very large piece of sugar paper on each table; on each piece, she has drawn the outline of an animal: one hen, two horses and three pigs.

Heather allocates each student to a group, then reminds the class that at the end of the previous lesson she had asked them to think of questions to ask Squealer. Before we move into the main activity, though, she wants to make sure that everyone is familiar with the genre, so she plays a short video clip of *Youth Question Time* (BBC 2009). Students respond in a variety of ways: some announce that the footage was boring, or unintelligible, or both, others offer comments on the target audience and the kinds of question that elicit interesting answers. Heather asks if in *Animal Farm* the animals have the opportunity to question Squealer. She emphasises that this is something she wants students to continue to think about during the lesson, not something that demands an immediate response. (This emphasis is important, in that she is positioning the activity in relation to the world of the novel and in relation to her students' reading of the novel.) Then, she draws attention to the image of the animal that she has outlined on the sugar paper—a different animal for each table. She explains that each group is to be the animal/character represented on their table—and that they will have the chance to question Squealer (the character who has been allocated to one of the six groups).

Before the *Animal Farm* version of *Question Time* can begin, though, the groups must prepare. In the guidance that Heather provides, what is envisaged is a logical, linear sequence of activities: first the students are to record on their sugar paper the main events of the novel so far, then to consider what they know of their character, and finally to formulate questions to put to Squealer. In practice, there are different approaches to the task. In the Boxer group, next to me, Adam[4] and Noreen are writing questions to Squealer while Jasmine and Maria seem to have responsibility for recording the key events. Nonetheless, there is dialogue across the group: Noreen and Adam read out their questions, facts are checked, Maria suggests further questions. In other groups, there are variations in the order in which tasks are being addressed and how this work is assigned to different individuals. This may be slightly different from what Heather had envisaged, but in every group all members are involved fully in the activity—and students are thinking about the novel in interesting, complicated ways.

In all groups, there is genuine collaborative engagement; in nearly all groups, there is close sympathetic identification with their allocated character (the one exception, from the evidence of what is written on the sugar paper, is the group that has been allocated Major's ghost). One material factor that supports and encourages such collaboration is, I think, the size of the sugar paper: because it is so big, it is possible for all four group members to have direct access to it as writers, more or less simultaneously—and this really does have a demonstrable effect on how the groups go about the task.

'What would Major do in your shoes?' asks Maria, before she writes the question on the sugar paper. It is a wonderfully probing question—a question that will create difficulties for Squealer. It is, therefore, evidence that Maria's group is preparing well for the next part of the lesson. That it comes at this moment, a good ten minutes into the activity, is, I think, a sign of the productivity of the activity—of the thinking that is going on, and of the potential of such collaborative activity. Is it a question that Boxer would ask? Perhaps not, given the extent to which Orwell's representation of the non-porcine animals denies them interiority or rational thought. I wonder, though, if this might be a strength of the activity, in that students are able simultaneously to explore what they know of the novel and its characters and to go beyond it, to brush it, in Walter Benjamin's phrase, 'against the grain' (Benjamin 1955/1970: 259).

Heather brings the class back together—and it is a bit of a struggle to achieve quiet, simply because there is so much energy being devoted to the group task. She gives students thirty seconds to allocate questions to each member of the group. They do this, very efficiently. The Squealer group take their seats at the front of the room. Heather brings the class to order, going into role as presenter of *Animal Farm Question Time*.

The first group to pose questions is the one representing Major's ghost. I remarked above that this was the one group where, on the evidence of the sugar paper, students were not showing any sign of identifying with their allotted character: the questions they had posed in writing were all those of a detached observer. But as Joe enters into dialogue with the Squealer group, he *becomes* Major's ghost—he enters into the role, and speaks with remarkable conviction and authority. The responses he receives from the Squealer group are equally remarkable. Each of its members adopts a formal register and a tone that is both superior and dismissive—somewhere between a headteacher and a politician, perhaps. They don't answer Joe's questions so much as lecture him on the virtues and glories of Comrade Napoleon.

We move on to Maria as Boxer, then Adam, also as Boxer. They ask apposite, searching questions. What is slightly scary is how dismissive the Squealer group is of other animals: their performance shows just how much they understand of the power relations on the farm and of how these inequalities are enforced in and through language. What is wonderful is the manifest enjoyment of all in inhabiting their roles. Next it is the turn of the Hens, who are very angry at the way they have been treated. Again, something slightly miraculous happens here. Students in the Hens' group develop a collective identity in the process of their confrontation with Squealer: they become visibly more supportive of each other, more prepared to argue their case, more involved in the story—and more articulate.

Heather orchestrates the debate very deftly, insisting on the rights of all to be heard. We hear from the Snowball group: Onur is magnificent—combative, aggressive and contemptuous towards Napoleon and Squealer as his lackey. What the Squealer group are very good at doing, *inter alia*, is refusing to answer the question—chiefly by attacking and undermining the questioners; but Sara, who is part of the Mollie group, has noticed this and is not prepared to let them get away with it. Mollie is the white mare whom Orwell represents as obsessed with her own looks, and with sugar. Sara-as-Mollie, on the other hand, has more pressing, more political interests. And this is another wonderful moment—a moment of learning: because Sara is involved in the role, because suddenly this argument matters to her, she expresses very clearly her analysis of what the Squealers have been doing—or failing to do. There is a profound understanding here of an aspect of language and power—of the enactment of power in the refusal to provide an answer.

With five minutes of the lesson remaining, Heather opens out the questioning to all comers. There is general outrage when one of the Squealers accuses Boxer/Noreen of being lazy. Heather brings the discussion to a necessary halt (necessary only because of time, not because of revolutionary activity among the animals). She asks each group to write a question that they would have liked to ask Squealer and didn't have the chance to ask, and the answer that they think Squealer would give. Then, almost as a sort of coda to the lesson, she asks how many of the animals that have been discussed today are still part of the farm (at the point that they have reached in their reading of the novel). Thus, the final move that students make, as the lesson ends, is a return to the text, the text that they can now explore from a different perspective. Heather's question invites the students to engage with the text as linear, developing over time (a series of events) while also considering it in a kind of continuous present, each moment of it simultaneously available to us.

Readers of this essay may feel that they have been lured here on false pretences. I promised to focus on the reading of the class novel, yet I have described a lesson in which little or no reading took place. Wasn't this something else entirely—a drama lesson, perhaps? What I mean by reading, however, is the process of meaning-making that is accomplished by people engaging with text(s). The students in Heather's lesson were actively engaged in making meaning: collaboratively, they were making sense of *Animal Farm*. My argument, therefore, is that this was a lesson in which a great deal of very sophisticated reading was accomplished—reading that was of both the word and the world (Freire and Macedo 1987).[5]

In the lesson, students explored Squealer's role in the novel, the characters of the other animals, the social relationships of the farm. They knew more about the novel—they understood it differently, and better—at the end of the lesson. They were involved in an exploration of how language operates to maintain, enforce and contest power relationships, both in the novel and in the world. But I want to make a further claim about the students' reading, a claim that the activities in which they participated involved them in a re-writing of the novel—and that it is this aspect of their work that is most exciting as a demonstration of their collective power as readers of complex texts (Barthes 1977). This dimension of the activity was introduced at the start, when Heather asked the class whether the other animals had the opportunity to question Squealer. Implicit in Heather's question is the recognition that the central activity of the lesson invites the students to go beyond the text and in doing so to interrogate it, to tease out the silences and absences in Orwell. This rewriting of the text is what happens when Maria-as-Boxer asks Squealer, 'What would Major do in your shoes?', when Onur-as-Snowball answers back to Napoleon, when Joe-as-Major's ghost berates the pigs for their betrayal of the revolution, when Sara-as-Mollie analyses the slipperiness of the Squealers' answers. Most poignantly and wonderfully, it is there when the Hens find a voice, when they, most unlike Orwell's poultry, speak truth to power.

Animal Farm Question Time challenged the unequal distribution of power on the farm. At the same time, it enabled the students to explore and interrogate their own relationships and identities, the social dynamics of the class. What enabled them to do both these things—and to do them safely—was that they were working in role. The question of what happens when students adopt roles, of how the process enables them to access resources of language, and also of thought and feeling, that might otherwise have seemed fairly remote from them, is worth dwelling on. The Vygotskian idea of the zone of proximal development is frequently encountered as a justification for particular forms of intervention (such as 'scaffolding') and to support arguments for the importance of 'more experienced others' in children's development.[6] In 'The Problem of Play in Development', an essay that is included as Chapter 7 of *Mind in Society* (1978), Vygotsky returns to the idea of the zone proximal development; this time, though, the term is used in a context that does not seem to have much to do with questions of instruction. Instead, it appears in a remarkable passage where Vygotsky argues for play as a centrally important contributor to development:

> … play creates a zone of proximal development of the child. In play a child always behaves beyond his average age, above his daily behaviour; in play it is as though he were a head taller than himself. As in the focus of a magnifying glass, play contains all developmental tendencies in a condensed form and is itself a major source of development.
>
> *(Vygotsky 1978: 102)*

Vygotky's claims for the productive possibilities of play, for what play enables children to do and to learn, seem to me to be directly relevant to what was going on in Heather's classroom. What enables her students to meet on common ground is not, as the inspectors proposed in 1978, a product of the literary quality of Orwell's novel. When Joe's group was exploring the character of Major, the students were assembling information from the text; they did this with varying degrees of diligence but without any particular commitment to the activity. When, on the other hand, Joe starts to question the Squealer group, he enters fully into the role of Major's ghost—and inhabiting the role gives him both access to different linguistic registers and a new kind of ownership over the text. Likewise, it is when the Hens enter into dialogue with Squealer that they construct a role for themselves, not as headless chickens but as mutually supportive mother hens. Their work in role seems to me to function as a penetrating interrogation of Orwell's tendency to represent the non-porcine inhabitants of the farm as hopelessly stupid, passive victims of the pigs.

I suggested above that the students were reading both the word and the world. The world that is being read is, in part, the adult world of political discourse. In conversation after the lesson, Heather considered that it had been a mistake to spend time watching the video clip of *Youth Question Time*. She realised that the students simply did not need to be inducted into the genre: they either were already knowledgeable or were perfectly capable of contributing to a formal debate without being presented with such a model. Here again, I would want to argue that it is the affordance of work in role that provides access to the genre. At the same time that this is happening, the students are engaged in another, considerably more complex, act of reading. Through their work in role, the students are exploring, rendering visible and holding up to scrutiny, the social relations of the classroom. In constructing the groups, Heather had allocated to the Squealer group four high-achieving, middle-class students whose interactions with other members of the class had, in previous lessons, betrayed more than a hint of arrogance. In the lesson, the Squealer group's preparations for *Animal Farm Question Time* had involved mining a thesaurus for suitably long, sonorous words with which to impress (and silence) their audience. There was a sense, therefore, in which the Squealer students were playing themselves. When the Hens assert their rights and when Sara-as-Mollie takes the floor to analyse exactly what is going on when the Squealers fail to provide answers to the other animals' questions, what is at issue is something of more immediate relevance than the covert hierarchies of the farm: the activity provides a means to challenge the social stratification of the class itself. This can be accomplished relatively safely because of the distance provided by role: Sara is, and is not, Mollie; the four students are, and are not, Squealer.

When Heather read a draft of this essay, she recalled the class's final work on *Animal Farm*:

> they took their work from the question time lesson further and wrote a persuasive speech in role as a character of their choice and performed it to the class. One student, Joe, created a name and a whole identity for a horse on the farm and read his speech in a cockney accent, walking around the classroom trying to rouse the crowd and convince them that they didn't need Napoleon. It was absolutely brilliant.
>
> (*Heather Wood, email correspondence, 28 June 2012*)

Joe's choice of accent is, it seems to me, inseparable from the meaning of his speech. It is the counterpoint to the Squealer students' use of the thesaurus: the horse is answering back.

Heather's students' reading of *Animal Farm* cannot be reduced to questions of reception or comprehension. On the contrary, the text is being constantly remade, in the readers' interests. These interests differ, and these different interests, all of which leave their mark on the text, are what make it unstable, complex, 'multiaccented':

The social *multiaccentuality* of the ideological sign is a very crucial aspect. By and large, it is thanks to this intersecting of accents that a sign maintains its vitality and dynamism and the capacity for further development. A sign that has been withdrawn from the pressures of the social struggle—which, so to speak, crosses beyond the pale of the class struggle—inevitably loses force, degenerating into allegory and becoming the object not of live social intelligibility but of philological comprehension.

(Vološinov 1929/1986: 23, original emphasis)

Animal Farm is reanimated, then, saved from becoming merely an object of 'philological comprehension', precisely because it has become 'entangled in the social relations' of the classroom.

Notes

1 These claims have been contested, of course, notably by Sarland in his very funny account of a less than uplifting shared experience of Steinbeck's *The Pearl* (Sarland 1991, 'On not finding yourself in the text').
2 I am very grateful to Heather Wood, both for giving me permission to write about the lesson and for the privilege of having observed it. The account that follows is one for which I take full responsibility—it is the lesson that I observed, not the lesson that Heather taught; the account relies heavily on the notes I took during the lesson, though it is also informed by the discussion that I had with Heather afterwards.
3 My emphasis on attending to the particular is at odds with the approach taken by the National Literacy Strategy:

> pupils in one school studying, for example, *Treasure Island* and *Animal Farm*, will, one way or another, have covered the same objectives by the end of the key stage as pupils in another school who have studied quite different texts.
>
> *(DfEE 2001: 14)*

4 Students' names have been changed to culturally appropriate pseudonyms.
5 This is, of course, a very different approach to reading than that which is to be found in the most recent version of the National Curriculum with which primary teachers have been confronted: it is not reducible to either 'word reading' or 'comprehension' (DfE 2012: 2).
6 For a fuller discussion of these ideas, see Daniels (2001), Chaiklin (2003) and Yandell (2007).

References

Barthes, R. (1977) *Image Music Text*, London: Fontana.
BBC (2009) *Youth Question Time*, London, Natural History Museum, 4 December 2009. Available online at www.youtube.com/watch?v=6OGZYleoboM, accessed 24 September 2012.
Benjamin, W. (1955/1970) *Illuminations*, Glasgow: Collins.
Brontë, C. (1847/1948) *Jane Eyre*, London and Glasgow: Blackie and son.
Burgess, M. (2003) *Doing It*, London: Andersen Press.
Chaiklin, S. (2003) The Zone of Proximal Development in Vygotsky's Analysis of Learning and Instruction. In A. Kozulin et al. (eds) *Vygotsky's Educational Theory in Cultural Context*, Cambridge: Cambridge University Press, pp. 39–64.

Daniels, H. (2001) *Vygotsky and Pedagogy*, New York & London: RoutledgeFalmer.

DES (Department of Education and Science). (1978) *Mixed Ability Work in Comprehensive Schools*, London: HMSO.

DfE (Department for Education). (2012) *National Curriculum for English Key Stages 1 and 2 – Draft: National Curriculum review*, London: DfE. Available online at www.education. gov.uk/nationalcurriculum, accessed 28 June 2012.

DfEE (Department for Education and Employment). (2001) *Key Stage 3 National Strategy: Framework for Teaching English: Years 7, 8 and 9*, London: DfEE.

Doecke, B., & McClenaghan, D. (2011) *Confronting Practice: Classroom Investigations into Language and Learning*, Putney, NSW: Phoenix.

Early, M., & Ericson, B. O. (1998) The Act of Reading. In B. F. Nelms (ed.) *Literature in the Classroom: Readers, Texts and Contexts*, New York: NCTE, pp. 31–44.

Freebody, P. (2003) *Qualitative Research in Education: Interaction and Practice*, London, Thousand Oaks, CA & New Delhi: SAGE.

Freire, P., & Macedo, D. (1987) *Literacy: Reading the Word and the World*, London: Routledge and Kegan Paul.

Haddon, M. (2003) *The Curious Incident of the Dog in the Night-time*, London: Jonathan Cape.

Lyons, M. (1999) New Readers in the Nineteenth Century: Women, Children, Workers. In G. Cavallo & R. Chartier (eds) *A History of Reading in the West*, Amherst & Boston: University of Massachusetts Press, pp. 321–343.

Orwell, G. (1945/1989) *Animal Farm: A Fairy Story*, London: Penguin.

Parr, G. (2010) *Inquiry-based Professional Learning: Speaking Back to Standards-based Reforms*, Teneriffe, Queensland: Post Pressed.

Richards, C. (2011) *Young People, Popular Culture and Education*, London & New York: Continuum.

Sachar, L. (2000) *Holes*, London: Bloomsbury.

Sarland, C. (1991) *Young People Reading: Culture and Response*, Buckingham: Open University Press.

Tillotson, K. (1954) *Novels of the Eighteen-Forties*, Oxford: Clarendon.

Tomalin, C. (2011) *Charles Dickens: A Life*, London: Penguin.

van de Ven, P.-H., & Doecke, B. (eds) (2011) *Literary Praxis: A Conversational Inquiry into the Teaching of Literature*, Rotterdam: Sense.

Vološinov, V. N. (1929/1986) *Marxism and the Philosophy of Language*, Cambridge, MA & London: Harvard University Press.

Vygotsky, L. S. (1978) *Mind in Society: The Development of Higher Psychological Processes*, Cambridge, MA & London: Harvard University Press.

Watt, I. (1957/1979) *The Rise of the Novel: Studies in Defoe, Richardson and Fielding*, London: Chatto and Windus.

Yandell, J. (2007) Investigating literacy practices within the secondary English classroom, or where is the text in this class? *Cambridge Journal of Education* 37.2, pp. 249–262.

14

TEACHING AND LEARNING FROM WILLIAM BLAKE THROUGH THE LENS OF CRITICAL LITERACY

David Stevens

As is undoubtedly the case with other great writers in an educational context, to teach Blake, I find, is to learn from him—and often this occurs through the agency of those taught. It is perhaps this feeling of reciprocity that accounts for Blake's greatness, and that of others of similar stature: a certain susceptibility to open-ended enquiry, with an apparently paradoxical combination of robustness on the one hand, allowing many ways in, yet always surviving with integrity; and uncertainty on the other, in the sense that Keats wrote of Shakespeare possessing 'negative capability ... that is when man is capable of being in uncertainties, mysteries, doubts without any irritable reaching after fact and reason'. With this in mind, I attempt in this chapter to build on previous writing on Blake in education (Blake ed Stevens 1995; Stevens 2000, 2011, 2012; Stevens and McGuinn 2004) to further illustrate the pedagogical possibilities around his work, focusing particularly on the poem 'London'. I also draw briefly on the insights of Blake's near-contemporaries Coleridge and Shelley, who although very different in many key respects from Blake, seem to me to offer profound and subtle perceptions into the nature of literature in the implicit context of teaching and learning. Crucially, too, I attempt to make positive use of the much more recent phenomena of critical literacy and critical pedagogy, inspired by Freire and followers, to illustrate how Romanticism—the spirit in which Blake, Coleridge and Shelley wrote—may be given a harder, more radical and contemporary edge appropriate to today's educational needs. To give perhaps a more vivid flavour of such things, I include also a few illustrative comments from a couple of recent occasions when I have explored 'London' with school students and pre-service English teachers.

That hard edge of reality is certainly present in Blake, throughout his work but especially in the crucial counterbalancing of 'experience' with 'innocence', and it is no accident that 'London', the poem I focus on here, is from the 'experience' part of his 'Songs of Innocence and of Experience'. For Blake, experience reminds us that all is not necessarily easy and well in the world, even if (in today's educational context) the classroom may afford some shelter from exploitative excesses and may even lead to a false sense of well-being:

> It is an easy thing to triumph in the summer's sun
> And in the vintage, and to sing on the wagon loaded with corn.
> It is an easy thing to talk of patience to the afflicted...
> To hear the dog howl at the wintry door, the ox in the slaughterhouse moan;
> To see a god on every wind and a blessing on every blast...
> It is an easy thing to rejoice in the tents of prosperity:
> Thus could I sing and thus rejoice: but it is not so with me.
> (Blake ed Stevens 1995: 139; from *Vala or the Four Zoas*)

This kind of reminder has always been part of the best of English pedagogy, I suggest. In so many English classrooms that I and others have experienced, especially through literary exploration but also including linguistic or thematic dimensions, serious issues are confronted—and often counterbalanced with a celebratory sense of what may be otherwise possible. But we need now to consider a little more deeply the nature of the development of English pedagogy, I suspect, particularly in terms of its relationship to both Romanticism and the critical pedagogy proposed by Freire and others.

'The significance of Romanticism for the development of English is well understood' (Peel 2000: 60); maybe, but what are the possible implications of such a tradition in terms of the critical context outlined above? The inescapable tension between social and individual aspects of life and culture, the prestigious place of the imagination, the nature of creativity and (loosely defined) spiritual growth, the credibility of all experience and feeling—including the darker side: all have direct and continuing relevance for English. There is not space here to examine in critical detail the nature of Romanticism in the English pedagogical tradition; nevertheless, some appraisal of the impact of Romanticism is required in the present context. Considering (and countering) the sense that what he saw as the Romantically conceived subject English had developed as a pale substitute for religious faith, David Holbrook pointed out that 'It is not a "religion": but it is a discipline in which we use language, to grope beyond language, at the possible meaning that life may have' (Holbrook 1979: 237). It is in this spirit that I work, but with a critical edge (as indeed did Holbrook, of course), drawing especially on critical pedagogy and thus, incidentally, relating pertinently to a version of personal growth through literature teaching so central to the Romantic English pedagogical tradition. Appropriately enough, Coleridge offers insight here, distinguishing between the 'unsatisfactory profession' of teaching (in his time, of course, but the relevance remains), and the balancing potential for a subversive alternative: fostering a 'buoyancy of spirit' through exploration of words as 'living powers' (Coleridge (1830) 1977: 315).

Because of this potential, teaching literature, especially, may in Freirean spirit blend critique and hope, criticality and celebration. For me, Freire's lifelong commitment to education as liberation—'...working against the myths that de-form us' (Freire 1997: 41)—is acutely apt in a social context damagingly obsessed with the mundane and merely instrumental (especially manifested in literature teaching in today's English classrooms, in England at least, where so often the meaning and effect of a poem are sacrificed to spotting elements of form). There is the hard edge of criticality there, but to read Freire attentively is also to witness a Romantic spirit at work:

> Born of a critical matrix, dialogue creates a critical attitude. It is nourished by love, humility, hope, faith, and trust. When the two 'poles' of the di-alogue are thus linked by love, hope and mutual trust, they can join in a critical search for something. Only dialogue truly communicates.
>
> *(Freire 1974: 40)*

In striking contrast, today's educational legislators talk in terms of 'delivering' a curriculum and aiming at pre-ordained 'targets', or, for teacher education at least, uniform and rigid 'standards'. By society's metaphors so shall you know it. Freire posed questions addressing the ultimate purposes of education itself. In particular, he criticised what he aptly termed the 'banking' model of teach-ing and learning: the unquestioning transmission of whatever goes for 'know-ledge'. Instead, he recommended actively democratic interaction, constructive criticality, acknowledgement of varied models of knowledge and insight, and, ultimately, the radical transformation of the world away from the debilitating profit motive. Of course, this vision is political; as Freire himself maintained, 'we are necessarily working against myths that deform us. As we confront such myths, we also face the dominant power because those myths are nothing but the expression of this power, of its ideology' (1997: 41). I think Blake would have agreed, as a skilled user of both the 'language of critique' to the 'language of possibility' (Freire 1974). It is precisely this combination that is vital: either one without the other would be severely deficient—wholly negative, or purely idealistic. The teacher's role is to balance these elements, managing the necessary dialectical tension between them. Seeing the word and the world (Freire's telling fusion) as new, open to critical insight *and* a sense of wonder, to critical distance *and* informed engagement, is absolutely fundamental here, and is at the heart of what Freire and his followers commend. It's also at the heart of 'London'.

That a sense of wonder at the nature of existence may be combined with a strongly critical and reflective standpoint, and that both these 'distanced' posi-tions may complement active, engaged immersion in social and cultural activity (including teaching and learning), are key ideas here. The tension is that between engaged involvement on the one hand, and critical, reflective distance on the other. This tension may lie at the heart of any creative act, including English (or indeed any) teaching. Involvement here is the motivating force, balanced by a sense of critical distance to give contextual understanding. The subject of English has special significance in its sharp focus on language—how it both expresses and conceals meaning, often simultaneously. However, such notions seem a far cry from the concerns and preoccupations of most English classrooms. Indeed, the dominant official educational discourse assumes an alienation from the ultimate purposes in any philosophical sense (Alexander 2007). Gibson has characterised this alienation as fundamentally 'a structure of feeling', echoing perhaps Blake's 'mind forg'd manacles' in 'London'. Gibson analyses this tendency as 'instrumental rationality', signifying

> a preoccupation with 'How to do it?' questions rather than with questions of 'Why do it?' or 'Where are we going?'. It is thus concerned with means rather than ends, with efficiency more than with consideration of purposes. In schools one manifestation is a stress on management and organisation at the expense of consideration of 'What is education for?'.
>
> *(Gibson 1984: 83)*

All this amounts to a potentially disastrous, alienating and dichotomous separation of means and ends, of activity and purpose, with the process spawning its own dubious justification and particular—often impenetrable—rationality. But there could be something far more positive at stake here: an awakened appreciation of the possibility of a new synthesis between celebratory and critical aspects of English pedagogy based precisely on conscious awareness of the nature of alienating thought and practice. As John Dewey had it, 'Every experience is a moving force. Its value can be judged only on the ground of what it moves toward and into' (Dewey (1938) 1997: 38).

One of my main concerns with contemporary education, including the generally laudable, even Romantic, emphasis on creativity, is that many of the strategies so readily endorsed could be used for negative ends: the context of values, within which any radically Romantic creativity must operate, is notably missing. In this sense too, it is important that both teachers and learners experience a sense of involvement in and ownership of the creativity in the classroom through what Gardner (1993) has called 'good work'. Anything else would clearly run counter to the very nature of creativity in education. The Chicago psychologist Csikszentmihalyi (1990) has conceptualised creativity as the experience of 'flow', or 'optimal experience', suggestive of engagement, empathy, connection and interplay; such a formulation sits comfortably with the critically Romantic model proposed here. Further characteristic symptoms, according to the 'flow' model, would include complete involvement in the activity through both intellect and feeling, immediate feedback through an intrinsic sense of the worth of the activity in and for itself, and an appropriate balance of challenge and capability. Interestingly, the notion of 'flow' as an essential ingredient of creativity corresponds to Romantic philosophies and provokes pertinent questions concerning the balance—and implied synthesis—between immersion and intellectually conscious critique.

So much depends on how successfully we may oppose as teachers the crippling, disempowering determinism so prevalent in the current climate. We need instead to foster a sense of purpose, and an underlying sense that human beings may work together to bring about change for the better. Blake again offers assistance here, in his insistence on a clear, all-encompassing sense of direction: such a sense informed his entire life's work and addressed fundamental concerns about our future and its values. In this sense any answers—even tentative ones—are essentially prophetic:

> Every honest man is a prophet; he utters his opinion both of private and public matters. Thus: if you go on so, the result is so. He never says, such a thing shall happen let you do what you will. A prophet is a seer, not an arbitrary dictator.
>
> *(Blake ed Stevens 1995: 46)*

This sense of participatory prophecy accords powerfully, as Blake's insights frequently do, with Freire, who endorsed a view of praxis encapsulated in 'the understanding of history as opportunity and not determinism' (Freire 1992: 77), maintaining elsewhere that,

> Education is thus constantly remade in the praxis. In order to *be*, it must *become*. ... Problem-posing education is revolutionary futurity. Hence it is prophetic (and, as such, hopeful). Hence, it corresponds to the historical nature of humankind. Hence, it affirms women and men as beings who transcend themselves, who move forward and look ahead, for whom immobility represents a fatal threat....
>
> *(Freire 1970: 65)*

Or, as Blake expressed it even more succinctly in his *Proverbs of Hell*, 'Expect Poison from Standing Water' (Blake ed Stevens 1995: 107). In the context of the current book especially, the centrality of literature in the English curriculum is, for me, crucial here—certainly not in opposition, or as hierarchically superior, to other aspects of English teaching, but rather in dynamic relationship with them. John Dewey, celebrating the liberating power of literature, lucidly stated what many English teachers still strongly feel, that

> Art breaks through barriers that divide human beings, which are impermeable in ordinary association. This force of art, common to all the arts, is most fully manifested in literature. Its medium is already formed by communication....
>
> *(Dewey 1934: 244)*

The uses of literature in teaching are at once profoundly intense and enormously wide-ranging. As the novelist Aidan Chambers maintains,

> I would go as far as to say that it is this particular use of language—the literary use that some have called 'storying'—that defines humanity and makes us human. ... this particular form of language and our skill in using it empower us in being what we are, and make it possible for us to conceive of being more than we are.
>
> *(Chambers 1985: 2–3)*

To return to Blake and the 'mind forged manacles' he hears so oppressively in alienated London: manacles they are, to all intents and purposes, but in seeing their 'mind-forged' nature the poet suggests the subtle connection between social reality and consciousness, objectivity and subjectivity, cause and effect. In effect this is a vivid evocation of what Habermas (1970) called the 'intersubjectively recognised subject', transcending the false, and unhelpful, dichotomy between 'outer' and 'inner' worlds and words, and between such traditions as the Romantic and the radically critical. The teaching of English could have as its central aim the liberation of this manacled world, and the starting point may well be the Blakean 'minute particulars' of the classroom, including the manacles, mind-forged or otherwise, to be found there. For Blake, as for us as English teachers,

> I must create a system or be enslaved by another man's.
> I will not reason or compare: my business is to create.
>
> (Blake ed Stevens 1995: 132)

It seems to me that Blake alludes to a tension at the heart of the process of education no less now than in his own time. On the one hand we have the creative possibilities expressed in 'Jerusalem':

> I give you the end of a golden string,
> Only wind it into a ball,
> It will lead you in at Heaven's gate
> Built in Jerusalem's wall.
>
> (Blake ed Stevens 1995: 140)

On the other hand, this sense of education as an opening out, carefully guided—taught, indeed—but ultimately relying on the autonomous activity of the learner, may be juxtaposed with Blake's awareness of the joyless, materialistic and deterministic approaches characteristic of the education processes around him. In particular, consider this description of the formal schooling of his day:

> But to go to school in a summer morn,
> Oh! It drives all joy away;

Under a cruel eye outworn,
The little ones spend the day
In sighing and dismay.

(Blake ed Stevens 1995: 183)

Matters have improved somewhat since Blake, himself largely unschooled, wrote this bleak description. And yet ... the stifling of the celebratory by means of initiative onslaught, intended or not; the strengthening of institutionalised education as a means of social control during the intervening two centuries—surely the tension remains powerfully apposite. Again, English and its allied arts subjects are frequently at the centre of this tension.

More recently, Richard Smith has made the point that to try to be systematic in understanding Romanticism would lead to frustrating failure, suggesting instead that

> ...the elements of the Romantic view that I want to emphasise are the opposite of the systematic. They are the creativity that consists in bringing reality into being, rather than faithfully representing it; the capacity to work with the protean and unstable; and—another dimension of moving beyond representation—the truth and knowledge that transcend the specific.
>
> (Smith 2008: 9)

Shelley's observation that 'man, having enslaved the elements, remains himself a slave' (in Wroe 2008: 339) finds an echo in Robert Witkin's central assertion introducing his aptly titled and influential book *The Intelligence of Feeling*:

> If the price of finding oneself in the world is that of losing the world in oneself, then the price is more than anyone can afford. ... The repression of subjectivity in our own age has served only to render its periodic outbursts sharper than ever.
>
> (Witkin 1974: 1–2)

Such sentiments themselves echo those of Blake in his own critical exploration of the nature of the repression of 'energy', and help to give a radical social dimension to Romanticism. Witkin, interestingly, goes on to link these ideas to the realities of schooling in terms of that central tenet of Romanticism, self-expression, noticing the

> ...ambivalent attitude in teachers with respect to self-expression ... both a positive necessity and a disturbing threat. He [the teacher] sees it as both creative and constructive on the one hand and as destructive and anarchical on the other. Self-expression is the fruit of the tree that conceals the serpent.
>
> (ibid: 34)

It's a thorny issue in creative pedagogy, elements of which pertain to both
Romanticism and critical approaches to teaching and learning. Witkin continues:

> The problem for the teacher, in his praxis, is how to marry both the im-
> pulse that bestows validity, and the context of legitimacy that denotes ac-
> ceptability, in the pupil's acts of self-expression. His stance with respect
> to both the creative process and the curriculum can be understood as an
> attempt to achieve just this.
>
> *(ibid: 35)*

Such insights, I feel, are relevant to my own recent teaching of Blake through
the lens of critical literacy. What has so often emerged has been young people's gathering appreciation of the link between Blake's concept of 'innocence' and an imaginative, creative and honestly critical understanding of the
world, and, correspondingly, the close resemblance of Blake's 'experience' to
a damagingly reductive, mechanistic literalness. A couple of illustrative examples may be timely here. Considering possibilities of teaching Blake with
PGCE (i.e. pre-service) English beginning teachers, focusing on 'London',
we were struck by the startling parallel between the image central to the
third stanza,

> And the hapless soldier's sigh
> Runs in blood down palace walls
>
> (Blake ed Stevens 1995: 73)

and the contemporary (i.e. 2014) art installation of a sea of poppies surrounding the Tower of London. I hadn't myself noticed this parallel—a particularly
perceptive student brought it to our attention—but the subsequent exploration
certainly yielded many insights along the lines of using critical literacy as a way
into Blake (and thus using Blake as a way into a critical appreciation of our own
world). For the art project itself alludes to the often uncomfortable relationship
between commemorating wartime sacrifice and suffering 'lest we forget', on
the one hand, and glorifying such experience (I use this word consciously here)
on the other. Blake's lines served powerfully to focus on this tension, and especially on the relationship of authoritarian power structures, emblemised in the
Tower/palace, and the suffering of 'hapless' individuals at their mercy. One of
these beginning teachers has since gone on to use the idea as a way into World
War One poetry appreciation. Another instance centred on the final emotionally culminating stanza of the poem presenting the plight of the 'youthful har-
lot', this time with a group of sixth-form (17- to 18-year-old) English literature
students.

> But most through midnight streets I hear
> How the youthful harlot's curse

Blasts the new-born infant's tear
And blights with plagues the marriage hearse.

(Blake ed Stevens 1995: 73)

Here, the poem allowed us an imaginatively fertile artistic context for consideration of young sex-workers in the UK and their exploitation by apparently 'respectable', individuals—a highly topical theme at the time. The non-literal power of Blake's lines enabled us to focus vividly and critically on this relationship in a way I suspect would have been much more laboured otherwise. Indeed, one student became very enthusiastic about Blake generally—both his writing and his art. She went on to write:

> There is always something particularly alluring in a figure with an immense talent which he chooses to use in a radical way. ... The arts world is littered with such people—they are said to be 'burned out' but these are the ones that will be always remembered. There is a saying 'shooting stars shine the brightest'.

I hope such experiences serve to give something of the flavour of the possibilities of critically aware literature teaching, albeit briefly, and in so doing build on the good work of Louise Rosenblatt, whose voice surely informs, consciously or otherwise, so much that is good in exploration of literature with students. In her seminal work *Literature as Exploration* (1970), Rosenblatt emphasised the role that readers of literary texts play as active constructors of meaning:

> Through the medium of words, the text brings into the reader's consciousness certain concepts, certain sensuous experiences, certain images of things, people, actions, scenes. ... The reader brings to the work personality traits, memories of past events, present needs and preoccupations, a particular mood of the moment, and a particular physical condition. These and many other elements in a never-to-be duplicated combination determine his response to the particular contribution of the text.

(Rosenblatt 1970: 30–31)

And that, it seems to me, is exactly what was happening in these brief encounters, and so many more like them.

I should like to round off this chapter by looking in a little more detail at 'London'. My purpose in this chapter has been to use the poem as richly emblematic of a dynamic and radical synthesis of the Romantic and the critical, in an educational context focusing on literature teaching. Indeed, the poet/narrator may be likened to a teacher, in effect, and in this sense the poem models positive reciprocity. Particularly striking in this respect is the dynamic combination of critical detachment from the observed situation, and passionate involvement in it—the detachment making possible a startling clarity of vision, balanced by the powerfully felt motivation to do something about it. Although part of the same oppressive world he depicts in the poem, Blake, by virtue of his poetic insight, is able to penetrate it critically; by doing this he implies a way forward. I am struck too by the evident fusion of senses, especially sight and hearing, and the way Blake plays so skilfully on the intense relationship between the particular—the three increasingly hapless figures of the chimney-sweeper, the soldier and the young prostitute—and the universal qualities their oppression denotes. Microcosmic and macrocosmic realities are evocatively fused here, in the same way that the English classroom may both reflect wider realities and form its own particular version. 'London' is in essence a radical study of urban alienation—spiritual, sexual, social and political—given startling immediacy through Blake's compressed poetic visionary imagination. But most of all I am interested in the 'mind forged manacles' Blake hears in all the sounds of London. Manacles they are, but in seeing their 'mind-forged' nature the poet suggests the subtle connection between social reality and consciousness, objectivity and subjectivity, cause and effect. In effect this is a vivid evocation of what Habermas (1970) called the 'intersubjectively recognised subject', transcending the false, and unhelpful, dichotomy between 'outer' and 'inner' worlds and words. The teaching of literature in English should, I suggest, have as its central aim the liberation of this manacled world, and the starting point may well be the minute particulars of the classroom—including the manacles, mind-forged or otherwise—to be found there.

References

Alexander, J. (2007) 'The uncreating word,' in Ellis, V., Fox, C., and Street, B. (eds) *Rethinking English in Schools.* London: Contunuum.

Berlin, I. (ed Hardy, H.) (1999) *The Roots of Romanticism.* London: Chatto and Windus.

Blake, W. (ed Stevens, D.) (1995) *Selected Works.* Cambridge: Cambridge University Press.

Chambers, A. (1985) *Tell Me: Children, Reading and Talk.* Stroud: Thimble Press.

Coleridge, S.T. (ed Richards, I.A.) (1977) *The Portable Coleridge.* Harmondsworth: Penguin.

Csikszentmihalyi, M. (1990) *Flow.* London: Harper Collins.

Dewey, J. (1934; this ed 1958) *Art as Experience.* New York: Capricorn.

Dewey, J. (1938; this ed 1997) *Experience and Education.* New York: Touchstone.

Freire, P. (1970; this ed 1996) *Pedagogy of the Oppressed.* London: Penguin.

Freire, P. (1974; this ed 2005) *Education for Critical Consciousness.* London: Continuum.

Freire, P. (1992; this ed 2006) *Pedagogy of Hope.* London: Continuum.

Freire, P. (1997; this ed 2007) *Pedagogy of the Heart.* New York: Continuum.

Gardner, H. (1993) *Frames of Mind: The Theories of Multiple Intelligences.* New York: Basic Books.

Gibson, R. (1984) *Structuralism and Education.* London: Hodder and Stoughton.

Habermas, J. (1970) *Towards a Rational Society.* Boston: Beacon Press.

Holbrook, D. (1979) *English for Meaning.* Windsor: NFER.

Rosenblatt, L. (1970) *Literature as Exploration.* London: Heinemann.

Smith, R. (2008) 'Proteus rising: re-imagining educational research.' *The Journal of Philosophy of Education* 42(1), 4–20.

Stevens, D. (2000) 'William Blake in education: a poet for our times?' *Changing English* 7(1), 55–63.

Stevens, D. (2011) 'Critically enlightened romantic values and English pedagogy: a response to Peter Medway.' *Changing English* 18(1), 45–56.

Stevens, D. (2012) 'Paulo Freire and the pedagogical traditions of the subject English.' *English in Education* 46(2), 121–134.

Stevens, D. and McGuinn, N. (2004) *The Art of Teaching Secondary English: Innovative and Creative Approaches.* London: Routledge Falmer.

Witkin, R.W. (1974) *The Intelligence of Feeling.* London: Heinemann.

Wroe, A. (2008) *Being Shelley.* London: Vintage.

15

ENGLISH LITERATURE AND DISCURSIVE CHANGES IN IRAN AFTER THE ISLAMIC REVOLUTION (1979)

Shirin Teifouri

Since the rising prominence of theoretical debate in the 1960s which caused an epistemological shift from textual interpretation to cultural critique on both sides of the Atlantic, the notion of 'literature' and the foundations of critical discourse have been dramatically transformed. Theoretical discourses and cultural studies of the post-1960s, as part of a larger agenda for social and political reformation, have been culturally translated, circulated, adapted, used or abused in different ways in different countries. This chapter asks whether the 'theory revolution' of the 1970s that transformed the state of English literature in Anglo-American universities had any impact on the direction of English literature in Iran after the Islamic Revolution (1979). At this time Iran was experiencing a different 'revolution' which resulted in closing doors to the West and making it extremely difficult to have cultural exchanges with English speaking universities.

What is taken for granted in the West is that European theory 'is being appropriated by universities all over the world' and it 'diffusion parallels the global spread of Western technology and capitalist economic organization' (Miller, 1999, 67). This perspective is institutionalized by the genre of Reader's Guides and anthologies of 'literary theory' written during the past decades. In *Modern Literary Theory: A Reader* (2001), for example, Philip Rice and Patricia Waugh write that contemporary critical theory has established itself 'comfortably in the everyday life of literary studies' (Rice & Waugh, 2001, 2). The globalized success of Reader's Guides and theory anthologies seems to confirm Miller's claim. They have penetrated the remotest marketplaces outside Western countries (even though with a considerable delay). However, the 'parallel' Miller draws between the appropriation of the American version of 'theory' and the global spread of Western technology 'all over the world' is actually more complex and circumscribed than it seems. The problem with such statements is not their accuracy but their certainty that theory's 'diffusion' and applicability is a smooth, one-way traffic from West to the rest.

Discursive change after the Islamic Revolution

The Iranian governmental change from the Pahlavi monarchy to Islamic Republic has unleashed a comparable process of 'discursive' change which has affected the state of English literature. Shortly after the Islamic Revolution the universities were closed for two years (1980–1982). This period was officially named 'Cultural Revolution' with the aim of changing the system of education from its 'Western' state to an Islamic one and making sure that the cultural policy of the education was based on religious values. The field of humanities, in general, and the English language and literature curriculum, in particular, was one of the areas modified by the Ministry of Science and Higher Education (now the ministry of Science, Research and Technology) in response to religious and socio-political changes in the country.

The English literature syllabus had to go through certain religious, political, and cultural filters, and academic staff had to take account of this process. The Western canon, like anything Western, was criticized and questioned by the first generation of the Revolution. The canon of English literature was self-evidently a product of 'Western' cultural values, transmitted in the language of Iran's principal political 'enemy'. The question of the Western canon became a complicated one, involving different political and theoretical challenges from those which resulted from the expansion of canon in the West itself. And yet, despite this ideological ferment, there was no sudden iconoclastic reversal; rather, a specific list of authors and works was selected to form a morally safer or less 'corrupting' body of material for Iranian students. Nevertheless, there were some attempts to modify textbooks. In 1986, for example, two Iranian professors of English literature compiled an abridged version of the Norton Anthology which excluded authors such as D. H. Lawrence because of his sexual explicitness. This book is still one of the textbooks used to teach the history of English literature in Iran (Sokhanvar & Honarvar, 1986).

Studying English literature in Iran: responses to the questionnaire

In the summer of 2008 I sent out a questionnaire which attempted to elicit fresh responses and address in a more systematic way the issue of what it meant to study English literature in Iran. I sent out twenty copies of a questionnaire by email attachment to male and female academics in different Iranian universities, and received back sixteen responses (five from women and eleven from men). The number of English literature staff is very limited in Iran, and in this regard, the number of female academics is even less. The sixteen respondents represent a significant sample of the whole. Participants are referred to by using alphabetical codes and their responses are cited as given, including occasional small slips of English grammar or idiom. The questionnaire was divided into three general areas: (1) Why do we read English Literature? (2) How do we read English literature? (3) What do we read?

Why do we read English literature?

The first issue the questionnaire brings to focus is the question of justification for studying English literature in Iran. What is the relevance of studying English literature to the lives of students in an Islamic country like Iran? Nearly all of the academics remarked that studying English literature/literature in English was an 'important' subject of study in Iran. An analysis of the reasons shows that literature is considered important in terms of its positive cultural and social impact on Iranian society and it can play a role in intellectual development of Iranian culture. Respondent [O] believes that

> The study of English Literature can help an Iranian Muslim scholar to understand her or his experience of her or his own cultural identity crisis. In my opinion the main problem with our identity is its paradoxical nature. We claim to be Muslims, at the same time we refer back to our ancient identity which is very respectful.

One of the unexpected subjects that emerged in the responses to this question was the 'Iranian identify crisis'. 'Literature is an expression of life', as [F] puts it, 'so we become aware of our own identity by comparison and contrast'. Respondent [I], with a PhD from a British university, makes a similar comment, explaining that going abroad made her more self-conscious about her own 'identity':

> I have come to believe that Iranians at the moment are suffering from an identity crisis. They don't know who they are. They are confused between their Aryan roots and their loyalty to the religion. The way I dress, and the way I am, I hope, will make them see that I am from a nation that has got a lot to say, and has an exceptionally rich cultural heritage.

In such a comparative analysis, the above answers highlight a kind of 'cultural vacuum' or 'cultural identity crisis' from which Iranian society is suffering. From this perspective, English literature is a way to remember 'cultural trauma' and is at the same time a cultural identity. The question of 'identity crisis' in the eyes of Iranian academics who are engaged in studying English literature has both a personal and a wider social application.

It can be argued that Iran's 'political isolation' and the power of Western media to distort the real picture of Iranian society into an incomprehensible mass of fanaticism and terrorism during the past decades, has motivated a revival in interest in the ancient kings of Iran (6th century BCE), such as Cyrus the Great and Darius, and in Iranian mythology. The dual conundrum of identity has both affected diasporic Iranians living in Western countries and people living inside Iran self-conscious and even obsessed with such paradoxes. In 'How Can One be Persian?' Marjane Satrapi (2006), the creator of *Persepolis* and an Academy Award-nominated Iranian-French artist, writes,

We are somewhere between Scheherazade's famed *One Thousand and One Nights* and the bearded terrorist, with his manic wife disguised as a pro. By way of flattery we are told that we are Persians, and that Persia was a great empire. Otherwise, we are Iranians. The Persians are in Montesquieu's writings and Delacroix's paintings, and they smoke opium with Victor Hugo. As for Iranians, they take American hostages, they detonate bombs, and they are pissed at the West. They were discovered after the 1979 Revolution (20–23).

As the above responses indicate, studying English literature in Iran not only is not in conflict with the lives of the Iranian students, but is considered as an 'important' consciousness-raising subject which gives them a kind of cultural identity, or at least enables them to reflect on their situation.

How do we read English literature?

It may be taken as a reasonably safe assumption that the theoretical upheaval of the post-1960s did not appear in Iranian academic and intellectual discourse until the late 1990s. In his article, 'Teaching Literary Criticism to Iranian University Students: Some Cultural Obstacles' (2009), Hossein Payandeh, a prominent literary critic and professor of English literature at Allameh University (Tehran), observes that, 'Until a few years ago, literary criticism was an optional course that students of Persian Literature could evade by taking a second course in physical education' (45). 'Even today', as Payandeh points out, 'literary theory and criticism is included neither in the core nor in the optional courses of postgraduate students reading for an M.A. or a Ph.D. in Persian Literature' (Ibid). Payandeh affirms that 'literary criticism is taught to students of foreign literatures (such as English Literature), simply because the first professors who decided what courses these students needed to take were all educated at Western universities and tried to emulate their programmes' (Ibid). As Payandeh puts it, literary criticism classes in Iran are often conducted through 'the single and authoritative voice of a professor who, in the literal sense of the word, "professes" to his audience the moral or social "message" of the text with very little or no participation in the discussion by his/her students' (38). In the time of assessment, students swallow indigestible words of other teachers and regurgitate them in their exam papers.

Such an educational paradigm can be described as what Paulo Freire called a 'banking' model—a process in which a commodity (knowledge) is 'deposited' by those who 'consider themselves knowledgeable' in the minds of those (students) who 'know nothing' (Freire, 2004, 72). 'Instead of communicating', as Freire puts it, 'the teacher issues communiqués and makes deposits which the students patiently receive, memorize and repeat' (Ibid). What normally happens in Iranian classrooms is that the students seek an 'ultimate' interpretation of texts without reflecting on who/what controls the conditions in which texts are circulated and interpreted. Such mind-colonizing educational strategies strip students of the ability to develop critical positions of their own and imprison them in a non-realistic and timeless relation to the world.

The lack of a democratic mentality to 'practice' critical thinking in Iranian culture and society is an important question which is also reflected in the responses in the questionnaire. The majority of the respondents confirm that at undergraduate level, especially poetry courses, instructors still rely on New Criticism's pedagogical system. Respondent [O] states that, 'In Iranian universities we mostly deal with teaching materials according to New Critical approaches'. This is confirmed by the comments of other academics: 'I use New Criticism because this approach sticks to the given text and considers understanding the first necessary step to appreciation' (Respondent B). On the other hand, the same academics approve of the importance of post-1960s thought and its relevance to Iranian society. The role of literary critical approaches in cultural and intellectual development in Iran runs like a motif through many of the comments: 'Many theoretical strategies of reading (especially cultural studies) could help Iranian intellectuals to adopt better tools to study their own cultures' (A). As [A] puts it, 'These approaches create a liberal atmosphere and encourage critical thinking in the class. They defy totalitarian strategies of reading that prescribe final, fixed, rigid, and "correct" meanings'. According to these approaches, students could see a literary text from various perspectives. The 'liberal atmosphere', 'critical thinking', 'totalitarian strategies', and 'various perspectives', emphasize a call for the subversive function of critical modes of reading. [I] asserts:

> Literary and cultural theory helps to map where the contemporary capitalist society stands at the moment, which is in turn an analytical metaphor to locate the Iranian culture in a bigger context and understand the issues involved in modernising the society, and decide whether to resist or accept globalization and postmodernity.

She continues that 'I have learned that we need to update our understanding of religion and Human Rights. We need reforms in our social context as well, because a healthy society is always experiencing ongoing reforms to better people's life and standards of living'.

Which approach, among the theoretical discourses of post-1990s, might have had the largest impact on Iranian academics? To find the answer the participants were asked to choose the critical approaches which they found influential in their research and teaching. According to the responses, I can divide the participants into two groups. The first group (nine out of sixteen) declare that they use a 'combination' of literary approaches in their teaching whenever applicable, and are reluctant to limit themselves to a particular approach. 'As a teacher', [K] asserts,

> I have to shift to the right approach to adapt it to the material I teach. It is important to decide for the right one, especially because the syllabi

are roughly decided by the Ministry of Science, Research and Technology, and the students who are going to take part in the MA examinations should be well prepared.

Besides the need to follow the pedagogical policy of those in authority, one needs to be 'eclectic' in order to prove his/her 'encyclopaedic' knowledge which is the route to success as a teacher in Iran:

> You cannot be theory-oriented or critical in Iran. Even in postgraduate courses the teachers keep their critical views for themselves, because they should play the role of an encyclopaedia in the class. One fact is that almost all students in Iran see books and teachers as neutral, truthful and reliable sources of knowledge and fail to see theories behind them. In Iran teachers and books are considered sacred. A teacher who seeks publicity avoids theory which could limit him to certain names, titles and concepts. For students the mark of good knowledge is not consistency and scrutiny, but encyclopaedic knowledge.

The pedagogic difference between conveying knowledge to students and teaching them how to think critically is brought into sharp focus here in the light of the students' own expectations. [N] notes:

> We do not have the same backgrounds (20th century philosophical, social and psychological) as the people do in a country like England; so I think we should do our best to make students familiar with the basic and preliminary ones which are found in the fields aforementioned.

Significantly, both [A] and [B] work in provincial universities in Iran. In contrast, the second group who are more theoretically committed are those with well-established positions at prestigious universities in Tehran and other large cities. While they also confirm using an eclectic methodology in their teaching, they state their preferences for critical modes of thinking most of which lay under the poststructuralist umbrella. By order of frequency, cultural materialism, Postcolonialism, feminism, and Deconstruction stand as the most influential approaches in this group's research and teaching. 'Cultural materialism is what our culture lacks', emphasizes [D] who teaches at Tehran University, 'so I deliberately use this approach'. A similar attitude comes out in the following remark by a female academic [E] at Islamic Azad University of Tehran:

> One does not need to go into a class and shout 'long live Marx'. Although I am a practicing Muslim, Marxist and cultural materialist theories as far as the ideas of 'social classes', 'economic base' and 'superstructures' are concerned, very well fit into my perspective into literature.

In this context, the potential of engaging with critical theory is radically circum-scribed by the cultural, religious, and ideological structures in which teaching and learning in the literature classroom takes place. With regard to the (ir)relevance of feminism and Postcolonialism to Iranian society, a male professor [B] at Shahid Beheshti University notes that: 'I encourage feminism and Postcolonialism in students' individual projects (theses). We live in an extreme patriarchal society. And like any other third-world country I find that postcolonial discourses are both meaningful and relevant'. Another male academic [O] asserts that,

> Studying feminism has made me aware of the difference in outlook toward women in Western cultures and Irano-Islamic culture, considering the role of women in society, family, etc. Regarding Post-colonialism it seems that we are culturally colonised with the power of mass media.

Still, he believes,

> None of these approaches apart from New Criticism can work out in our society. If I want to choose two approaches which are difficult to handle with an Iranian identity I choose Feminism and Post-colonialism. I some-times refer to these approaches in free discussions about literature rather than doing research on them. Feminism is the most problematic approach to practice in Iran.

The word 'feminism' seems to be kept in a more private sphere. A parallel can be drawn to the comments of a female academic [G] at Shiraz University who affirms the controversy which feminist discourses might arouse among her read-ers and colleagues: 'Feminism and Freudian approaches require me to revise my language to adjust to the sensibility of Iranian readers and other colleagues … you need to observe the cultural reservations to survive as an Iranian academic'. Another female participant [I] explicitly states that, 'Unfortunately, as a nation we have learned never to speak our minds and our children have learned this as well. So when it comes to politics, our people are reduced to either self-censorship or dishonesty'.

As is noted in the above responses, any 'practice' of theory requires a demo-cratic society which should allow pluralistic discourses to challenge each other. In a conversation between Michel Foucault and Gilles Deleuze (1972), Foucault reminds us the false binary opposition between theory and 'practice': 'Theory does not express, translate, or serve to apply practice: it is practice' (Foucault, 1972, 3–10). As Foucault observes, theory is not a detached, objective and in-dependent form of knowledge, but an active critical engagement with power and social/cultural and political structures. Similarly, Judith Butler has empha-sized that, 'Theory takes place every time a possibility is imagined, a collective self-reflection takes place, a dispute over values, priorities, and language emerges' (Butler, 2004, 175–176). An example, as suggested by Butler, casts more light on this argument: 'Feminist literary criticism is never fully distinct from feminism as a movement. Feminist theory would have no content were there no movement, and the movement, in its various directions and forms, has always been involved in the act of theory' (175). A cultural translation of 'theory' in Iran is a challenging task. This is the reason why Iranian academics such as Payandeh and those who participated in my survey find it hard and often 'hopeless' to teach literary criticism to Iranian university students.

What should we read?

Respondents to the questionnaire were asked to suggest five books which they would consider essential reading for Iranian students embarking on the study of English literature (that is, literature in English). Respondents were divided, and some thought the question itself to be divisive. [H] believes that, 'I guess this is the question that "they" have answered. They sent us their anthologies such as Norton or Oxford'. [C] states, 'there are over 500 "essential" texts—any five I name would be purely random'. [J] affirms that it is a 'difficult question ... Iran + Islam + English Literature is a bizarre mixture unless one transcends the differences and thinks in a universal language of humanity, what I have tried to do'. [I] declares: 'I'd never recommend a certain book as a must read. This is a wrong fashion established in Iran that students think there are certain books that are more important than others. I think this is one of the many things our students need to Unlearn'.

Except for four participants, others did name books (not necessarily five) which included both literary works of Western canon and textbooks. Table 1 presents the composite list, in no particular order; where a book was nominated more than once, that figure is given in brackets.

'Essential reading' for Iranian students of English literature

Dante, *The Divine Comedy* [2]
Homer, *The Iliad* [2]
Shakespeare, *Hamlet* [2]
Jane Austen, *Pride and Prejudice* [3]
Emily Brontë, *Wuthering Heights* [3]
Mark Twain, *Adventures of Huckleberry Finn* [2]
Joseph Conrad, *Heart of Darkness* [2]
Norton Anthology of English Literature (Ed. M. H. Abrams and Stephen Greenblat) [2]
M H Abrams, *A Glossary of Literary Terms* [2]
David Lodge, *Modern Criticism and Theory: A Reader* [2]
Karen Lawrence, Betsy Seifter, and Lois Ratner, *McGraw Hill Guide to English Literature* [2]

At the same time the respondents were asked to give their reasons for their choices. What they acknowledged is the aesthetic and thematic quality of the works rather than any political or social function. Respondent [K] asserts that, 'I think that a firm background in the classics would empower the students to continue their literary activities on their own and have a vaster knowledge of the social historical factors shaping the present literature. It would make them independent critics'. Putting emphasis on 'the majors', [C] believes that, 'They (ancient classics) are all important because most of the great English writers were immersed in them and their influence can be seen in the literature both super-ficially (references, allusions) and profoundly (thematic, structural)'. It is obvious that there is no explicit call for canon change as the most frequent books are the very classics which have been the subject of dispute in the West. This, too, forms part of the web of paradox and irony in which this whole subject is caught.

Conclusion

I return to the quotation by Alfred Lord Tennyson which opens this chapter—to the 'changes' which some parts of the 'earth' might have seen, taken for granted, and now possibly consider as old-fashioned. At the same time, on the other parts of the 'earth', such changes might not have happened, or might be taken as evil; or the changes themselves might be of a quite different kind.

The study of English literature at university level in Iran is circumscribed by a number of limitations. Some of these limitations are common to other countries and cultures—uneven quality of language teaching, shortage of books and other materials, lack of funding for professional development—while others are more local and derive from Iranian history and social structures. The most we can conclude is that the relative stasis of methodology in teaching English literature and theory is a product of circumstances which form part of the political history of Iran over the past thirty years.

The result of the questionnaire shows that there is a gap between what the Iranian academics wish for and what they actually do in their classes and re-search. A feminist or psychoanalytic approach, for example, may be cultivated as a personal preference, or shared in private discussion groups, but this makes its influence hard to evaluate. Although 'brand names' such as Derrida, Foucault, Habermas, etc., have made 'Theory' marketable in Iran's publishing business in the past decades, critical theory has not been 'practically' adopted by English departments especially in the undergraduate curriculum. In graduate courses any use of theory could only be directed outwards as an accessory method. New Criticism has remained the dominant approach and this means that Iranian stu-dents can work independently from the West and Western culture.

Despite all these, the result of my questionnaire confirms that the Iranian academics consider the 'practice' of the critical theories in a democratic soci-ety as transformative and necessary step to resolve the current intellectual and pedagogical crisis in twenty-first century Iran. Critical theory might have not been culturally or politically established in the Iranian curriculum, but it has at least provoked debates about the necessity of critical and democratic thinking in teaching not only English but Persian literature. If the theoretical development of the second half of the twentieth century helped to open the doors for the 'other' to Western students of English literature, the intrinsically differential perception of 'us' by 'them' and of 'them' by 'us' is the way forward to fill in the gaps and meet the missing discourses in Iran.

References

Butler, J. (2004) *Undoing Gender*. New York: Routledge.

Foucault, M. (1977) 'Intellectuals and power: A conversation between Michel Foucault and Gilles Deleuze', in *Language, Counter Memory, Practice: Selected Essays and Interviews*, ed. Donald F. Bouchard. 205–217. Ithaca: Cornel University Press. First published in *L'Arc* 49 (1972): 3–10.

Freire, P. (2004) *Pedagogy of the Oppressed*, 30th anniversary edition. trans. MB Ramos. New York: Continuum Press.

Miller, J. H. (1999) *Black Holes*. Stanford: Stanford University Press.

Payandeh, H. (2009) 'Teaching literary criticism to Iranian University students: Some cultural obstacles'. *The Journal of Teaching Language Skills (JTLS) of Shiraz University*, 1.1: 38–47.

Rice, P. and Waugh, P. (2001) *Modern Literary Theory*, 4th ed. London: Arnold.

Satrapi, M. (2006) 'How can one be Persian?', in *My Sister, Guard Your Veil; My Brother, Guard Your Eyes: Uncensored Iranian Voices*, ed. Lila Azam Zanganeh. 20–23. Boston: Beacon Press.

Sokhanvar, J., and Hooshang H. (ed.) (1986) *An Abridged Edition of the Norton Anthology of English Literature*. Tehran: Vahid Pub.

PART III

Rationales for teaching literature

16

REASONS FOR READING

Why literature matters[1]

Gabrielle Cliff Hodges

The role of teachers in encouraging reading

The first phase of the 'Teachers as Readers' research, funded by the Esmée Fairburn Foundation and the United Kingdom Literacy Association (UKLA), drew on data generated by 1,200 primary teachers in England. They responded to a questionnaire about their personal reading habits, their knowledge of children's literature and their use of literature in the classroom. The data seemed to suggest a narrowness of scope, both in terms of knowledge about literature and how it might be taught (Cremin *et al.*, 2008a,b). The research team, although acknowledging that the situation in primary schools might have been more subtle than their findings alone suggest, offer possible reasons why the data are dispiriting:

> This complex picture, while no doubt influenced by technological and childhood changes, is also arguably shaped by the recent and widely recognised professional focus on tests and targets. Pressured by the need to ensure curriculum coverage of nationally set objectives, many perceive that teachers in England may have reduced opportunities for independent reading for pleasure and neglected *the reason for reading in the first place*.
>
> (Cremin et al., *2009, p. 11* my italics)

Subsequent phases of the 'Teachers as Readers' project have therefore been expressly designed to extend teachers' awareness of their own practices as readers, deepen their knowledge about children's literature and explore children's reading beyond the school, understanding the potential value of all three for classroom teaching and learning (Cremin *et al.*, 2014, 2015). Two constant aims have been to help young people become engaged readers who read purposefully with confidence and enthusiasm and to research the connections between young people's reading at school and at home. The intentions appear to have been to restore teachers' and students' enjoyment of reading for its own sake and to rescue literature from its subservient role of providing extracts for linguistic analysis in the classroom or being used as a mere stepping off point for literacy work.

Although 'Teachers as Readers' was a primary phase project, a different report—this time cross-phase—offers similar conclusions. *English at the Crossroads* (Ofsted, 2009), explores how the English curriculum in both primary and secondary schools in England appeared to have changed in the three-year period between 2005 and 2008. Drawing on 242 inspections of schools as well as other evidence from National Strategy evaluations, discussions with teachers and assessment data, the reports states:

> The current survey found that schools, especially in the primary phase, devoted a considerable amount of time to reading. However, few had developed a clearly articulated policy, based on a detailed understanding of how pupils become readers. They used many initiatives and strategies but often in a fragmentary way ... Therefore, although there was a great deal of activity related to reading, it was not always integrated effectively or directed sufficiently at producing enthusiastic, independent readers.
>
> *(ibid., p. 23)*

More recently, another cross-phase Ofsted report on the teaching of English suggests that 'too few schools [give] enough thought to ways of encouraging the love of reading' (Ofsted, 2012, p. 5). If schools' response to this criticism has been lukewarm, it may be because of the pressure they are under to demonstrate quality via data-based evidence of students' measurable attainment in tests. The quality of students' engagement in reading and reading for pleasure, however, is not readily susceptible to being measured and converted into data the same way. That does not mean it cannot be planned or form part of a teacher's pedagogy; but what it does require is research-based evidence to justify it:

> While the profession undoubtedly wants to avoid 'measuring the pleasure', volitional reading demands careful nurturing, ongoing invitations to engage, imagine and be inspired. A planned reading for pleasure pedagogy is needed, based on evidence and principle.
>
> *(Cremin, 2016)*

In 2012, the Education Standards Research team at the Department for Education (DfE) produced a report on reading for pleasure, designed to offer teachers just such research-based evidence. However, it is strongly informed by quantitative research, and it may be that we need to pay equal attention to qualitative research in order to deepen our understanding of some of the multifarious things that happen when people read, not least when they read literature, and recognise how such understanding develops teachers' pedagogy (Cliff Hodges, 2016). I return to this point later on. First, however, I discuss one or two relevant policy documents.

Rationales for literature detected in policy documents

One policy document in which a rationale for storytelling and literature is expressly included is the final report on a government-commissioned independent review of the primary curriculum (Rose, 2009). It states:

> The powerful, not to say unique, contribution to children's enjoyment and comprehension of language—and to their emotional development—from deep engagement with storytelling and regular exposure to excellent literature is recognised throughout early years and primary education. This tradition should be strongly upheld alongside the direct teaching of reading and writing.
>
> (ibid., p. 58)

However, if we analyse the language of this statement, values inscribed in the rationale emerge. 'Exposure' is an odd choice of word to collocate with literature; it is more commonly used in connection with danger, extreme heat or cold, infection or radiation! Ironically, it therefore suggests something against which young people might need protection. Literature is also here presented as a 'tradition' to be 'upheld', with all the implications of status and power those two words connote. Furthermore, it is to be experienced 'alongside' the teaching of reading, rather than as an integral part of the process. Later in the report, there is another suggested rationale for reading: that children 'decode familiar and unfamiliar words so effortlessly as to be able to concentrate fully on the meaning of the text, which is the goal of reading' (ibid., p. 61). Here, the human dimensions of enjoyment, comprehension and emotional development suggested earlier are no longer in evidence.

The English National Curriculum includes a statement about the importance of subject English as a whole, suggesting that reading, in particular, offers students 'a chance to develop culturally, emotionally, intellectually, socially and spiritually. Literature, especially, plays a key role in such development' (DfE, 2014). These are substantial claims but their potential for interesting discussion has been eclipsed by the DfE's simultaneous decree that in the English Literature General Certificate of Secondary Education (GCSE) examination, the only post-1914 fiction or drama allowed must be from the British Isles (DfE, 2013), thus eliminating longstanding favourites such as *To Kill A Mockingbird*, *Of Mice and Men* and *A View from the Bridge*, all of which offer readers precisely 'a chance to develop culturally, emotionally, intellectually, socially and spiritually' that the National Curriculum espouses.

The Arts Council—a national development agency for the arts in England—in a consultation document on children's literature, takes a less prescriptive stance. Here the importance of literature lies in its potential to nourish and enrich young people's lives:

> We see children's literature as the touchstone for a healthy and sustainable literary culture. Children's writers and illustrators reach readers at

their most dependent and travel with them through to young adulthood and beyond. This reading is among the most important—transforming—undertaken in any reader's life.

(Arts Council England, 2003, p. 3)

The idea of authors and young readers as fellow travellers, on different but companionable journeys, is an interesting one. It suggests an element of choice and direction, of young readers actively engaging in the culture of reading, not merely being exposed to literature.

However, the statement which arguably brings the best of all the above together comes from Robin Alexander's *Children, their World, their Education: Final Report and Recommendations of the Cambridge Primary Review* (2010). It is, perhaps, no coincidence that Alexander's statement occurs in a chapter which itself forms a rationale, entitled 'What is primary education for?'. Before attempting an answer to this vast question, Alexander defines the terms he will use. Of the word 'aim' he writes, 'An *aim* we take to be a broad statement of purpose, a road to travel rather than the terminal point represented by those *objectives* which translate aims into specific actions' (Alexander, 2010, p. 195). One of the twelve aims he lists is 'Exciting the imagination'. Children's imaginations need to be excited, he writes, in order that children can:

> ... advance beyond present understanding, extend the boundaries of their lives, contemplate worlds possible as well as actual, understand cause and consequence, develop the capacity for empathy, and reflect on and regulate their behaviour ... We assert the need to emphasise the intrinsic value of exciting children's imagination. To experience the delights—and pains—of imagining, and of entering into the imaginative world of others, is to become a more rounded person.
>
> *(ibid., p. 199)*

Although the statement is all-encompassing, and the goal of becoming 'a more rounded person' debatable, the above could nevertheless form part of a rationale for reading literature. The word 'exciting' is telling, not least because it is here used as a verb, as befits its meaning which is, literally, *setting in motion*.

Rationales for literature emerging from research

Having explored briefly how rationales for literature are represented in a selection of policy documentation, I next touch on some of the research conducted into young people as readers during the last three decades or so in England to see what purposes, if any, are suggested for their reading of literature. By the time they reach their teenage years, most young people in England are able to read, so the need for a clear rationale for reading literature remains strong.

Over thirty years ago, Alastair West undertook a fascinating piece of research exploring the different ways in which three secondary schools influenced their students' reading development. In two linked articles for *The English Magazine*, he reported some of his key findings, for example:

> All three schools placed a high valuation upon reading in their rhetoric, but only one had discovered ways of giving that high valuation any structural form within the working practices and social relations of the institution.
>
> *(West, 1986, p. 7)*

In that one school—Baydon—students exercised choice over their wider reading with their choices validated in assessed coursework and their progress as readers explicitly and informatively reported. Engagement and achievement in reading were noticeably higher than in the other two schools even though the latter were more socially advantaged. Although West offers some criticisms of the way in which teachers at Baydon were possibly somewhat limited by predominantly liberal humanist views, and thus not particularly diverse in the way they taught literature, he nevertheless notes that:

> Baydon was a school that organised itself for readership. All the social aspects of readership—how people become readers and how readers behave—were acknowledged at Baydon and built into their working practices.
>
> *(West, 1987, p. 18)*

This position chimes with the aims of 'Teachers as Readers' and, indeed, with some aspects of the two Ofsted reports mentioned earlier, but what West's study also has at its very heart—fuelled, no doubt, by the intense literary theory debates that Terry Eagleton (1983) describes as going on at that time—is a sense of what the teachers in all three schools thought that reading literature was for, espousing as they did a 'liberal humanist view that literature contributes to the individual's moral and emotional education by facilitating a greater understanding of the self, the world and others' (West, 1986, p. 5). Although such a position would not—either then or now—be universally shared (any more than Alexander's notion above of imaginative engagement leading to a more rounded person), in this instance it was nevertheless acknowledged overtly as a set of values informing the teachers' work and, as such was available for scrutiny and debate.

It is not uncommon for reading research to include questionnaires as an important data collection method (Benton, 1995a,b; Clark and De Zoysa, 2011; Clark and Foster, 2005; Hall and Coles, 1999; Hopper, 2005). These questionnaires—often more quantitative than qualitative—seldom include questions about young people's reasons for reading, though. Where they do, the type of questioning and subsequent analysis of data can be limited. Clark and Foster's research for the National Literacy Trust—*Children's and Young People's Reading Habits and Preferences: The Who, What, Why, Where and When* (2005)—does attend to the question of why young people choose to read. However, respondents are told to tick as many statements as they wish from a fixed number of options to complete the sentence 'I read because...' rather than being given freedom to articulate their own reasons. The options are:

> it is a skill for life; it will help me get a job; it teaches me how other people live and feel; it helps me understand more of the world; it is fun; it helps me find out what I want/need to know; it gives me a break (escapism); I have to; it helps me understand more about myself.
>
> *(Clark and Foster, 2005, p. 109)*

How these options were arrived at and the values which underpin them remain unexamined in the report, as does the decision to allow respondents to tick as many as they want rather than just one. Furthermore, the subsequent data analysis is purely statistical with no accompanying explanations. For example, the research finds that:

> ... the majority read because it is a skill for life and will help them find what they need/want to know. Almost half the pupils also said that reading is fun and that it will help them get a job. Two-fifths of pupils read because it helps them understand the world better and because it teaches them how other people live and feel; a third of pupils read because it is a form of escape. However, a fifth said that they read because they have to.
>
> *(ibid., p. 24)*

What we gain, therefore, is *knowledge* about what options young readers have selected rather than deeper *understanding* about *why* young people read. Moreover, six years on, the National Literacy Trust is still relying heavily on survey-style research (Clark and De Zoysa, 2011); even while attempting more sophisticated analysis, the authors acknowledge its limitations:

> Cross-sectional data, such as the ones used in this brief paper, are only of limited use in investigating the ins and outs of complex relationships. While the models show relationships in terms of preceding and succeeding influences, they are only a temporal snapshot and the causal nature of this relationship associating enjoyment, attitudes and behaviour with attainment cannot be asserted from these data. Causality is no doubt complex in that enjoyment, attitudes, behaviour and attainment reinforce one another and longitudinal data is therefore clearly necessary as a next step to explore possible causal relationships in this already complex interplay of variables.
>
> *(ibid., pp. 21–22)*

If we *do* want to acquire deeper *understanding* about *why* young people read, it can be instructive to explore theories arising from different kinds of critical literature, as I do in the next section, as well as considering what may be learnt from qualitative research.

Rationales for literature emerging from theory

In this section I turn to theorists who have influenced my own thinking about reading and literature and whose ideas offer starting points for renewed debate. Louise Rosenblatt's *Literature as Exploration* (1938/1995) and *The Reader, the Text, the Poem* (1978/1994) are still often cited today. Her theories were developed during many years' teaching in universities in the United States. There are several potentially crucial pedagogical implications of her ideas. One of her arguments, for example, is that whether an efferent or aesthetic reading occurs—or a mixture of both—depends on the stance adopted by the reader. Rosenblatt's notion of the imagined work which is created as a result of the transaction between text and reader but which is not the same as either of them, emphasises the distinctiveness of each person's reading and, likewise, throws into question the hegemony of the *text*, lending support instead to the notion of authorised *readings*. Nevertheless, these readings are still dependent upon the text, usually with attendant awareness of the text's author as well as its literary and historical contexts. Text and author therefore exert some force on the reading process but neither is the ultimate arbiter of any 'correct' reading. Nor is that what literature is for. Rosenblatt suggests, very importantly, that the reading created in the transaction between the reader and the text, be seen as an event in time, susceptible to revision in the light of other such 'events', which jostle with it, whether constructed by different readers or by the same reader re-reading the same text at a different time. However, these events have some purpose:

> The reader, reflecting on the world of the poem or play or novel as he conceived it and on his own responses to that world, can achieve a certain self-awareness, a certain perspective on his own preoccupations, his own system of values.
>
> *(Rosenblatt, 1978/1994, p. 146)*

This notion of the reading process as both dynamic and reflexive is a key point of connection between Rosenblatt's ideas and Wolfgang Iser's. While Iser's work is situated within a largely philosophical tradition of literary theory, his ideas have been influential in education because they offer theoretical justification for the kinds of practice many literature teachers strive to achieve, especially in classrooms where literary study is seen as a democratic entitlement for all students, not merely for those who seek to pursue it voluntarily at the post-compulsory stage. In his preface to *The Act of Reading: A Theory of Aesthetic Response* (1978), Iser states what might well stand as a key aim for many literature teachers, namely to facilitate intersubjective discussion of individual interpretations (Iser, 1978, p. x). In classrooms where teachers seek to encourage individual students' readings of texts and increase their power as critical readers of literature, such an invitation is welcome. Continuing to outline the rudiments of his theory, Iser summarises how he perceives the relative roles of author, reader and text:

> As the reader passes through the various perspectives offered by the text and relates the different views and patterns to one another he sets the work in motion, and so sets himself in motion, too.
>
> *(ibid., p. 21)*

His argument that readers are motivated and that reading is creative sits comfortably with Alexander's desire to excite the imagination. A further implication of Iser's notion of the realised, or virtual, work accomplished by each reader is that the text therefore cannot be the same as its meaning, a misconception that has often bedevilled literary work in secondary English classrooms, not least where the end has been a public examination and it becomes all too easy to revert, under pressure, to the quest for single meanings and right answers. But two major questions remain, notably what are texts for and what is the motivation required by any reader to set the reading process in motion? Iser's answer is that textual realisations have a reality which complements lived reality in the world. Referring specifically to the idea of reading a literary text, Iser argues that it offers readers the opportunity to 'transcend the limitations of their own real-life situation; it is not a reflection of any given reality, but it is an extension or broadening of their own reality' *(ibid., p. 79)*. The idea of transcendence is imbued with connotations of higher rather than different values. In *The Redress of Poetry* (1995), Seamus Heaney offers a similar but essentially more democratic suggestion about literature, in this case poetry:

> Its projections and inventions should be a match for the complex reality which surrounds it and out of which it is generated … As long as the coordinates of the imagined thing correspond to those of the world that we live in and endure, poetry is fulfilling its counterweighting function.
>
> *(Heaney, 1995, p. 8)*

Despite the difference in values, however, Heaney and Iser share a commitment to the motivating function of literature: its potential for readers to recognise the distinctions and connections between real and imagined worlds.

Another influential thinker in this field is Robert Scholes. His career as researcher and teacher of English in American universities spans more than half a century and, like Rosenblatt, his theories stem from the exigencies of the classroom. In *Textual Power: Literary Theory and the Teaching of English* (1985), he argues that 'reading and writing are important because we read and write our world as well as our texts, and are read and written by them in turn' (Scholes, 1985, p. 9). Textual power therefore affords readers the ability to *reflect* on the world as well as to *act* within and upon the world. Three key facets of textual power are: reading, interpretation and criticism. It is criticism, according to Scholes, which brings the student to maturity because, like writing itself, it is 'a way of discovering how to choose, how to take some measure of responsibility for ourselves and for our world' (*ibid.*, p. 73), but all three processes—reading, interpretation and criticism—involve readers shuttling back and forth between their texts and the worlds in which they live their daily lives. This dynamic is what Scholes believes to be the purpose of textual study. He uses the science fiction of Ursula Le Guin by way of exemplification:

> When science fiction really works it does not domesticate the alien but alienates the domestic. It takes us on journeys where we meet the alien and find that he is us. If Le Guin is right, it is only after such a voyage of alien-ation that we might hope to be reconciled to our own humanity.
>
> (*ibid.*, *p. 128*)

Where Iser suggests reading literature as a way of *transcending* reality and Heaney offers the idea of it serving a *counterweighting* function to reality, Scholes argues that literature offers readers *reconciliation* with that reality. To that end, he is em-phatic about the part teaching plays in the development of readers. Scholes also contends, however, that textual study is incomplete if students are not writers as well as readers. For Scholes, learning the craft of writing and reading through actively practising both is essential for the acquisition of textual power.

Writers' perspectives

In the final part of this chapter, I want to take up the notion of connections bet-ween writers and readers to see what both suggest might be reasons for reading in the first place. Two threads in particular seem to bind them: one is the notion that writing and reading literature, if nothing else, are acts of imagination to explore possible worlds and reflect on actual worlds; the other is the notion that writing and reading literature are specifically human activities which have at their heart what it means to be human in all its diversity and commonality.

For example, an often-cited critic, reader, teacher and writer of children's lit-erature is Aidan Chambers. The opening chapter of *Booktalk: Occasional Writing on Literature and Children* (1985) is an address to the 1981 meeting of the Interna-tional Association of School Librarianship called 'The role of literature in chil-dren's lives'. In it, he rehearses ideas with which many will already be familiar, especially about the vital role of narrative in people's lives. Here it is interesting to recall specifically what he has to say about what reading literature is for. At the heart of his argument lies a belief that:

> ... it is this particular use of language—the literary use that some have called 'storying'—that defines humanity and makes us human. I would say that this particular form of language and our skill in using it empower us

in being more what we are, and make it possible for us to conceive of being more than we are.

(Chambers, 1985, p. 2)

For Chambers, then, the power which stems from reading literature not only has the potential to enable us to *be* more than we are, but also to conceive that we *might be* more than we are. Literature is a means by which to think, not a medium through which we are told what to think. Reading literature is therefore both an aesthetic and an intellectual pursuit. As Jerome Bruner so aptly said of narrative, in *Actual Minds, Possible Worlds* (1986), it places readers in the position of 'subjunctivising reality' (p. 26), of not only reflecting on what *is* or what *was*, but also asking what *might be*. It is indeed *multimodal*, exciting the imagination so that readers recognise *actual* worlds and, simultaneously, create *possible* worlds.

In a more recent book, *Reading and the Reader* (2013), Philip Davis, explores reading in the twenty-first century in not dissimilar terms. He writes from his perspective as a university professor of literature interested not only in how literature students read but also how ordinary readers read, for example those with whom he works and researches in community reading groups. His argument is, essentially, that reading literature is a way of *thinking* about reality, focusing closely on the way reading can act as 'a holding-ground for the contemplation of experience' (Davis, 2013, p. 16). He elaborates:

> Most of us cannot become formal thinkers, as philosophers are trained to be ... but for those who wish to use thinking to get above themselves whilst *still* remaining within themselves, it is reading which serves as the trigger for such reflection and as a space for such contemplation. We need the activation of these second selves, or second lives and levels, both on the page and in our minds when reading it.

(ibid., p. 25)

Davis's notion of a holding-ground—the part of a sea-bed where a ship's anchor can gain purchase—seems an apt metaphor for reading since it suggests a space for contemplation where not only readers, but writers, too, whose work is written to be read may spend time in reflection and thought.

Novelist and playwright, David Almond, expands on this idea of the relationship between reader and writer in the 'Afterword' to his play, *Wild Girl, Wild Boy* (2002):

> Any good story, no matter how controlled it appears on the page, is not a tame trapped thing. It still has wildness in it, a yearning to break free of its neat lines and numbered pages. And it does break free. It leaps from the page, and moves far beyond the control of the author, as soon as a reader begins to read it.

(Almond, 2002, p. 88)

When a story takes the form of a play, the process is particularly striking. Watching rehearsals for *Wild Girl, Wild Boy*, Almond observes:

> As soon as the lines were spoken, they became something new—at once very like and very unlike the way I'd heard them in my mind. And each time they were re-spoken, they changed again. I saw what happened in silence in a reader's mind happening in a stage-like space before me.
>
> (ibid., p. 89)

Almond's experience as audience for the play he himself has written is a reminder of the recreative potential of *all* literary experiences. Such ideas about reading as an imaginative act, in which the forces exerted by text and writer have the potential to excite corresponding forces in the reader, offer powerful rationales for working with literature in the classroom.

The notion of literary reading and writing as specifically human endeavours affords a further rationale. Beverley Naidoo is a writer who insists on this point in every aspect of her work. In her acceptance speech when awarded the Carnegie Medal for *The Other Side of Truth* (2000), she said:

> In my writing, I have always aimed to reveal the impact of the wider society and its politics on the lives of my young characters … Literature is a bridge into other worlds. It offers a route into exploring our common humanity.
>
> (Naidoo, 2001)

The Other Side of Truth is a novel whose story is triggered by the turmoil of political events in Nigeria in the 1990s. Its central character is Sade, daughter of a courageous Nigerian journalist, who with her young brother is smuggled into the United Kingdom when their mother is shot dead. The novel is dedicated to 'all young people who wish to know more', an acknowledgement that much as young readers of literature might enjoy venturing into the realms of the imaginative, equally they want to know about the here and now—the human condition—and, crucially, to journey back and forth between the two.

Young readers' perspectives

In my research over the last two decades or so, I have spent a great deal of time asking young people in the early years of secondary schooling about their personal reading habits, especially—but by no means exclusively—their reading of literature (Cliff Hodges, 2016). There is not space here to outline the research in great depth, but I will end with a few excerpts from what one particular group of twelve-and thirteen-year-old students wrote and said. The data below come from their personal reading histories—'rivers of reading' as we came to call them (Cliff Hodges, 2010)—or from their contributions in semi-structured group interviews. Their perspectives seem to lend weight to some of the ideas outlined above. While the students diverge widely as readers, interested in an extraordinarily varied range of reading matter, they concur on a number of points, specifically that reading literature excites the imagination and prompts them to reflect on themselves as human beings as they shuttle back and forth between literature and life. For example, one girl wrote about some of her favourite genres:

> I mostly read thrillers, sci-fi, horror, fantasy and some true life stories, I love all these books because it distracts me, takes me away to somewhere else and even though you know most of it is never going to happen there is still hope and possibilities. The stories tell me that if I don't feel like I am fitting in then there are others that feel the same way even if they are not all real (Andie[2]).

She understands the distinction between real*ism* and real*ity* and enjoys the *distraction* reading enables; however, she simultaneously acknowledges that its *attraction* is closely bound up with the business of her daily life, offering the chance to reflect actively on both possible and actual worlds. The books she lists as her all-time favourites bear out her eclectic taste with choices ranging from Michelle Magorian's Second World War romance, *A Little Love Song* (1991), to Kevin Brooks' bleak and gritty *The Road of the Dead* (2006). Further evidence of her deep engagement with her reading emerged when she later discussed *The Road of the Dead* in the group interview. She ventured that she often becomes quite emotionally involved in what she reads and in this case even found herself (in her words) 'actually grieving' for the murdered girl, Rachel. Her use of the term 'grieving' suggests quite a complex stance towards Rachel, not merely imagining her predicament but engaging affectively with the way she is represented so as to feel a sense of grief at her death.

Another young reader, Abigail, wrote about how much she enjoyed *Molly Moon's Incredible Book of Hypnotism* (2002) by Georgia Byng, the first in a series which is itself about a young girl imagining other worlds:

> I have read all the Molly Moon books. I thought, if I tried hard enough I could hypnotise people too. I also wrote to the author and received my very first (hand written) letter, from an author (Abigail).

Abigail enjoys exercising her imagination, in this instance exploring what might happen in a world where you could hypnotise people, but also pragmatic enough to write to the author. In a separate comment, she wrote about enjoying Louise Rennison's Georgia Nicolson series: 'They are fab. Really can relate to them and have brought me closer to my best friend', further evidence of her ease in moving between the world of her texts and the world of her life and her awareness that, as Scholes has it, '… we neither capture nor create the world with our texts, but interact with it' (Scholes, 1985, p. 111). Later, in discussion with me, she elaborated on the appeal of the Georgia Nicolson series:

> ... me and my best friend, Denise, we read, we read them at the same time and we sit in tutor rooms laughing at each other's books and we've got a real link through the books (Abigail).

Like Andie, Abigail enjoys a wide range of types of reading including fantasy. In her interview she said she was reading J. K. Rowling's *Harry Potter and the Half-Blood Prince* (2005) for the third time, clearly gaining aesthetic pleasure from her reading of Rowling's work.

> I love the way that the author kind of makes up these things that no one else knows about and no one else has any idea how she comes up with them ... You know they're not real and you know they can't happen and it's not possible, because it's, yeah, just fictional, but it's so real the way she writes it and you can just imagine it happening, like behind some wall somewhere or something (Abigail).

Those last few words are an interesting variation on the idea of transactional reading: the author's text and the reader's imagination working together to create a fantastic reading event but tantalisingly other-worldly, just out of reach 'behind some wall somewhere'.

In the same group interview, Tom had this to say about *The Hobbit* (1937), a book that he had really enjoyed:

> I sort of connect to it in a different way because it's completely fantasy, like there's no way it could happen, but you don't have to connect to it in a real way (Tom).

Tom appears to be quite comfortable with the notion that it is possible to enjoy fantasy for intrinsic pleasure without having to justify any links with the actual world. He is widely read and has strong views about what he likes and dislikes, and why. He hated *Skellig* (1998) because 'It didn't have anything meaty in it, didn't have any substance', but enjoyed mystery detective books by writers such as Dashiell Hammett and Raymond Chandler which he described as both interesting and exciting. When discussing the current popularity of spy stories, he shrugged off the fact that it might be to do with concerns about terrorism and such like. A keen reader of Robert Muchimore books and Charlie Higson's young James Bond series, he suggested:

> Everyone likes to imagine it—I mean no one likes to say—everyone likes to imagine themselves as a spy (Tom).

As well as enjoying different types of fantasy, many young readers—as Naidoo says—want to know more, and not just about the here and now. Lily wrote that Judith Kerr's *When Hitler Stole Pink Rabbit* (1971) really helped her understand what happened in the Second World War. Michael Morpurgo's *Twist of Gold* (1993), a novel about two children who leave their mother dying during the nineteenth century Irish potato famine and undertake a journey across America to find their father, she found to be '... amazing. I read it six times'. The commitment involved in re-reading a book so many times is interesting: writers like Kerr and Morpurgo certainly offer knowledge for readers to take away from their novels, but the aesthetic process is clearly also an enjoyable aspect of repeated re-reading.

Charlie had read *An Ordinary Man: The True Story behind Hotel Rwanda* (Rusesabagina and Zoellner, 2006). He was still, however, trying to make connections between the book and his life's experiences. He was a keen reader of Chris Ryan and Andy McNab's Special Air Service (SAS) style of fiction, but *Hotel Rwanda* was very different. In the group conversation I had with him, he started by asking me:

> ... have you see the film *Hotel Rwanda?*... I've read a book on it ... I read the book before the film and it was just shocking ... some of the things that happened it was just unbelievable. It's just how, it's that we had peacekeepers over there and we just stood back and watched and we couldn't intervene (Charlie).

Charlie is an exceptionally keen reader especially of adult literature. He was one of the few members of the group who also said he read the newspaper quite thoroughly. His family got the *Daily Mail* and the *News of the World* on Sundays, and he said, 'I always start off on the back page ... go through about fifteen pages and then I'll turn over to the front again and I'll go sort of inwards like that'. He also enjoyed many different sports and with his friend Steve attended the local branch of the Army Cadet Force. Interestingly, his incredulity at the events in *Hotel Rwanda* seemed to stem from reading at the limits of his human understanding. His known world had collided with his reading about an almost impossibly brutal situation, not only beyond his grasp but beyond the scope of United Nations peacekeepers as well. The book was forcing him to readjust and re-evaluate. Despite his penchant for adult literature and fluency with the written word, here it appears his skills were not enough:

> ... the only film I've seen that was better than the book was *Hotel Rwanda*. The film was really good, because the book you just sort of, it was quite difficult to understand how hard it must have been but once you see the film you could see all the emotions on people's faces (Charlie).

Mehmet found Mark Haddon's *The Curious Incident of the Dog in the Night-Time* (2003) powerful in a rather different way. I had said I was interested in the power that words on the page can have to make people cry or laugh. He extended this point:

> I mean I don't think it's always just a physical reaction. I think it's kind of like—it's gonna sound like a bad thing—a mental scarring for life. Like ... some books can make you think completely differently about something, like when I read *The Curious Incident of the Dog in the Night-Time* I thought completely differently about people with Asperger's and it made me ... realise how hard their life is actually. 'Cos when you're reading a book you, you feel it from their point of view (Mehmet).

This idea that the effects of reading literature stay with you well beyond the duration of the reading is not uncommon. Although the power of texts to linger is seldom cited as an argument for reading literature, it is often an outcome of doing so, not least where the literature provokes thought about moral, social or spiritual issues. Freya had read Gabrielle Zevin's *Elsewhere* (2005), the story of a young adult girl killed in a road accident narrated from an imagined place 'beyond the grave':

> This was a really good book. It certainly made me wonder. It's almost like this book carried on after I finished it. I thought about it a lot more than any other book (Freya).

Continuing to mull over a book after you have finished reading provides ideal conditions for another reason for reading: active and critical reflection of the kind advocated by Scholes. Interestingly, both Lily and Abigail, on separate occasions, suggested that they had begun to enjoy interpreting and critically analysing their school reading. The way Abigail put it was:

> Last year, in Year 7, our English teacher, I think she really got me to think about our books differently ... I've always enjoyed reading, but like I used to just read a book and like the story, but now I kind of read more into it, think about what they're doing and maybe their past or what you think's gonna happen. Yeah, I just see them differently now, I'm looking for things (Abigail).

Lily made a similar point, describing one such text as having a 'second meaning ... it was kind of like one story and then if you looked deeper into it there was a separate story in it'.

These young readers, then, like the many others I have interviewed over the past few years, do not have a homogenous or fixed position on what reading literature is for. They differ in what they read as well as whether, where and when. What they share, however, is having reasons for reading in the first place, distinctive though those reasons might be, whether to know more, to entertain themselves, to imagine, feel and reflect. If educators and researchers neglect the reasons for reading—for reading and studying literature in particular, which has been my concern here—an opportunity is missed to build on what is possibly one of the most powerful and important elements in the process.

Notes

1 An earlier version of this chapter was published in the form of an article in the United Kingdom Literacy Association (UKLA) journal, *Literacy*: Cliff Hodges, G. (2010). Reasons for reading: Why literature matters. *Literacy*, 44 (2), 60–68. Some sections have since been expanded further in Cliff Hodges, G. (2016). *Researching and Teaching Reading: Developing Pedagogy through Critical Enquiry*. London: Routledge.
2 All the students' names have been changed to ensure anonymity.

References

Alexander, R. (ed.) (2010) *Children, their World, their Education: Final Report and Recommendations of the Cambridge Primary Review*. London: Routledge.

Almond, D. (1998) *Skellig*. London: Hodder Children's Books.

Almond, D. (2002) *Wild Girl, Wild Boy*. London: Hodder Children's Books.

Arts Council England. (2003) *From Looking Glass to Spyglass: A Consultation Paper on Children's Literature*. London: Arts Council England.

Benton, P. (1995a) Conflicting cultures: Reflections on the reading and viewing of secondary school pupils. *Oxford Review of Education*, 21 (4): 457–469.

Benton, P. (1995b) Recipe fictions ... literary fast food?: Reading interests in year 8. *Oxford Review of Education*, 21 (2): 99–111.

Brooks, K. (2006) *The Road of the Dead*. Frome: Chicken House.

Bruner, J. (1986) *Actual Minds, Possible Worlds*. Cambridge, MA: Harvard University Press.

Byng, G. (2002) *Molly Moon's Incredible Book of Hypnotism*. London: Macmillan's Children's Books.

Chambers, A. (1985) *Booktalk: Occasional Writing on Literature & Children*. Stroud: Thimble Press.

Clark, C. and De Zoysa, S. (2011) *Mapping the Interrelationships of Reading Enjoyment, Attitudes, Behaviour and Attainment*. London: National Literacy Trust. Retrieved 10 May 2016 from: www.literacytrust.org.uk/assets/0001/0025/Attainment_attitudes_behaviour_enjoyment-Final.pdf.

Clark, C. and Foster, A. (2005) *Children's and Young People's Reading Habits and Preferences: The Who, What, Why, Where and When*. Retrieved 10 May 2016 from: www.literacytrust.org.uk/research/Reading_Connects_survey.pdf.

Cliff Hodges, G. (2010) Rivers of reading: Using critical incident collages to learn about adolescent readers and their readership. *English in Education*, 44 (3): 181–200.

Cliff Hodges, G. (2016) *Researching and Teaching Reading: Developing Pedagogy through Critical Enquiry*. London: Routledge.

Cremin, T. (2016) *Reading: Re-asserting the Potency of the Personal*. [Web blog post]. Retrieved 15 May 2016 from: http://cprtrust.org.uk/cprt-blog/reading-re-asserting-the-potency-of-the-personal/.

Cremin, T., Bearne, E., Mottram, M. and Goodwin, P. (2008a) Primary teachers as readers. *English in Education*, 42 (1): 8–23.

Cremin, T., Mottram, M., Bearne, E. and Goodwin, P. (2008b) Exploring teachers' knowledge of children's literature. *Cambridge Journal of Education*, 38 (4): 449–464.

Cremin, T., Mottram, M., Collins, F. and Powell, S. (2014) *Building Communities of Engaged Readers*. London: Routledge.

Cremin, T., Mottram, M., Collins, F., Powell, S. and Drury, R. (2015) *Researching Literacy Lives: Building Communities between Home and School*. London: Routledge.

Cremin, T., Mottram, M., Collins, F., Powell, S. and Safford, K. (2009) Teachers as readers: Building communities of readers. *Literacy*, 43 (1): 11–19.

Davis, P. (2013) *Reading and the Reader*. Oxford: Oxford University Press.

Department for Education (DfE). (2013) *English Literature GCSE Subject Content and Assessment Objectives*. London: DfE.

Department for Education (DfE). (2014) *National Curriculum in England: English Programmes of Study*. London: DfE. Retrieved 16 May 2016 from: www.gov.uk/government/publications/national-curriculum-in-england-english-programmes-of-study.

Eagleton, T. (1983) *Literary Theory*. Oxford: Basil Blackwell.

Haddon, M. (2003) *The Curious Incident of the Dog in the Night-Time*. London: Jonathan Cape.

Hall, C. and Coles, M. (1999) *Children's Reading Choices*. London: Routledge.

Heaney, S. (1995) *The Redress of Poetry*. London: Faber & Faber.

Higson, C. (2005) *Young James Bond Series*. London: Penguin Books.

Hopper, R. (2005) What are teenagers reading? Adolescent fiction reading habits and reading choices. *Literacy*, 39 (3): 113–120.

Iser, W. (1978) *The Act of Reading: A Theory of Aesthetic Response*. Baltimore: John Hopkins University Press.

Kerr, J. (1971) *When Hitler Stole Pink Rabbit*. Glasgow: William Collins.

Magorian, M. (1991) *A Little Love Song*. London: Methuen.

Morpurgo, M. (1993) *Twist of Gold*. London: Egmont.

Naidoo, B. (2000) *The Other Side of Truth*. Harmondsworth: Penguin.

Naidoo, B. (2001) *Acceptance Speech Carnegie Medal Winner*. Retrieved 15 May 2016 from: http://booksforkeeps.co.uk/issue/130/childrens-books/articles/other-articles/the-other-side-of-truth.

Office for Standards in Education (Ofsted). (2009) *English at the Crossroads: An Evaluation of English in Primary and Secondary Schools 2005/08*. London: Ofsted.

Office for Standards in Education (Ofsted). (2012) *Moving English Forward: Action to Raise Standards in English*. London: Ofsted.

Rennison, L. (1999) *Confessions of Georgia Nicolson Series*. London: Picadilly Press.

Rose, J. (2009) *Independent Review of the Primary Curriculum: Final Report*. London: Department of Children, Families and Schools.

Rosenblatt, L.M. (1938/1995) *Literature as Exploration, 5th ed*. New York: Modern Language Association of America.

Rosenblatt, L.M. (1978/1994) *The Reader the Text the Poem: The Transactional Theory of the Literary Work*. Carbondale: Southern Illinois University Press.

Rowling, J.K. (2005) *Harry Potter and the Half-Blood Prince*. London: Bloomsbury.

Rusesabagina, P. and Zoellner, T. (2006) *An Ordinary Man: The True Story Behind Hotel Rwanda*. London: Bloomsbury.

Scholes, R. (1985) *Textual Power: Literary Theory and the Teaching of English*. New Haven: Yale University Press.

Tolkien, J.R.R. (1937) *The Hobbit*. London: George Allen and Unwin.

West, A. (1986) The production of readers. *The English Magazine*, 17: 4–9.

West, A. (1987) The limits of discourse. *The English Magazine*, 18: 18–22.

Zevin, G. (2005) *Elsewhere*. London: Bloomsbury.

17

THE TEACHER'S CONUNDRUM

Literature for adolescents in a standards-obsessed world

Marshall A. George and Melanie Shoffner

Conversations with colleagues around the English-speaking world make it clear that educators at all levels—primary, secondary, and tertiary—are faced with the challenge of an increasingly standards-obsessed world. The United States' widespread adoption of the Common Core State Standards for English language arts (CCSS) has led to major shifts in curriculum and teaching, similar to those seen under the Australian Curriculum, the UK's National Curriculum, and New Zealand's Literacy Standards, including curricular alignment to standardized tests, reduced literary choice, and lack of instructional variety. Under the CCSS, for example, students are directed to read increasingly complex texts across grade levels and to engage in writing and speaking tasks that are grounded in evidence from literary and informational texts while focusing on the reading of literature and informational (nonfiction) texts. A list of exemplar texts (known as CCSS Appendix B) is provided with the Standards themselves, naming such texts as Alcott's *Little Women, Narrative of the Life of Frederick Douglass,* and Winston Churchill's 'Blood, Toil, Tears and Sweat: Address to Parliament on May 13th, 1940' for grades 6 through 8; Anna Quindlen's 'A Quilt of a Country,' *Metamorphoses* (both Ovid and Kafka), and Voltaire's *Candide* for grades 9 through 10; and Orwell's 'Politics and the English Language,' Dostoevsky's *Crime and Punishment,* and Molière's *Tartuffe* for grades 11 through 12. The concept of text complexity, as well as the seeming emphasis on nonfiction texts, has met with mixed responses from ELA practitioners and scholars, in part because teachers' autonomy over curricular choices is increasingly limited. In the US, this is especially true when choosing literature for study in the ELA classroom, resulting too often in the exclusion of adolescent/young adult literature.

Also known as young adult literature, adolescent literature is defined as books written for and about young people between the ages of 11 and 18 (Cole, 2009; Groenke & Scherff, 2010; Stover, 1996). Such literature connects to young adult readers through recognizable language and meaningful subject matter while also providing a point of entry for diverse students, a population recognizably absent from the canonical texts frequently taught. According to Hinchman and Moore (2013), 'Youths do well when they read what they find interesting and valuable and when they connect what they are reading to their personal lives, other texts, and their knowledge of the world' (p. 445).

In this chapter, we argue for the inclusion of young adult literature in middle and high school ELA classrooms as meaningful fiction that engages, affirms, and connects to adolescents. Rather than a genre that disrupts the goals of college and career readiness—one of the primary stated intents of the CCSS—we posit that literature written specifically for adolescents (ages 12 through 18) supports teachers' efforts to engage students in the study of the critical literacies needed for college, career, and life in the 21st-century. Following an explanation of the Common Core State Standards, we continue with an exploration of adolescent literature which positions it as both meaningful literature for academic study and literature which simultaneously aligns with standards and addresses concerns that have emerged from the field. We then suggest ways in which teachers might engage in informal professional learning to stay abreast of the rapidly expanding world of adolescent literature in order to incorporate it into their classrooms.

The standards

For the first time in US history, curricula in the vast majority of America's public schools are now aligned to a common set of standards. Since 2010, 42 states, 4 territories, the District of Columbia, and the Department of Defense Education Activity (DoDEA) have adopted the Common Core State Standards (CCSS), impacting approximately 82% of US students (Shanahan, 2015). Sponsored by the National Governors Association (NGA) for Best Practices and the Council of Chief State Officers (CCSO)—and influenced by 'policy makers, politicians and the general public' (Zancanella & Moore, 2014, p. 273)—development of the CCSS began in 2009; non-educational entities, like the Bill and Melinda Gates Foundation, were also involved in the standards development (providing $35 million in support of the project), marking a clear intrusion of private interests in public education (Zancanella & Moore, 2014). In the following year, the standards were adopted and implemented fairly quickly after their completion, thanks in part to the Federal Race to the Top (RTTT) program that rewarded states for doing so. Perhaps not surprisingly, the adoption and implementation of these standards have led to a great deal of controversy.

According to the Common Core Standards Initiative website (2016), the CCSS in English language arts build on many states' existing standards with three key shifts: emphasizing increasingly complex texts across grade levels; requiring that students demonstrate reading/writing/speaking skills by citing evidence from literary and informational texts; and building knowledge through the reading of nonfiction/informational texts. These shifts have been met by mixed responses from English educators (Alsup, 2013; Glaus, 2014; NCTE, 2012; Ostensen & Wadham, 2012; Shanahan, 2015). The primary CCSS document is supplemented with additional materials, one of which is Appendix B, a list of texts intended primarily 'to exemplify the level of complexity and quality that the Standards require all students in a given grade band to engage with. Additionally, they are suggestive of the breadth of texts that students should encounter in the text types required by the Standards' (CCSS, 2010 Appendix B, p. 2). While there are a few works of young adult literature from the 1960s and 1970s on the grades 6 to 8 list, with the exception of *The Book Thief* (Zuzak), there are no works of adolescent literature at all on the Appendix B lists for grades 9 to 12. One contributing factor may be that the median year of publication of all texts on the list is 1915 (Glaus, 2014); practically nothing published in the 21st-century is found for any grade level in Appendix B.

While the CCSS-ELA standards have been discussed from many different perspectives (e.g., Alsup, 2013; Aquino-Sterling, 2014; Burns & Botzakis, 2012; Gamson, Lu & Eckert, 2013; Maloch & Bomer, 2013; Moller, 2013), the expressed concerns can be summarized as the following:

- The emphasis on informational or nonfiction texts may lead to a de-emphasis on literary fictional texts.
- The concept of text complexity as it is found in the CCSS document is problematic and leads to the exclusion from the curriculum of many valuable literary works.
- While intended to be a resource only, the inclusion of Appendix B as a list of exemplar texts has led to the exclusion of many texts, including works of adolescent literature, from the ELA curriculum.
- The importance of local context, student interest and engagement, and the affective aspects of reading has been ignored in the CCSS and accompanying documents.

Each of these has implications related to the inclusion (or, in reality, the exclusion) of adolescent/young adult literature in middle and, especially, high school ELA curriculum.

Common core quandaries

Informational texts

The CCSS (2010) utilize the term *informational texts* broadly, including biographies, autobiographies, 'books about history, social studies, science, and the arts ... technical texts, including directions, forms, and information displayed in graphs, charts, or maps...[and]...digital sources on a range of topics' (p. 31). The documents seem to suggest that in elementary grades, students should spend half of their time reading literary texts and the other half reading informational texts. In grades 7 through 12, that percentage is no longer balanced, with 70% of reading time focusing on informational/nonfiction texts and 30% on literary ones. Alsup (2013) has pointed out that this split leads to a clear 'devaluing of traditional fiction, particularly longer novels, which take significant class time to read' (p. 181). She has suggested that,

> some secondary educators are deciding that reading long fictional works may not be the best use of time if student experience with multiple, interdisciplinary, 'complex texts' is the goal, particularly for middle and high school readers who are urged in the CCCS to read more nonfiction than fiction narrative.
>
> *(p. 181–182)*

In contrast, Shanahan (2015) has argued that the CCSS call for an increased emphasis on expository/nonfiction texts does not discourage the teaching of literature, reminding teachers that 'the text division refers to a student's entire school day or school year,' (p. 586) as students are also expected to engage in reading in social studies and science classes, primarily informational texts. Maloch and Bomer (2013) pointed out that, 'if we expect our students to write for any number of purposes, we must provide and teach around texts of varying kinds so that they have models and mentors for their own composing' (p. 213). Similarly, Fisch and Chenelle (2016) have lauded the use of nonfiction to enhance the teaching of literature, saying, 'Rather than just a Common Core mandate crowding out the literary texts we love, informational text can serve as the on-ramp to meaningful learning and engagement with both literature and the world' (p. 31).

Thus, there are two competing viewpoints about the emphasis on informational texts in the Common Core State Standards; generally speaking, the increased study of informational texts is seen to either detract from or enhance the study of literary fiction. While we understand that the standards clearly call for reading informational texts in multiple content areas, we have seen, in practice, that many school leaders and even classroom teachers interpret the standards to be primarily focused on ELA, leading to an ELA curriculum that includes increasingly less literary fiction and more nonfiction/informational texts. We believe that the ELA curricula should be well-balanced and inclusive, incorporating a variety of types, topics, authors, genres, formats, and, not least, text complexity. This leads to the next major criticism of the CCSS.

Text complexity

When discussing text selection, writers of the CCSS hold that the texts used in K through 12 education have declined in their level of sophistication in recent years. The concern cited is that, because students have not been required to read complex texts in high school, they are not prepared for the demands of reading required texts in college. The standards are necessary, in part, to raise that level by including increasingly complex texts. (NB: Gamson, Lu, & Eckert (2013) have challenged this claim and the research cited in the CCSS in a rigorous study of their own examining texts used in schools across grade levels.)

According to Hiebert (2012), 'Since text complexity has not been directly addressed in either state standards or reading programs over the past 25 years, considerable confusion exists about what text complexity means' (p. 12). The CCSS defines text complexity as 'the inherent difficulty of reading and comprehending a text combined' (NGA/CCSO, 2010b, p. 43). The documents identify 'three equally important parts' of a 'tripartite system' (Appendix A, p. 4) that establish the level of a text's complexity: quantitative dimensions, qualitative dimensions, and reader and task considerations. In other words, a text considered for use in the classroom must be analyzed by looking at its Lexile level (a qualitative analysis of structure), levels of meaning, use of language, the knowledge demands needed to comprehend the text, and the context and relevance of the text to the readers.

While some educators believe that this is an even-handed way of judging the complexity of specific texts (Glaus, 2014; Shanahan, 2014), others have argued the inability of such standardized measures to determine appropriately difficult literature for specific readers. As Gamson, Lu, and Eckert (2013) explained,

> text complexity, though important, is only one dimension of what makes for an excellent, robust, and engaging reading program. One hazard of focusing too intently on the CCSS notion of text complexity is that it ushers us into a rather rarified atmosphere, where Lexile rank—or any static single standard—becomes all important.
>
> *(p. 389)*

As interpreted by many school administrators, rather than allowing teachers to emphasize additional factors when choosing texts for their students—such as student engagement, thematic connection or community relevance—the CCSS require teachers to focus primarily on text complexity, which comprises a narrow list of criteria that may or may not accurately reflect the needs of student readers. The emphasis on close reading, for example, is one outcome of the focus on text complexity alone. While the close reading of sophisticated texts may prepare students for the rigors of college reading, Hinchman and Moore (2013) have expressed concern that engaging students solely in the close reading of increasingly complex texts will likely lead to students struggling to do just that, 'whether it's due to the texts challenging linguistic or conceptual demands or the students' abilities to perform particular close reading tasks. English language learners, striving readers, and students with special needs are especially vulnerable' (p. 445).

Text selection

The CCSS do not expressly direct teachers to incorporate specific texts within certain grade levels. Rather, the opening lines of Appendix B (2010) of the CCSS state that, the following text samples primarily serve to exemplify the level of complexity and quality that the Standards require all students in a given grade band to engage with. Additionally, they are suggestive of the breadth of texts that students should encounter in the text types required by the Standards. The choices should serve as useful guideposts in helping educators select texts of similar complexity, quality, and range for their own classrooms. They expressly do not represent a partial or complete reading list.

(p. 1)

Nevertheless, in our work with schools and districts, we have found Hiebert's (2012) assertion to be quite accurate: 'In some educational contexts, the exemplar texts from Appendix B have been embraced as the new curriculum' (p. 6). Indeed, a search of resource catalogues for ELA-related resources and materials makes clear that educational publishers have created CCSS aligned materials that draw almost exclusively on titles from the lists in Appendix B. This is certainly true, for example, for the EngageNY materials that are widely used across the state of New York (see www.engageny.org/resource/grades-9-12-ela-curriculum-map).

A blind adherence to Appendix B as ELA curriculum, however, ignores the importance of choosing texts and, as a result, creating curriculum that responds to the needs of adolescent students. One concern is the lack of diversity represented by the exemplar texts. With the increasing diversity of student populations in the US, one would expect the ELA curriculum to respond accordingly. For example, in 2015, English language learners (ELLs) accounted for 9.1% (4.4 million) of students in public K through 12 schools (National Center for Educational Statistics). However, 'the vast majority of the CCSS exemplars were written by white authors and feature white characters. There are few books about underrepresented groups, only a handful written by cultural insiders, and even fewer that offer underrepresented groups' perspectives on history or the present' (Miller, 2013, p. 60).

A last concern is the apparent exclusion of modern fiction, such as adolescent literature, as acceptable texts for the ELA classroom. A reliance on the texts listed in Appendix B 'will preclude students' opportunities to engage in close reading of relevant contemporary texts, those that youths find motivating and engaging because the contents align with present-day experiences and that prepare them for the reading demands of today's society' (Hinchman & Moore, 2014, p. 445). Additionally, Miller (2014) has suggested that the lists in Appendix B have 'the potential to secure the marginalization of YAL from ever entering the 9–12th-grade language arts classroom or the AP literature classroom' (p. 45), given the lack of adolescent literature offered as exemplar texts for all grade levels.

Literature for adolescents

As ELA teachers work to implement the CCSS, they must increasingly strive to compact their curriculum. This is not a straightforward cause and effect issue, of course, since curriculum responds to multiple factors. However, the CCSS do require ELA teachers to add more nonfiction texts and to ensure that the adopted texts are sufficiently complex; moreover, teachers lose additional instructional time in order to provide more CCSS-aligned test preparation for students, in addition to the actual number of instructional days lost to test taking. One casualty of ELA curriculum compacting is almost assuredly the number and variety of literary texts included in the curriculum, affected by the numerical increase of nonfiction texts and the questionable definition of text complexity (Glaus, 2014; Miller, 2014). At the secondary level, this often translates to the inclusion of fewer works of adolescent literature.

While the CCSS acknowledge that students' motivation, knowledge, and experiences should be considered as an important element in selecting texts (Appendix A, 2010, p. 9), quantitative and qualitative measures are more often considered the most important when determining text complexity criteria rather than being held equal with reader and task considerations. Adolescent literature is a strong fit with the Common Core expectations, however, 'because it can meet the standards for quantitative and qualitative measures of complexity at the same time as it meets the needs of readers and the tasks in which they must engage' (Ostensen & Wadham, 2012, p. 7).

In implementing the CCSS, we have the chance to consider why canonical texts tend to hold more importance in the ELA classroom and what unintended consequences those texts may support for readers. For example, relying solely on canonical texts may reinforce particular perspectives about what constitutes quality reading which may, in turn, continue to shape and privilege certain beliefs around reading. Such a perspective has the potential to reinforce a colonizing ideology in which students leave school with a reading canon that is situated in an 'official knowledge [type]' ideology (Miller, 2014, p. 53). As Ostensen and Wadham (2012) have reminded us, there may be value in choosing more traditional texts but 'the research base and assumptions underlying the new standards actually make a compelling case [to include] more young adult titles in the classroom' (p. 5). Moreover, 'students benefit and gain in cultural capital when teachers choose texts wisely, because texts can be catalysts for particularized knowledge and human experience, and as students transact with the world around them, change can happen' (Miller, 2013, p. 82).

Within the fields of English and Literary Studies, the scholarly study of adolescent literature has been a growing area over the past 50 years. When it adopted its position statement *Research and Scholarship Focusing on Adolescent/Young Adult Literature*, The Conference on English Education (CEE) of The National Council of Teachers of English (NCTE) (2007) affirmed that 'adolescent/young adult literature is a recognized and important area of scholarship and research not only in English and literacy education, but also in multiple disciplines' and that 'research and scholarship focusing on adolescent/young adult literature should be included in the preparation and certification of teachers of English language arts.'

In the past two decades, the inclusion of adolescent literature has become increasingly common in the high school ELA classroom but, despite its many benefits for adolescent readers, the genre is still not found as frequently as canon-ical texts (Applebee, 1993; Connors & Shepard, 2012; Stotsky, 2010). Teachers are often hesitant to integrate young adult literature into the ELA curriculum, as demonstrated by Miller's (2014) study of Advanced Placement English teachers, because they believe adolescent literature is not as rigorous as more canonical texts. However, the concept of rigor as exclusive to canonical texts (or informa-tional texts, for that matter) is a problematic one.

Like any literary genre, adolescent literature offers a range of quality—however one may define the term—but 'a considerable body of young adult literature can withstand the test of close literary scrutiny' (Soter & Connors, 2009, p. 62). Santoli and Wagner (2004), in reviewing adolescent literature's potential in the ELA classroom, noted that 'the breadth and depth of young adult literature are equal to any other genre today and that the recurring life themes of love, death, loss, racism, and friendship contained in the classics are also present in young adult literature' (p. 68). Indeed, the presence of those consistent themes in adolescent literature clearly connects young adult literature to the ELA class-room; if we value the study of themes developed in canonical literature, we must extend the value of study of those same themes to any other work of literature. In doing so, young adult literature offers a more accessible entry into often difficult thematic material. As Ostensen and Wadham (2012) have argued,

> Classic literature has an important place in the ELA classroom, but when decisions are made about which texts to use to support the Common Core, consideration should be given to Rosenblatt's (1995) warnings that readers must find something familiar to connect with in a text and that too much struggle can alienate them from its meaning.
>
> *(p. 6)*

Relevance is certainly not the only reason to incorporate adolescent literature into the ELA curriculum; equally important qualities are literary sophistication and complex social issues (Soter & Connors, 2009). With high-interest, textually complex young adult literature, content can be matched with complexity for adolescent readers, which both calls attention to adolescent development and identity (Lewis & Dockter, 2011) and addresses many of the same literary ele-ments found in canonical literature (Santoli & Wagner, 2004). Textually com-plex young adult literature also speaks to Rosenblatt's (1995) description of the 'human experience' found in stories, supporting engagement and creative acti-vity between reader and text. With such engagement, students find an answer to their question of 'why do we have to do this?' through the explorations and connections that develop during and after reading (Glaus, 2014).

For example, adolescent literature encourages students to experience the world around them in ways that authenticate their own life experiences. When students see their realities mirrored in text, they can negotiate toward or against the expe-rience of the characters they find there (Hagood, 2002) and come to terms with pieces of their own identities. Eliminating a barrier to students' comprehension consequently increases the opportunity for deeper study of the text, supporting students' development in a range of outcomes. Moreover, the 'use of familiar teenage characters and settings ... often mirrors what students know from their own experience, making the texts less demanding in terms of what prior knowledge students need to bring to the reading' (Ostensen & Wadham, 2012, p. 10).

At issue, then, is how to develop ELA teachers' use of adolescent literature in the secondary classroom. The recently revised NCTE Standards for Teacher Preparation (NCTE, 2012b) indicate that ELA teacher preparation programs must ensure that preservice teachers build content knowledge, as well as content pedagogical knowledge, related to adolescent literature. The assumption, then, is that ELA teachers will take this knowledge into their classrooms in order to effectively integrate young adult texts into their curriculum.

Developing teacher understanding of literature for adolescents

Teachers in the US who have gone through initial certification programs with NCTE national recognition (through NCATE or CAEP) should have some knowledge of adolescent literature, either through a dedicated course or as additional content in an associated course. Many career teachers may have entered the classroom prior to that NCTE requirement, however. Having developed an understanding of adolescent literature during their preparation is not a guarantee of inclusion, however, since teachers may struggle to keep current with the ever-growing field of young adult literature. This lack of familiarity means teachers are less likely to incorporate adolescent literature into the ELA classroom when they have the opportunity to do so.

One answer to developing teachers' knowledge in any area once they enter the classroom is professional development (PD). The purposes for continuous learning are many and varied; however, Tan, Cheng, and Teng (2015) have identified five main reasons that teachers engage in PD:

> (1) keeping discipline knowledge current, (2) staying abreast of the latest changes in educational landscape through networking with other like-minded teachers, (3) role modeling life-long learning, (4) motivating themselves to stay passionate in teaching, and (5) fulfilling the responsibility of being a professional.
>
> *(p. 1590)*

Professional development—like university courses in YA literature or in-service workshops on pedagogical strategies with adolescent texts—is one way for teachers to develop their knowledge of adolescent literature. However, understanding the many constraints under which teachers operate—from time and money to access and opportunity to curriculum revision and test preparation—we are hesitant to advocate formal professional development as the only way to learn about adolescent literature. Instead, we posit three informal avenues for teachers to engage in professional learning of adolescent literature that may positively impact their ability to incorporate young adult literature into the classroom: membership in professional associations (such as ALAN, NCTE, and ILA), engagement with social media (such as blogs, Twitter, GoodReads, and Facebook), and participation in faculty book clubs. Each of these avenues is well-aligned with the purposes for professional development suggested by Tan, Cheng, and Teng (2015).

Professional associations

When Jim Burke (2012) urges ELA teachers to join 'the great conversation' afforded by membership in professional associations such as NCTE, he joins others (Christenbury, 2006; Maxwell & Meiser, 2010) in lauding the usefulness of reading journals from those associations, attending local, regional, and national conventions and conferences, and participating in virtual communities made available by the associations. Two professional groups in the United States focus exclusively on reading, teaching, and studying literature written for adolescents and young adults: the Assembly for Literature for Adolescents of the National Council of Teachers of English (ALAN) and The International Literacy Association's Special Interest Group Network on Adolescent Literature (SIGNAL). Both organizations are made up of classroom teachers, librarians, professors, authors, publishers, and others interested in adolescent literature. ALAN supports 'communication and cooperation among all individuals who have a special interest in adolescent literature, presents programs and conferences on this subject, promotes and increases the number of articles and publications devoted to it and integrates the efforts of all those with an interest in this literature' (ALAN, 2016). Similarly, SIGNAL is 'dedicated to the celebration, research, and promotion of Young Adult Literature' (SIGNAL, 2016).

The journals of both groups, *The ALAN Review* and *SIGNAL Journal*, are peer-reviewed publications with a mix of scholarship, practical ideas, book reviews, and pieces contributed by adolescent literature authors. We see professional journals as an invaluable resource for teachers, offering teachers a tangible way of deepening their understanding of adolescent literature while expanding their instructional approaches to it in the classroom. In a recent conversation, for example, a third year 10th grade ELA teacher told Marshall, 'I so look forward to my *ALAN Review*. Every issue provides me with new "must reads," teaching and curriculum ideas, and new ways of thinking about books that I have already read or teach.'

In addition to *The ALAN Review* and *SIGNAL*, other NCTE journals such as *Voices from the Middle* (focused on middle grades ELA) and *English Journal* (focused on high school ELA), as well as ILA's *Journal of Adolescent and Adult Literacy*, are important resources for ELA teachers. In addition to these journals, NCTE and ILA both offer digital and print resources for teachers on their websites, publishing and selling books specifically geared to teaching ELA, which includes the teaching of adolescent literature.

Moving beyond journals to attend conferences is another important offering made by possible through professional organizations. The NCTE Annual Convention each November, the annual ALAN Workshop held two days after NCTE, and the ILA annual conference held each summer provide opportunities to network with colleagues and peers, learn from fellow teachers' presentations, meet adolescent literature authors, and browse acres of books and resources in the exhibit hall. When Nicole deGuzman (2016) attended the ALAN Workshop for the first time, she found it more than worthwhile:

> It's hard to forget the contagious buzz of the workshop room, the combined brilliance of so many talented educators, writers, and others coming together, buzzing with a common purpose. It's been an uphill battle at my school to deliver more young adult lit to actual young adults, a battle I'm still fighting. At ALAN, I got a break and a breath I barely knew I needed, in a haze of camaraderie I didn't know existed. At ALAN, I got a vital renewal in the belief that YA literature matters.
>
> *(p. 1)*

Social media

The ubiquity of social media provides teachers with an easily accessible means by which to support their continued professional development once they enter the classroom (Rodesiler, 2014); by extension, teachers can leverage different forms of social media to develop their learning about adolescent literature. The connections formed online offer opportunities for teachers to participate in meaningful dialogue, collaborative problem solving, and supportive reflection which, in turn, can support their professional learning (Beach, 2012).

One example is extending conversations begun at professional conferences via online communities, such as NCTE's Connected Community and ILA's *Literacy Daily Blog*. Rather than leaving behind the thought-provoking interactions that often occur during face-to-face meetings, teachers can use social media as a 'bridge' (Nobles, Dredger & Gerheart, 2012) to continue those conversations once they return home. Personal online communities can also be used for professional purposes. Through Facebook, teachers can stay connected to colleagues they meet who are interested in issues of adolescent literature in a space designed for the sharing of information. Through Twitter, teachers can create connections to and gather information about adolescent literature: following authors like Patrick Ness or Laurie Halse Anderson, exploring hashtags like #YASaves or #YAfiction, engaging in Twitter chats about adolescent literature.

Blogs that address adolescent literature directly also offer opportunities for teachers to learn more about reading and teaching young adult literature. A recent post on the blog *Literacy and NCTE*, for example, asked why teachers can't assign happy books (2016), citing arguments for and against YA literature being too dark for adolescent readers, while *Dr. Bickmore's YA Wednesday* blog covers different topics related to adolescent literature each week, from novels that address school shootings to reading young adult nonfiction. Sites that connect readers also allow teachers to develop and extend their understanding of adolescent literature. Goodreads (2016), for example, is a type of virtual library that allows members to search for books, post reviews and comment on other's reviews, as well as create groups, hold discussions, and examine lists—all focused on adolescent literature.

Book clubs

Book clubs offer another means of informal professional development. By reading and discussing a common novel, teachers within a school or district can engage in collaborative learning around adolescent literature. In effect, teachers can participate in a version of the literature circles they so often implement in their own classrooms: 'small, peer-led discussion groups whose members have chosen to read the same story, poem, article or book' (Daniels, 2002, p. 2). When regarded as such, teachers are not only reading potential texts *for* their classroom but modeling the type of engagement with literature they expect *in* their classroom.

While book clubs need have no specific organization, we offer one example for context. Over a five-year span, Marshall worked to build book clubs with teachers in three New York City middle schools to build their content knowledge of adolescent literature (George, 2000, 2003, 2004). While the majority were English language arts teachers, social studies and science teachers, administrators, school psychologists, and school counselors joined the group, as well. At the beginning, these book clubs were for faculty and staff only. However, after students indicated their interest, they were invited to join the community of readers (George, 2004).

These book clubs met monthly during lunch. Some of the reading selections were recently published works that had received significant praise in the field (i.e. winners of the Printz, Newbery, Coretta Scott King, Young Adult Choice, and Pura Belpre Awards); others were titles considered 'classics' in the world of adolescent literature that few had read (i.e. *The Chocolate War, Annie on My Mind, The Outsiders*). Discussions blended the perspectives of readers and teachers, supporting conversations about the literary nature of the texts as well as potential curricular and pedagogical possibilities. These conversations were extended and enhanced when students joined the book club.

In terms of professional development, everyone involved felt a 'culture of literacy and literature' in the school, where teachers and students felt comfortable sharing their 'independent reading lives' (George, 2004, p. 24). More specifically, the English teachers involved in the book clubs began incorporating more adolescent literature in their classrooms, built larger classroom libraries, and implemented book clubs or literature circles in their own classrooms.

Conclusion

Teachers are in the best position to choose texts that meet the learning needs of the students in their classes. Reaching beyond the limited (and problematic) lists of texts provided in the CCSS Appendix B allows teachers to implement their professional understandings of students, grade level, curriculum, and pedagogy to support meaningful learning. Adolescent literature should be part of teachers' professional understanding, just as informal ways of learning should be part of teachers' professional development. In learning about adolescent literature, ELA teachers are learning about viable texts for their classrooms that are well-suited to the demands of our standards-obsessed world:

> With the wide expansion of young adult literature today, it is possible to the meet the Common Core State Standards with books that are sophisticated and complex while having new conversations about text complexity and its various forms. Textually complex young adult literature is a vast and growing resource for cultivating student readers, but only if we recognize it in this manner.
>
> *(Glaus, 2014, p. 414)*

References

Alsup, J. (2013). Teaching literature in an age of text complexity. *Journal of Adolescent and Adult Literacy 57*(3), 181–184.

Aquino-Sterling, C. (2014). Speaking and listening in a new key: Discursive performances in light of common core. *Voices from the Middle 22*(1), 30–35.

Beach, R. (2012). Research and policy: Can online learning communities foster professional development? *Language Arts 89*(4), 256–262.

Beach, R., Thein, A.H., & Webb, A. (2012). *Teaching to exceed the English language arts Common Core State Standards: A literacy approach for 6–12 classrooms.* New York: Routledge.

Bickmore, S. (2016). *Dr. Bickmore's YA Wednesday.* Retrieved August 3, 2016 from www.yawednesday.com/.

Burns, L.D., & Botzakis, S.G. (2012). Using the *Joy Luck Club* to teach core standards and 21st century literacies. *English Journal 101*(5), 23–29.

Cole, P.B. (2009). *Young adult literature in the 21st century.* New York: McGraw Hill.

Common Core State Standards Initiative. (2016). *Key Shifts in English Language Arts.* Retrieved March 28, 2016 from www.corestandards.org/other-resources/key-shifts-in-english-language-arts/.

Conference on English Education of the National Council of Teachers of English (2007). *Position Statement on Research and Scholarship Focusing on Adolescent/Young Adult Literature.* Retrieved June 1, 2016 from www.ncte.org/cee/positions/yaliterature.

Creemers, B., Kyriakides, L., & Antoniou. P. (2013). *Towards the development of a dynamic approach to teacher professional development. Teacher professional development for improving quality of teaching.* Amsterdam: Spring Netherlands.

Daniels, H. (2002). *Literature circles: Voice and choice in book clubs and reading groups* (2nd ed.). Portland, ME: Stenhouse.

Davis, M. (2016). Why can't teachers assign happy books? *Literacy and NCTE: The Official Blog of the National Council of Teachers of English.* Retrieved August 3, 2016 from http://blogs.ncte.org/index.php/2016/08/cant-teachers-assign-happy-books/.

deGuzman, N. (2016, February). Reflections on ALAN workshop from a first time registrant. *ALAN Newsletter*. Retrieved June 1, 2016 from www.alan-ya.org/reflections-on-alan-workshop-from-a-first-time-registrant/.

Fisch, A., & Chenelle, S. (2016). Using nonfiction to enhance our teaching of literature. *English Journal 105*(40), 31–36.

Gamson, D.A., Lu, X., & Eckert, S.A. (2013). Challenging the research base of the Common Core State Standards: A historical reanalysis of text complexity. *Educational Researcher 42*(7), 381–391.

George, M.A. (2000). Researching the implementation of faculty book clubs in an urban middle school. *The ALAN Review 28*(1), 22–25.

George, M.A. (2003). Professional development for a literature-based middle school curriculum. *The Clearing House 75*, 327–331.

George, M.A. (2004). Faculty-student book clubs create communities of readers in two urban middle schools. *Middle School Journal 35*(3), 21–26.

Glaus, M. (2014). Text complexity and young adult literature: Establishing its place. *Journal of Adolescent & Adult Literacy 57*(5), 407–416.

Goodreads. (2016). *About Goodreads*. Retrieved August 3, 2016 from www.goodreads.com/.

Groenke, S.L., & Scherff, L. (2010). *Teaching ya lit through differentiated instruction*. Urbana, IL: NCTE.

Guthrie, J.T., & Wigfield, A. (2000). Engagement and motivation in reading. In M.J. Kamil, P.B. Mosenthal, P.D. Pearson, & R. Barr (Eds.), *Handbook of Reading Research* (Vol 3, pp. 406–424). Mahwah, NJ: Erlbaum.

Hiebert, E.H. (2012). The CCSS text exemplars: Understanding their aims and use in text selection. *Reading Today 30*(3), 6.

Hinchman, K.A., & Moore, D.W. (2013). Close reading: A cautionary interpretation. *Journal of Adolescent & Adult Literacy 56*(6), 441–450.

Ladson-Billings, G. (2006). Yes, but how do we do it? Practicing culturally relevant pedagogy. In J. Landsman, & C.W. Lewis (Eds.), *White Teachers/Diverse Classrooms: A Guide to Building Inclusive Schools, Promoting High Expectations, and Eliminating Racism* (pp. 292). Sterling, VA: Stylus.

Maloch, B., & Bomer, R. (2013). Informational texts and the Common Core State Standards: What are we talking about anyway? *Language Arts 90*(3), 205–213.

Miller, sj. (2014). Text complexity and 'comparable literary merit' in young adult literature. *The ALAN Review Winter*, 44–55.

Moller, K.J. (2013). Considering the CCSS nonfiction literature exemplars as cultural artifacts: What do they represent? *Journal of Children's Literature 39*(2), 58–67.

National Center for Education Statistics. (2015). *Fast Facts: English Language Learners*. Institute of Education Sciences. US Department of Education. Retrieved from https://nces.ed.gov/fastfacts/display.asp?id=96.

National Council of Teachers of English (2012a). *Resolution on Teacher Expertise and the Common Core State Standards*. Retrieved May 22, 2016 from www.ncte.org/positions/statements/teacherexpertise.

National Council of Teachers of English (2012b). *NCTE/NCATE Standards for Initial Preparation of Teachers of Secondary English Language Arts, Grades 7–12*. Retrieved June 4, 2016 from www.ncte.org/library/NCTEFiles/Groups/CEE/NCATE/ApprovedStandards_111212.pdf.

National Governor's Association Center for Best Practices & Council of Chief State School Officers. (2010a). *Common Core State Standards*. Washington, DC: Authors.

National Governor's Association Center for Best Practices & Council of Chief State School Officers. (2010b). *Common Core State Standards for English language arts & literacy in history/social studies, science, and technical subjects: Appendix B.* Washington, DC: Authors.

Nobles, S., Dredger, K., & Gerheart, M.D. (2012). Collaboration beyond the classroom walls: Deepening learning for students, preservice teachers, teachers, and professors. *Contemporary Issues in Technology and Teacher Education 12*(4). Retrieved from www. citejournal.org/volume-12/issue-4-12/english-language-arts/collaboration-beyond-the-classroom-walls-deepening-learning-for-students-preservice-teachers-teachers-and-professors.

Ostensen, J., & Wadham, R. (2012). Young adult literature and the common core: A surprisingly good fit. *American Secondary Education 41*(1), 4–13.

Rodesiler, L. (2014). Weaving contexts of participation online: The digital tapestry of secondary English teachers. *Contemporary Issues in Technology and Teacher Education, 14*(2). Retrieved from www.citejournal.org/volume-14/issue-2-14/english-language-arts/weaving-contexts-of-participation-online-the-digital-tapestry-of-secondary-english-teachers.

Shanahan, T. (2015). What teachers should know about Common Core: A guide for the perplexed. *Reading Teacher 68*, 583–588.

Stover, L.T. (1996). *Young adult literature: The heart of the middle school curriculum.* Portsmouth, NH: Boyton/Cook.

Tan, A.L., Chang, C.H., & Teng, P. (2015). Tensions and dilemmas in teacher professional development. *Procedia-Social and Behavioral Sciences 174*, 1583–1591.

Zancanella, D., & Moore, M. (2014a). The origins of the Common Core: Untold stories. *Language Arts 91*(4), 273–279.

Zancanella, D., & Moore, M. (2014b). The origins and ominous future of the US Common Core standards in English language arts. In A. Goodwyn, L. Reid, & C. Durrant (Eds.), *International Perspectives on Teaching English in a Globalised World* (pp. 199–209). New York: Routledge.

18

DEVOLVING ENGLISH LITERATURE IN SCHOOLS

'Non-standard' approaches to the literature curriculum

Gary Snapper

Following reactionary reform of the national curriculum and examination system in England in 2014, and in the light of a widening gap between the politics of England on the one hand and Scotland and Wales on the other, this chapter explores ideas of devolution, and international difference and diversity, in relation to an increasingly centralised, standardised and nationalist literature curriculum, using Scottish writer and critic Robert Crawford's work on the power relationships between Scottish and English literature as a starting point. The prescriptive canonical nationalism of the literature curriculum in England, and its associated narrow assessment regime, are contrasted with the devolutionary potential of the study of literature in the International Baccalaureate diploma, which offers the opportunity for exploration of a wide range of different types of literature and language internationally, and a variety of modes of learning and assessment, within a framework of teacher and student choice. Finally, the chapter argues that moving away from the standard structures of the narrowly defined literature curriculum can open up opportunities for teachers and students to hear a broader range of voices, and to explore a broader range of ideas about literature in society—considerably broader than those which syllabuses generally allow or encourage.[1]

Devolution, difference and diversity

The issue of devolution in the UK—the devolving of political powers away from England to Wales, Scotland and Northern Ireland, and possibly also from London to the English regions—is a longstanding one, and one which, following the Scottish independence referendum of 2014 and the British EU referendum of 2016, is more charged than ever. Political and cultural differences between the regions and countries of the UK have become more apparent in recent years as greater powers have been devolved, in particular, to the national governments of Scotland and Wales, giving those countries a stronger voice with which to represent their differences from England and express the cultural diversity of the UK. Questions of national identity have been given urgency by the growing political division (broadly) between the increasingly outward-looking left-wing nationalism of Scotland and Wales on the one hand, and the increasingly inward-looking neo-liberal conservatism of England on the other.

Nowhere is national difference and diversity in the UK felt more than in *language*. In Scotland, Wales and Ireland, standard English is in tension with other national languages—Welsh, Gaelic, Scots—and each of those languages has, in recent decades, successfully mounted a challenge to standard English both in the education system and in public life more generally, embedding linguistic and cultural diversity in the system. In England, meanwhile, increasingly conservative education policies have sought to de-privilege non-standard forms of the language, for instance through a hardening attitude to the use of dialect in oral work in the classroom and a highly prescriptive approach to the teaching of grammar.

In the other countries of the UK, too, recent decades have seen an exuberant celebration of national difference, linguistic diversity and political challenge in and through *literature*. This is perhaps particularly the case in Scotland—and notably through the work of such celebrated writers as Edwin Morgan, Tom Leonard, Liz Lochhead, James Kelman, Alasdair Gray and Irvine Welsh. The work of these writers constantly plays on the border between Scots and English, and between the standard and the non-standard or demotic—and their characters and themes challenge definitions of and attitudes to nationality, class, language—and literature—in a way which reflects their allegiance to a culture whose identity is defined partly by its *difference* from England and English, by positing a different way of being British.

The Scottish poet and critic Robert Crawford (Professor of Modern Scottish Literature at the University of St Andrews) writes about this aspect of Scottish literature in his book *Devolving English Literature* (2000), from which the title of this essay is borrowed. He identifies what he calls a consciously 'barbarian' tendency in the literature of the 'Anglo-Celtic archipelago':

> There is a widespread wish in recent poetry to be seen as in some manner barbarian, as operating outside the boundaries of standard English and outside the identity that is seen as going with it. Such a wish unites post-colonial writers such as Les Murray and Derek Walcott with writers working within the 'Anglo-Celtic archipelago.' It joins the post-colonial and the provincial ... For most creative users of the English language today, one of the fundamental questions is how to inhabit that language without sacrificing one's own distinctive, 'barbarian' identity.
>
> *(p. 300)*

In invoking post-colonialism and notions of standard and non-standard English, Crawford hints here at his broader theme in the book—the traditional and continuing dominance of 'standard English' conceptions of 'English Literature'. In his introduction, he writes:

> Much attention has been devoted to the question of how we might define, select, or construct the entity known as 'literature'. Until very recently, it seemed the word 'English' was left unexamined.
>
> *(p. 2)*

> The development of the subject 'English Literature' has constantly involved and reinforced an oppressive homage to centralism. As such, English Literature is a force which must be countered continually by a devolutionary momentum.
>
> *(p. 7)*

He also suggests that 'Scottish Literature ... offers the longest continuing example of a substantial body of literature produced by a culture pressurised by the threat of cultural domination' (p. 8).

Literature and curriculum in the UK

It's interesting to reflect on Crawford's ideas here in the light of a key pronouncement about English Literature in schools by the recent Education Secretary in England, Michael Gove (in a speech given to Conservative Party Conference on October 5th 2010):

> We need to reform English. The great tradition of our literature—Dryden, Pope, Swift, Byron, Keats, Shelley, Austen, Dickens and Hardy—should be at the heart of school life. Our literature is the best in the world—it is every child's birthright and we should be proud to teach it in every school.

Gove's absurdly unverifiable claim that 'our literature is the best in the world'— 'our' apparently meaning canonical literature written in English, in England (with the exception of Swift), by white people and before the 20th century— clearly exemplifies Crawford's claim about English Literature's 'centralism'.

In this speech, Gove spelled out the principle which was to inform his revamp of the English curriculum in England in 2014—culminating in 'rigorous' GCSE English Literature exams in which all students (aged 16) must be tested, in terminal examinations only, on a complete Shakespeare play, a complete Victorian novel, a selection of Romantic poetry and a work of modern British literature. Non-British literature is specifically banned from the exam, in a direct attempt to remove works such as *Of Mice and Men* and *To Kill a Mockingbird* (until recently almost universally taught at this level but now considered too 'easy' by the government) from the high school English curriculum. Furthermore, the requirement to teach literature 'from different cultures and traditions' has also been removed.[2]

The reformed curriculum at this level does not expressly *forbid* the teaching of any particular texts, but the reality of a crowded curriculum in a high-stakes national examination system, in which both teachers' and students' performance are measured by exam results, is that only the specified exam texts are likely to be taught between the ages of 14 and 16. Furthermore, the range of texts that might be chosen in each of the specified categories is limited to the few texts set by the examination boards (and inevitably almost all the literature set is English rather than more widely 'British').

It has also become clear that the pressure to prepare students to cope with tough exams on the pre-20th century canon at GCSE has led in many schools to a reduction in the diversity of modern literature being studied *before* the age of 14—although there *is* a requirement at this stage to teach some 'seminal world literature written in English'—a re-formulation of the previous 'literature from different cultures and traditions' (presumably felt to be too much an expression of multiculturalism).

At A Level (the course studied by the majority of students in England, Wales and Northern Ireland who stay at school from 16 to 18), the situation in England with regard to English Literature is similar, although a little more diverse. Most students now study only eight texts, at least half of which must be pre-20th century, including Shakespeare. The other texts may be modern, and at least one must be a 21st-century text. The emphasis is still pretty firmly on English literature from England and certainly does not include more than the occasional nod to regional or world literature. American writers *are* permitted at this level and feature occasionally on the syllabus, as, more rarely, do writers in English from outside the UK such as Arundhati Roy. Literature in translation is rarely taught, and indeed officially discouraged where (as for almost all texts studied) students are assessed on their understanding of the writer's use of language.

Devolving English literature

In the light of all this, Crawford's reflections on the need to 'counter the force' of English Literature through 'devolutionary momentum' seem to speak directly to us as teachers of English Literature—in the UK, certainly, but also in other English-speaking countries around the world where prescriptive and standardising approaches to curriculum and assessment are being imposed. The idea of 'devolving' English literature, with its political—and even (as Crawford suggests) post-colonial—associations, suggests a number of possibilities which might help us to re-state an alternative vision for literature teaching in schools.

First, there is the idea of *redeployment* and *self-determination* contained in devolution: the devolution of the teaching of English Literature to teachers. Greater freedom to choose texts and topics, and to follow one's interests and the interests and needs of one's students; and a greater emphasis on teacher assessment and a variety of different (non-standard(ised)) curricular modes and outcomes to free us to some extent from the centralist tyrannies of the prescribed set text and the terminal examination.

Second, there is the idea of *decentralisation* and *internationalism* suggested by devolution: the acknowledgement that we live in a complex and diverse world in which crude nationalisms are unhelpful, nations do not operate in isolation and understanding local and global issues and relationships is essential. With this in mind, the study of 'non-standard' literatures—regional and multicultural—world literature and literature in translation might be repositioned as at least as important as the standard(ised) national canon or literary heritage.

Third, there is the *cultural and political challenge* to the status quo offered by devolution—the post-colonial spirit of it—offering us the opportunity to put cultural and literary politics more centrally and more explicitly into our teaching. As English teachers we have traditionally prided ourselves on the humaneness of our discipline, and the *texts* that we teach frequently open up important political and cultural issues in powerful ways—from racial prejudice and colonialism in Shakespeare, say, to the gender and environmental politics of Atwood. But what about the politics of *literature* as a form or concept—and perhaps particularly the politics of *English* literature (as Crawford suggests)? What about the theoretical questions of social, cultural and linguistic function and value that courses in English Language, Media Studies and Cultural Studies often deal with, but which standard approaches to English Literature tend to sidestep?

The International Baccalaureate

One model for such devolution is offered by the International Baccalaureate (IB), an international diploma for students aged 16 to 19, taught in some schools and colleges in the UK as an alternative to A Level, and similarly by institutions in many other countries around the world as an alternative to national systems at this level.

I taught the IB for some years at a comprehensive school in England, and continue to be involved in the IB through curriculum development work for the IBO, the organisation which manages the diploma worldwide. The IB Literature syllabus (known now as 'Language A: Literature') allowed me and my colleagues to experience and experiment with all three aspects of devolution suggested above. The syllabus offers a freedom in course construction and an approach to assessment radically different from the A Level course; and the focus of the IB on internationalism—as well as its pre-disposition to broad, comparative and thematic learning—means that, within the English syllabus, one is encouraged to move well beyond the constraints of narrow nationalism and atomistic reading, and engage with broad cultural themes.

The chief vehicle for 'devolutionary momentum' in the IB English syllabus is the 'Works in Translation' unit, assessed through written coursework. For this unit, we could choose to teach virtually any writers in the world, as long as they *didn't* write in English. Although many schools stick to Euro-centric material—Chekhov, Ibsen and so on—there is also a strong tradition of choosing more adventurously here. Seeing this as an opportunity to broaden students' experience, and to engage with international issues, we decided to develop a three-text study of post-colonial African literature.

The centrepiece of the African unit was *I Will Marry When I Want*, the 1977 play by the Kenyan writer Ngugi wa Thiong'o, now Professor of English and Comparative Literature at the University of California, living in exile in the United States. After having written a series of well-known novels in English, Ngugi, around 1970, abandoned English as his literary language and started writing in his native Gikuyu in order to re-establish an African literary tradition for African audiences. He worked with a community centre in a working-class town near Nairobi to write and produce *I Will Marry When I Want*—a community drama—which allowed ordinary people to tell their story and express their views, notably about the way they felt they had been betrayed by Daniel Arap Moi's neo-colonial government following independence from Britain. The play was immediately banned, and Ngugi was held in prison for a year without trial by Arap Moi.

Ngugi later wrote grippingly in his book *Decolonising the Mind* (1986) about this sequence of events, including the process of writing, rehearsing and performing the play, and his reasons for doing what he did—a section of the book we read together in class. Students were fascinated by the real-life political drama which lay behind the fictional politics of the play, and enjoyed re-interpreting the play with their new understanding of the social and political contexts of the play's rehearsal, performance and aftermath. Later, students wrote letters, 'in role' either condemning or defending the play, giving evidence drawn from the play, Ngugi's commentary on it and the historical background.

In other parts of the book, Ngugi expands on the idea of English Literature as a tool of colonialism by exploring, for instance, how the British colonial regime suppressed indigenous art forms and promoted British culture, notably Shakespeare in the theatre:

> The oppressed and exploited of the earth maintain their defiance: liberty from theft. But the biggest weapon wielded and actually daily unleashed by imperialism against that collective defiance is the cultural bomb. The effect of a cultural bomb is to annihilate a people's belief in their names, in their languages, in their environment, in their heritage of struggle, in their unity, in their capacities, and ultimately in themselves.
>
> *(p. 3)*

This is one of many aspects of Shakespeare as a literary phenomenon that conventional literary study doesn't often give students the chance to consider. Ngugi also deals powerfully with the idea of drama as a physical and political act, and its potential as a major cultural force in the community—another issue that conventional literary study doesn't often touch on.

The explicit combination of literature and politics, both the politics within the literary text *and* the politics surrounding it, raised a variety of important issues in the classroom about the way in which literature functions in society, the relationships between literature, culture, language and power and the cultural politics of a post-colonial world. In particular, this work enabled us to look in a very concrete way at the way in which the value of English Literature is in many ways culturally specific and contested in sometimes very political ways—a type of work perhaps more often associated with university than with the school study of literature.

From Africa to Scotland

Another devolutionary element of the IB programme is the 'Options' unit, which gives the teacher complete freedom to put together a thematic unit without reference to any list of set texts, authors or other requirements, and (in recent years) with the option of incorporating non-fiction, film, graphic novels and so on. The unit is assessed by internal oral assessment and tasks can be negotiated with individual students.

I decided on a thematic unit that enabled students to build on some of the issues covered in the African study and look at some of the ways in which literature, culture and politics might interact nearer to home. Thus—returning to Crawford's suggestion that 'Scottish Literature offers the longest continuing example of a substantial body of literature produced by a culture pressurised by the threat of cultural domination' and his idea of the 'barbarian' in modern English literature—I decided to explore with students some of the cultural and linguistic tensions and questions of national identity that exist within Britain as manifested in 20th-century literature from Scotland, Ireland, Wales and England.

Whilst I chose single authors for three of the texts (Seamus Heaney, Dylan Thomas and Tony Harrison), I also wanted to take the opportunity to experiment with teaching a wide range of inter-related shorter texts as distinct from the atomistic study of a whole self-contained text which is the dominant mode of most literary study at this level. For the Scottish text, I therefore devised a short anthology of contemporary Scottish literary texts, focusing on a sequence of poems, short stories, essays and extracts from longer works by James Kelman, Irvine Welsh, Liz Lochhead, Tom Leonard, Alasdair Gray and Edwin Morgan, as well as some Scots ballads and classical poetry.

The starting point for this study was James Kelman. Beginning with some of his *very* short stories, in *The Burn* (1991), we looked at some of the ways in which he experiments with narrative voice, looking particularly at 'The Hon' ('The Hand'), a 350-word story in the form of a vernacular anecdote which begins:

> Auld Shug gits oot iv bed. Turns aff the alarm cloak. Gis straight ben the toilit. Sits doon in that on the lavatri pan. Wee bit iv time gis by. Shug sittin

ther, yonin. This Hon. Up it comes oot fri the waste pipe. Stretchis right
up. Grabs him by the bolls.

(p. 123)

Here we see Kelman experimenting in miniature with the Scots dialect
narrator—a line of experiment which reaches its culmination with his controversial Booker-prize winning novel, *How Late It Was, How Late* (1994), in which
the entire novel has a third-person Scots dialect narrator, and in which the voice
of the narrator and the voice of the main character, Sammy, seem to merge into
each other:

> Sammy had stopped, he turned to the tenement wall and leaned his fore-
> head against it feeling the grit, the brick, he scraped his head along it an
> inch or two then back till he got that sore feeling. The thing is he was go-
> ing naywhere, nayhwere. So he needed to clear his brains, to think; think,
> he needed to fucking think. It was just a new problem. He had to cope wit
> it, that's all. that's all it was. Every day was a fucking problem. And his was
> a new yin.

(p. 37)

How Late It Was, How Late is a powerful work about class and power in society, in
which we become privy to the moving inner life of a traumatised working-class
Scotsman, and yet when it was awarded the Booker Prize, many were outraged
because of the frequent swearing throughout the novel. One of the judges, Rabbi
Julia Neuberger, threatened to resign, arguing that the novel was 'a disgrace'. In
class, as well as looking in detail at these short stories and extracts from Kelman's
work—focusing on issues about narrative voice, viewpoint and dialect—we
looked at newspaper articles about Kelman and the Booker prize incident, read
a lengthy essay by Kelman about his work (1992) and watched a video of a TV
documentary about Kelman.

In both the video and the essay, Kelman movingly talks about his mission to
legitimise the working-class Scots narrative voice in English literature, pointing
out that throughout the history of the novel, all third-person narrators have been
standard English and therefore middle or upper class: dialect voices only appear
in dialogue, and always mediated by a standard English voice. Later in the video,
a Black South African writer talks about the way in which Kelman's champi-
oning of the suppressed voice in literature inspired Black South African writers
during the struggle against apartheid—creating another link between this work
on Scotland and the African unit previously studied.

The discussion which took place in class as a result of these few but highly
concentrated stimuli was urgent and thoroughly engaged. Students were particularly taken with the idea of the voices that literature suppresses, the potential
exclusivity of literature—which in turn raises fundamental questions about literature, education and society, and, more specifically, about the literature which

is legitimated by the teaching of English. A range of questions about language, literature and culture arose, too: about the nature of swearing; about literary prizes; about the differences between spoken and written language, and between literary and non-literary language; about whether you could use non-standard English to narrate a novel without making it incomprehensible; about exactly whose voice a third person narrator actually *is*; about who is represented in and by literature; and so on. There was also an interesting discussion—crucial in relation to Kelman's work—about who the intended readership of the novel was: wouldn't it just be read by middle-class literary types like me?

We went on to look further at a variety of issues through other short pieces or extracts, including the history of the English language (taking the opportunity to look at some Anglo-Saxon, and medieval Scots and English), and the implications of Scots as a separate language from English; the definition of dialect, and Kelman and Welsh's bi-dialectalism—swapping between standard and non-standard English writing; the ironic imposition of non-standard language on to standard literary forms, as for instance in Morgan's 'Glasgow Sonnets'; questions of stereotype and national identity; and so on.

Devolutionary momentum

I suggested earlier that Crawford's idea of devolution might be applied through challenges to the 'centralism' enshrined both in the prescriptive controls of English Literature syllabuses and examinations, and in the cultural exclusions of the idea of English Literature. Clearly, the programme described above— enabling the study of a diverse range of international literature and a wide variety of standard and non-standard uses of language and literary forms, and allowing diverse approaches to curriculum and assessment—is in striking contrast with more conventional and standard(ised) approaches to the literature curriculum, and in particular with the current extremely centralist model of the literature curriculum in England.

So what kind of 'devolutionary momentum' did we build up through all this? And what did these devolved freedoms offer us? I'd argue that including the kind of non-standard, devolutionary work on literature I've described can free teachers and students to listen to a wide range of voices and ideas, and explore a wide range of issues, of a different kind from those encountered through the standard forms of the school literature syllabus and examination, perhaps helping students to access and gain ownership of the critical discourses of literary study at a higher level.

Using the freedom to combine conventional set text study with the study of short texts and extracts, and to explore a range of literature from different cultures, languages and dialects, we covered a lot of literary ground, making links between a wide range of texts (from medieval to contemporary), and a lot of international ground too. At the same time, we did a lot of close reading and talked a great deal about language and form: working with short texts and extracts focuses attention on language in a very concentrated and different way from working with longer whole texts.

Students learnt a lot about *literature*, too, I felt, rather than about single literary *texts*—partly because I also used the freedom to explore literature in a more explicitly theoretical, socio-political way than literature syllabuses often allow or encourage. This opened up stimulating lines of discussion, particularly in the area of literature's connections with language, class, culture, politics and so on—issues not often tackled in the English Literature classroom in schools, and yet motivating for many students, addressing, as they do, aspects of cultural and social power, identity and value which concern them very directly.

This idea of making the politics of power, identity and value explicit in the literature curriculum recalls the work, in US universities, of Gerald Graff in 'teaching the conflicts' in the 'culture wars' (1992), and of Robert Scholes in developing students' 'textual power' (1985).[3] As Scholes writes in *The Rise and Fall of English* (1998):

> Eliminating the political is the fond hope of those nostalgic for ... cultural homogeneity ... But we cannot do it now and still be responsible educators. Responsibility here must take the form of establishing a disciplinary framework strong enough to allow the political full play in the study of textuality. By being responsible in this way, we will not suppress the power and beauty of language that have always been our concern. We will simply resituate them in a more rhetorical and less literary discipline of thought and study.
>
> *(p. 153)*

Notes

1 An earlier version of this essay appeared in the NATE magazine *English Drama Media* (June 2008).
2 These reforms do not apply to Scotland or Wales, where a more progressive model still applies and there is additional emphasis on the national literature of those countries. See Elliott (2014), however, for a fascinating account of the recent national politics of the literature curriculum in both England and Scotland. See also Coles (2013) for a discussion of the role of canonical literature in current reforms.
3 See Snapper (2014) for a fuller discussion of the relationship between the discourses and modes of school and university English.

References

Coles, J. (2013) 'Every child's birthright'? Democratic entitlement and the role of canonical literature in the English National Curriculum', *The Curriculum Journal*, 24:1, 50–66.

Crawford, R. (2000) *Devolving English Literature*, Edinburgh: Edinburgh University Press.

Elliott, V. (2014) 'The treasure house of a nation? Literary heritage, curriculum and devolution in Scotland and England in the 21st century,' *The Curriculum Journal*, 25(2), 282–300.

Graff, G. (1992) *Beyond the Culture Wars*, New York: Norton.

Kelman, J. (1991) *The Burn*, London: Martin, Secker and Warburg.

Kelman, J. (1992) *Some Recent Attacks*, Stirling: AK Press.

Kelman, J. (1994) *How Late It Was, How Late*, London: Martin, Secker and Warburg.

Scholes, R. (1985) *Textual Power*, New Haven: Yale University Press.

Scholes, R. (1998) *The Rise and Fall of English*, New Haven: Yale University Press.

Snapper, G. (2014) 'Student, reader, critic, teacher: issues and identities in post-16 English literature', in A. Goodwyn, L. Reid and C. Durrant (eds) *International Perspectives on Teaching English in a Globalised World*, London: Routledge.

Wa Thiong'o, N. (1986) *Decolonising the Mind*, London: Heinemann.

19

CREATING READERS

Improving the study of literature by improving recreational reading habits

David Taylor and Aaron Wilson

Introduction

In this chapter we consider ways in which schools and parents can work together to promote students' recreational reading in order to raise academic outcomes related to the study of literature. We present a framework for thinking about the promotion of recreational reading and we provide illustrations of some of the approaches parents in a recent case study took using that framework.

Firstly, we acknowledge that recreational reading is different from, and has a complex relationship to, academic literary reading. In respect of reading for academic purposes we take a disciplinary literacy stance premised on the idea that as students advance through their schooling years, the texts (and the knowledge and strategies required to read and write those texts), become increasingly more sophisticated and subject-specialised (Shanahan and Shanahan, 2008) due to the different norms that discipline communities have established for representing, communicating, evaluating and defending ideas (Moje, Overby, Tysvaer and Morris, 2008). The reading that students are required to do in English language arts is very different from the reading they will do in mathematics, science and the social sciences; texts, reading tasks and reading purposes all differ markedly across these disciplines. An important implication of disciplinary differences is that we cannot assume that what a student learns about reading in one subject will necessarily be useful in another subject. This may be liberating for English teachers who, it would seem, should be held no more responsible for preparing students to read the specialized forms of representation typical in physics classrooms than physics teachers should be for supporting students to read Shakespearean texts. Another implication, more salient to the present chapter, is that recreational reading outside of the classroom has a more complex relationship to literary reading than we might normally think.

Disciplinary norms and expectations are articulated as outcomes in subject-based curricula. In the New Zealand English Curriculum, and in English language arts programmes internationally, a highly valued outcome is students who become lifelong readers of complex literary texts across a variety of historical, national and ethnic traditions (Lee, 1995; Ministry of Education, 2007) and who are able to make 'warrantable interpretations' about the meaning, effectiveness and aesthetic value of such texts (Lee and Spratley, 2010: 10). These outcomes are operationalized in high stakes assessments such as external examinations held at the end of Year 12 in NZ for example where students are expected to write essay length responses to prompts such as:

- Analyse how one or more important events were used to highlight the idea of control or manipulation in the written text(s).
- Analyse how the beginning and/or end of the written text(s) emphasised the writer's purpose.
- Analyse how the use of 'opposites' or contrasts helped you understand one or more themes in the written text(s).

In what ways then can recreational reading contribute to the achievement of outcomes such as these? Given the sophisticated and specialised nature of reading for the academic purposes of appreciating, analysing and critiquing literary text, we see wide recreational reading as a necessary but not sufficient condition for developing literary reading outcomes at school. Put another way, while we acknowledge that having a history of extensive reading outside of the classroom does not guarantee that a student will excel in literary reading tasks at school, it certainly helps.

The literature shows that wide recreational reading out of school is associated with a range of social and academic outcomes. Wide reading has social and psychological benefits for young people including the development of self-expression and problem-solving skills. Reading can provide young people with enjoyment, enrichment, information and identity (Moje et al., 2008). In our view these should be regarded as valued outcomes in themselves.

That wide reading out of school is associated with reading achievement in school is important if not surprising. After all, it is widely accepted that engagement with text should be central to the development of reading proficiency; there is no skills-only approach that can substitute for extensive reading (Schoenbach, Greenleaf, Hurwitz and Cziko, 1999). Moreover, repeated practice is an important principle of learning in general (Bransford, Derry, Berliner, Hammerness and Beckett, 2005; Darling-Hammond and Bransford, 2005) and reading mileage is associated with reading fluency, vocabulary development and, in turn, with comprehension (Allington, 2014).

Reading is also associated with academic outcomes that include but are not limited to academic reading achievement; reading supports cognitive development and reading proficiency is a key predictor of academic success generally (Kirsch et al., 2003; PISA, 2013). Personal reading in particular has a strong correlation with success at school (Chamberlin, 2013; Moje et al., 2008; Mullis, Martin, Foy and Drucker, 2012; PISA, 2013; Sullivan and Brown, 2013; Wylie, Hodgen, Hipkins and Vaughan, 2008). This is not limited to the most likely areas such as comprehension, vocabulary and spelling but is also linked to other curriculum areas (Moje et al., 2008; Mullis et al., 2012; Sullivan and Brown, 2013). For example, in drawing on longitudinal data from the 1970 British Cohort Study, Sullivan and Brown (2013) found that reading for pleasure had a powerful influence on cognitive development and after controlling for socioeconomic status and parents' reading behaviour, they found reading regularly for pleasure between the ages of 10 and 16 led to an advantage of 9.9 percentage points in mathematics. If recreational reading is associated with achievement in mathematics, it seems reasonable to think it would be even more strongly associated with literary reading achievement! A more recent longitudinal study from Aotearoa New Zealand similarly found that a 16-year-old's enjoyment of reading significantly predicted how well he/she was doing at school and the likelihood of him/her remaining at school until the end of high school (Wylie et al., 2008).

Research about the Summer Learning Effect (SLE) has contributed much to what we know about students' out of school reading practices, and the relationship of those practices to academic achievement. The SLE is a well-documented phenomenon that refers to the gains or losses in reading level students experience over the summer holidays when they are not at school (Allington et al., 2010; Heyns, 1978). In early research into SLE, Heyns (1978) established that the level of change over summer in a student's reading, as measured on standardised tests, could be indicated by the volume of reading they did over this time. Heyns found that one month's achievement gain was made for every four books read over summer. Despite analysing a wide range of data about children's experiences during the summer vacation period, the only factors associated with achievement gains were the number of books read, the amount of daily leisure reading and the frequency of library use. More recently interventions to address SLE have continued to support these findings. Allington et al. (2010) found similarly that when 9- to 14-year-olds from high-poverty elementary schools were given the opportunity to self-select books to take home over three summers the SLE was limited by comparison with the control group.

Moje et al. (2008) in their seminal article, 'The complex world of adolescent literacy' identified that students' recreational reading involved reading such a very wide range of texts 'that it was difficult to choose just which ones to include' (108). Some studies have found that even reading texts with little resemblance to school texts can promote cognitive development in ways that would, ultimately, have a positive effect on student achievement (Chamberlin, 2013; Mullis et al., 2012; Sullivan and Brown, 2013). However, Moje et al. found that only reading novels regularly outside of school could be shown to have a positive impact on achievement as measured by school grades. This may be because students' reading of other types of texts may happen too infrequently to be beneficial to school achievement or it may be some texts are too different from texts found in schools to help student achievement.

Despite the well-known benefits of wide reading, a decline in reading as students reach high school has often been observed (Guthrie, Alao and Rinehart, 1997; Sullivan and Brown, 2013). A common claim in the literature is that this is not due to a lack of ability but a lack of desire to read. Alvermann (2003) refers to this as 'aliteracy' and interprets this as arising from a lack of engagement brought about by low self-efficacy. This problem is likely to become cyclic as students' lack of reading further undermines their identities as readers, lowering engagement even further and eroding their sense of confidence.

So, how to disrupt this spiral? Given that recreational reading can increase student achievement, it is important to consider the conditions which promote or restrict this type of activity. Home factors are crucial here as it is beyond the school gates that the sites of recreational reading will often be found. Three cycles of PIRLS testing over 20 years have found a continued strong positive association between reading achievement and home experiences that foster literacy learning (Mullis et al., 2012). To understand these home factors which are attributed with successfully promoting an environment for personal reading and reading engagement we have developed a framework or typology for thinking about ways to promote reading out of school. The framework proposed here is to consider strategies to promote reading as falling into the following categories: access, engagement and modelling. The use of this framework helps to understand how different strategies can promote personal reading and subsequently to identify from which strategies a child might benefit. Below we explain each of the aspects of the framework and illustrate this with examples of actions that families of Year 9 (approximately 13 years old) students took to promote recreational reading.

The intervention was led by David, the first author, in the school at which he normally taught and was the topic of his Masters of Education thesis. Eight families with a child in Year 9 participated in the intervention. Participants included six mothers, one father and one grandmother. Between them they were working with three girls and six boys. The intervention consisted of a series of informal meetings where David and the families shared ideas about promoting recreational reading, using the framework to structure the approaches. The purpose of this chapter is to illustrate the kinds of actions parents and family members took, rather than to present a detailed and scholarly analysis of the effects of the intervention.

The most common goal stated by the participants was to encourage reluctant readers to increase their volume of reading. It should be noted that while participants were encouraged to see all text types as 'valid' reading, most chose novels as the focus of their intervention.

Access

The provision of a text-rich environment, through the use of libraries, purchasing books and the provision of newspapers and magazines, has been linked strongly to student engagement in reading (Heyns, 1978; Jesson, McNaughton and Kolose, 2014; Mullis et al., 2012). Access to texts, often measured by the number of books in a home, is a key commonality amongst many students who achieve well in measures of reading proficiency (Chamberlin, 2013; Kirsch et al., 2003; Mullis et al., 2012; Sullivan and Brown, 2013). Conversely early school leavers in Aotearoa New Zealand are more likely to come from homes with fewer than 100 books (Wylie et al., 2008). There are a number of ways that students can access texts but if they, or their family, are unaware of these sources or not utilising them, it will narrow the range of reading material from which a student might find texts appropriate to their interests and reading level. This may, particularly over time, have a negative effect on their engagement in reading.

The participants typically identified finding a text their child would like as an issue. A particular challenge for the parents of one struggling reader was finding text which was interesting to a 13-year-old but at an appropriate level for their reading ability.

Families employed a range of strategies to help their children access texts. One common approach was to take a trip to the local library. One family successfully employed a 'quick grab' strategy at the public library: 'She didn't want to get any books and was just going to wait for me. I said, "Look, let's just get a stack", and in one minute grabbed about eight random books'.

Other families found books of a popular film were effective. One father reported, 'I bought the DVD online, and I said to him: "Do you want to watch it when it turns up?" "No, no, no, I've got to read the book first. Want to read the book"'.

Others found that their child was more motivated to access and read e-books. One family made regular visits to the library and though the boy would usually get some books out they noticed early on in the intervention that the books sat unread. Their big breakthrough was when the father downloaded the public library application that allows a borrower to take out e-books. He sat with his son who led the process of downloading the application for the library's catalogue and e-books onto his own iPad. The father said this 'worked great, he was really engaged with getting the app downloaded and searching through the available online books'. As a result of this new way to access the books, the boy had returned to being a voracious reader. The father said it was 'ballistically good'. 'Now we can't get the iPad off him—he's reading all the time'.

There are two standout things about the strategies families used to provide their children with access to reading texts. Firstly, the approaches taken had to be tailored to the individual child. Approaches that were effective for one child were not necessarily as effective for others. Secondly, access alone was not always enough; some of the children already had access to a wide range of reading materials that they considered to be interesting and worth reading, yet the books were often left gathering dust. Families also had to consider ways of engaging their children in their reading.

Engagement

The provision of a text-rich environment is a relatively passive support. When it comes to parental engagement with reading activities, it is the active interaction between parent and child that supports personal reading. This can cover a range of activities, including, but not limited to: reading to a child, asking questions about a text, encouraging the formulation of questions about a text, having the child summarise a text and re-reading for understanding (Chamberlin, 2013; Cook-Cottone, 2004; Janiak, 2003; Kim, 2009; Roberts, Jurgens and Burchinal, 2005; Sullivan and Brown, 2013; Wigfield et al., 2008). The 2010/11 PIRLS cycle found that 90% of parents of high-achieving 10 year-old students in Aotearoa New Zealand said that they read to their child while only 55% of parents of low-achieving students said that they read to their child; this differential of 35% was amongst the highest in the world (Chamberlin, 2013).

This category includes anything a parent does to promote engagement in a text once one has been found. The primary strategies tried by participants to promote reading engagement centred around establishing routines for set reading and reading related activities, and trying to have discussions about what the children were reading.

At the start of the intervention, only one family had specific reading routines they used at home, but at the conclusion, there were five families using such routines to promote reading. One mother began regularly reading a Dutch novel to her daughter, stopping to address comprehension and issues from the text as they went. She commented that 'the reading itself is fabulous, apart from the fact that we talk about the story (we always do, so nothing new here), her Dutch vocabulary is expanding by the day'. Another family implemented a half-hour of reading time each weekday evening with no technology available. While this was hard to maintain at times, they kept returning to it and over time the girl started to read more.

In another family, it was the grandmother who was participating and her focus was on developing her relationship with her two grandsons. As she was not the primary caregiver, she had limited time with them but wanted it to be special time. She established what she called 'a very nice routine' where she and her two grandsons would light an outdoor brazier and all sit around 'in blankets, under the stars' and discuss what they were reading—and why—over a cup of cocoa.

Establishing routines like these did not help all families to reach their goals. One family intended to have a technology-free family reading time in the evening, but it transpired that the parents themselves were the ones who found this hardest as they needed to use computers and phones for work they were doing. Another family's effort to implement technology-free reading times was a 'strategy that backfired' because the daughter 'chose to have lights off and go to sleep'.

All but one of the families found that having discussions about their child's reading was a challenge as attempts to talk more about books could easily seem contrived or interrogative. One family reported a challenge in engaging more by trying to balance questioning without seeming overbearing, with backing off and letting the reading happen naturally. One mother found herself repeatedly asking her daughter 'about what she was reading and what was happening' and concluded that 'I think I am putting her off reading for life'. Even when she tried to take a more 'low key approach', she thought it felt 'awfully forced' and in the end her daughter said, 'Mum, back off'.

Modelling

The third important aspect which contributes to successfully promoting personal reading is the modelling of a positive disposition or attitude towards reading exhibited by parents, families and communities. Data from the last PIRLS cycle (Mullis et al., 2012) highlight the importance of these attitudes. Using seven items to collect parents' attitudes to reading, they determined that parents who agreed with four statements, registered 'agreed a little' for the other three and read daily for enjoyment were deemed to 'like reading'. Those who 'disagreed a little' with four statements and read monthly for enjoyment were categorised as 'do not like reading'. Parents in between these positions were placed in a 'somewhat like reading' category. When student achievement data were overlaid it revealed that the average for students who had parents who like reading was significantly higher than those whose parents did not like reading (535 as opposed to 487). In fact, when looking at the individual data from all 43 countries in the PIRLS 2010/2011 cycle, the children of parents who 'like reading' outperform those who 'somewhat like reading', who in turn outperform those who 'do not like reading' in each of the 43 participating countries. With such a clear pattern, it is hard to ignore the case for parental disposition, as expressed by liking reading, being a reliable indicator of student engagement and performance.

In understanding why this link exists, the PIRLS analysis suggests that the majority of children learn effective literary practices from the modelling, as well as the direct engagement, that occurs in the home (Mullis et al., 2012). This parental and family disposition is a powerful osmotic process: '[y]oung children who see adults and older children reading or using texts in different ways are learning to appreciate and use printed materials' (116). This supports the findings of Kloosterman, Notten, Tolsma and Kraaykamp (2011) in their longitudinal study of parental practices and student academic performance that students who have been 'socialised' into reading have an advantage over those who have not. Baker concurs, suggesting that positive parental disposition is a 'critical mechanism' in promoting children's reading (2003: 90). Finally, the PIRLS report suggests that '[b]eyond modelling, parents or other caregivers can directly support reading development by expressing positive opinions about reading and literacy. Promoting reading as a valuable and meaningful activity can motivate children to read' (116).

Therefore, in considering the key factors that contribute to the promotion of recreational reading, parental disposition towards reading, as evidenced by modelling reading and expressing positive values and beliefs about reading is crucial.

This category covers behaviours that demonstrate a positive disposition towards reading and includes a caregiver making their own reading visible to children, discussing their own reading and generally showing that they value reading. No participant specifically chose any modelling strategies to try and address the issue they had chosen to work on with their children. Nevertheless, there were strategies used in the course of the intervention, and it is interesting to note that at the conclusion of the intervention, all participants who were still involved unanimously agreed that their own modelling of reading was very important to the process of encouraging their children to read.

As mentioned above, some families used discussion of their reading as a way to encourage the children they were working with to discuss their own reading. As well as the conversational benefits already outlined, this has the advantage of demonstrating to children how one might go about talking about a book whilst also implicitly conveying a belief in reading being a valid activity. For the mother from Family 1, this was also an effect of talking about her daughter's books: 'by talking about her books it tells her it's worthwhile—valued'. She also found that discussing her own reading with her daughter gave increased value to reading. The mother of Family 7 also found that discussing her own reading was positive for encouraging her son: 'I've been reading a lot more and talking to him about what I've been reading, so that's good. Sometimes around the dinner table I'll pipe up and say "I read this in my book today…" and he'll say [something about his book]'. Both of these families used modelling alongside their other strategies and both had very good success with encouraging their reluctant readers to get into good reading habits. The grandmother from Family 2 also reported that sharing her own reading contributed to making the time spent with her grandchildren 'a very positive experience'. As the research literature makes clear, parents liking reading is a strong indicator of student performance in standardised reading tests. In all three of these cases, the families reported having regular, positive conversations about reading with the children involved.

Conclusion

Students with low reading mileage and a limited knowledge of books are going to struggle to be successful in the study of literature. Recreational reading is therefore an important way for students to prepare themselves to engage successfully with the discipline of literary analysis. While this is important throughout a child's schooling, the drop off in recreational reading at the start of high school is a barrier to success in this discipline in the senior school years. This intervention suggests that working individually with parents, and using the access, engagement and modelling frame, can be effective in getting reluctant readers to engage with the kinds of reading that will support their future success in the study of literature.

References

Allington, R. L., McGill-Franzen, A., Camilli, G., Williams, L., Graff, J., Zeig, J., … Nowak, R. (2010) Addressing summer reading setback among economically disadvantaged elementary students in *Reading Psychology*, *31*(5): 411–427.

Alvermann, D. (2003) Seeing themselves as capable and engaged readers: Adolescents and re/mediated instruction. www.learningpt.org/pdfs/literacy/readers.pdf.

Baker, L. (2003) The role of parents in motivating struggling readers in *Reading & Writing Quarterly*, *19*(1): 87–106.

Chamberlin, M. (2013) *PIRLS 2010/11 in New Zealand: An overview of national findings from the third cycle of progress in international reading literacy study (PIRLS)*, Wellington: Ministry of Education.

Cook-Cottone, C. (2004) Constructivism in family literacy practices: Parents as mentors in *Reading Improvement*, *41*(4): 208–216.

Guthrie, J. T., Alao, S. and Rinehart, J. M. (1997) Literacy issues in focus: Engagement in reading for young adolescents in *Journal of Adolescent & Adult Literacy*, *40*(6): 438–446.

Heyns, B. (1978) *Summer learning and the effects of schooling*, New York: Academic Press, Inc.

Janiak, R. (2003) Empowering parents as reading tutors: An example of a Family School partnership for children's literacy development in *Annual Meeting of the American Educational Research Association*, Chicago, IL.

Jesson, R., McNaughton, S. and Kolose, T. (2014) Investigating the summer learning effect in low SES schools in *Australian Journal of Language and Literacy*, *37*(1): 45–54.

Kim, J. (2009) How to make summer reading effective. www.summerlearning.org/resource/collection/CB94AEC5–9C97–496F-B230–1BECDFC2DF8B/Research_Brief_03_-_Kim.pdf.

Kirsch, I., De Jong, J., LaFontaine, D., McQueen, J., Mendelovits, J. and Monseur, C. (2003) *Reading for change: Performance and engagement across countries*, Paris: OECD.

Kloosterman, R., Notten, N., Tolsma, J. and Kraaykamp, G. (2011) The effects of parental reading socialization and early school involvement on children's academic performance: A panel study of primary school pupils in the Netherlands in *European Sociological Review*, *27*(3): 291–306.

Moje, E. B., Overby, M., Tysvaer, N. and Morris, K. (2008) The complex world of adolescent literacy: Myths, motivations, and mysteries in *Harvard Educational Review*, *78*(1): 107–154.

Mullis, I. V. S., Martin, M. O., Foy, P. and Drucker, K. T. (2012) *PIRLS 2011 international results in reading*. The Netherlands: International Association for the Evaluation of Educational Achievement.

PISA. (2013) *PISA 2015 draft reading lieteracy framework*, Paris: OECD.

Roberts, J., Jurgens, J. and Burchinal, M. (2005) The role of home literacy practices in preschool children's language and emergent literacy skills in *Journal of Speech, Language, and Hearing Research*, *48*(2): 345–359.

Sullivan, A. and Brown, M. (2013) *Social inequalities in cognitive scores at age 16: The role of reading* (No. 10), London: Centre for Longitudinal Studies, Institute of Education, University of London.

Wigfield, A., Guthrie, J., Perencevich, K., Taboada, A., Lutz Klauda, S., McRae, A. and Barbosa, P. (2008) Role of reading engagement in mediating effects of reading comprehension instruction on reading outcomes in *Psychology in the Schools*, *45*(5): 432–445.

Wylie, C., Hodgen, E., Hipkins, R. and Vaughan, K. (2008) *Competent learners on the edge of adulthood: A summary of key findings from the competent learners @ 16 phase*, Wellington: Ministry of Education.

20

THE NATIONAL CURRICULUM FOR ENGLISH IN ENGLAND, EXAMINED THROUGH A DARWINIAN LENS

Andrew Goodwyn

The context in England

Secondary schools in England are once more grappling with a revised National Curriculum for English [NCE] and revised examinations at ages 16 and 18. However, the rationale for the compulsory study of English as a subject, and specifically literature, as dictated by the Department for Education (July 2014, all references are to the web site, DfE, 2016) contains the familiar statements *'Through reading in particular, pupils have a chance to develop culturally, emotionally, intellectually, socially and spiritually. Literature, especially, plays a key role in such development'*. One stated aim is that all students will *'appreciate our rich and varied literary heritage'*. Although there is some tokenistic attention to the idea of 'world literature' the overall aim, expressed at Key Stage Four (KS4, for students aged 14 to 16), is that students should *'read and appreciate the depth and power of the English literary heritage'*, making it clear what 'our' means above, it is a nationalistic project for England.

The NCE was recently revised with the Programmes of Study for Key Stage 3 (students aged 11 to 14) being published in September 2013, those for Key Stage 4 in July 2014. Since its inception in 1988, these documents are statutory although this term is losing its force as so many schools are now exempt from following the NC, for example Academies and Free Schools.

A critical analysis of the National Curriculum for English, particularly at KS4 in relation to Literature

The overarching theme of this NCE is a very nationalistic project, operating a reductively narrow view of an English Literary Heritage, hardly a surprise, but the analysis here sets out to demonstrate how fiercely nationalistic the NCE has become when the need for global understanding is surely increasingly profound. The NCE's concept of Literature is as an *Englishising* artefact, not as a source of important knowledge for young people about life and culture. Secondly this NCE, and related documents, are infused with *a-more-formal-past model of English,* that is a politically nostalgic view that English as a subject was once taught more formally with more emphasis on spelling and correctness and 'serious' literature. Thirdly, this theme is also informed by the surveillance culture that is typified by Ofsted inspections, performance league tables, high stakes testing and the performance management of teachers (Goodwyn, 2010).

The documents for both Key Stages open with this 'Statement of Purpose', the numbers are inserted for the subsequent analysis.

English—Key stage 4

Purpose of study

(1) English has a pre-eminent place in education and in society. (2) A high-quality education in English will teach pupils to speak and write fluently so that they can communicate their ideas and emotions to others and through their reading and listening, others can communicate with them. (3) Through reading in particular, pupils have a chance to develop culturally, emotionally, intellectually, socially and spiritually. (4) Literature, especially, plays a key role in such development. (5) Reading also enables pupils both to acquire knowledge and to build on what they already know. (6) All the skills of language are essential to participating fully as a member of society; pupils, therefore, who do not learn to speak, read and write fluently and confidently are effectively disenfranchised.

1   English has a pre-eminent place in education and in society.

'English' means the school subject or discipline of 'English' not the language and it is notable that no justification for this statement is made. However, this statement 'works' on a variety of levels, not least because subject English, since 1988 (but equally since 1888) has had constant attention, as have its teachers and its place in the nationalistic project of England. 'English' has frequently been described as the most important subject on the curriculum as it was in 1988, it was also the first subject to be 'Nationalised' as Kenneth Baker (conservative Minister of Education), the 'architect' of the National Curriculum, required that it be the first subject to be so treated (Cox, 1992).

2   A high-quality education in English will teach pupils to speak and write fluently so that they can communicate their ideas and emotions to others and through their reading and listening, others can communicate with them.

The term 'high quality' implies an alternative 'low quality' education in English which is an indirect reference to the current surveillance culture, a regime of high stakes testing, performance league tables and frequent and deeply powerful inspections, all factors (we are told) intended to ensure high quality teaching. The expectation that pupils should become fluent speakers as well as writers is welcome, especially as the status of Speaking and Listening has, arguably, been considerably lowered as its formal assessment is no longer required.

3 Through reading in particular, pupils have a chance to develop culturally, emotionally, intellectually, socially and spiritually. Literature, especially, plays a key role in such development.

This familiar claim has no attempt made to substantiate it and certainly no argument put forward as to the particular power of 'Literature'. If we interpret the term 'reading' quite broadly and then the word 'Film' was substituted or 'Television' or 'The Internet', then there would be no loss of probability that such influence on pupils was possible. In terms of pupil interest and engagement there would be much more likelihood, perhaps, of such impact upon them. One notable change from the previous NCE has been the almost total removal of all references to, for example, the importance of the moving image or multi-modal texts, from the NCE at any Key Stage, this is another feature of the return to a more-formal-past model of English.

However this claim for Literature's power and importance has merit and certainly English teachers themselves are very much believers (Goodwyn, 2012, 2016). The fact that Literature is the first word in the sentence might lead to the ambiguity that what was meant was 'literature' with a small 'l', it becomes clear later that it has a capital 'L' and also almost exclusively (not quite) means the English literary canon.

4 Reading also enables pupils both to acquire knowledge and to build on what they already know.

Although quite an innocuous statement, this is a curious comment as it would surely be equally the case to put the word 'Writing' in place of Reading? Or Speaking and Listening'? However, there is an implication, that I would accept, that the term 'reading' here follows on from the use of the word 'Literature', implying to me, that this is 'Literary reading', to me a very specialised form of both reading and knowledge. I will elaborate on this below in terms of a Darwinian perspective. I will also acknowledge here that an emphasis on Literary Reading [LR] makes sense because it is a dominate activity in the subject of English. Whereas it might clearly be argued that almost all school subjects involve reading, the predominant mode of such reading would be both non-literary and, generally, to gain information. The final phrase marks a distinct shift and interesting coda, linking back forcefully to the implicit message from 'high quality education in English' stating:

5 All the skills of language are essential to participating fully as a member of society; pupils, therefore, who do not learn to speak, read and write fluently and confidently are effectively disenfranchised.

There are a number of interesting elements to this very declamatory statement. At a simple level it is not actually true. However desirable it would be for all citizens to be able to 'speak, read and write fluently and confidently' it is clear that not all do and yet they do function in society; no one would argue that this mode of low-level functionality is desirable, who could? However, the implicit message of the statement which is contained in the negative framing of the sentence; by ending the statement with the idea that somehow pupils could be disenfranchised is implying that those responsible for the positive 'enfranchising' of the pupils might be ineffective, they might, then, be the agents who prevent their pupils from fully participating in society. The use of 'therefore' is especially prominent in implying an authority is being claimed against those would seek to disenfranchise pupils. The implied reader is an English teacher being informed, in no uncertain terms, that she will be subject to close scrutiny to ensure that the state's version of 'high quality English' is delivered.

If we adjust the sentence to make it essentially a positive statement, it is not elegant but it might be phrased as:

As all the skills of language are essential to participating fully as a member of society pupils, therefore, who learn to speak, read and write fluently and confidently are effectively enfranchised.

This rephrasing illustrates very clearly that the convolutions of the current and statutory statement are very much part of the rhetoric of surveillance. This language is strongly mirrored in the new (2014) specifications for the GCSE examinations (these are the major examinations for all students aged 16), there is no space here to give detail. The NCE thus proposes a very *Englishing* model of literary reading, a narrow, nationalistic rationale for studying literature.

Darwinian literary theory: a radical new paradigm?

This section explores three key theories, introducing *Darwinian literary theory*, partly through a consideration of the failure of *post-modernism* and the relative importance for English teachers of *critical literacy*.

Darwin was an idealist as well as a scientist, so although he stated matter of factly:

Man still bears in his bodily frame the indelible stamp of his lowly origin.
(Darwin, 1981, vol 2, p. 405)

He also stated that:

As man advances in civilisation, and small tribes are united into larger communities, the simplest reason would tell each individual that he ought

> to extend his social instincts and sympathies to all members of the same nation, though personally unknown to him. This point being once reached, there is only an artificial barrier to prevent his sympathies extending to the men of all nations and races.
>
> *(Darwin, vol 1, pp. 100–101)*

And

> The disinterested love for all living creatures, the most noble attribute of man.
>
> *(1871, vol 1, p. 105)*

Literature is a specialised form of knowledge and may be considered an outcome of the 'adaptive mind', a complex and controversial concept, one element of its definition, from an evolutionary psychological perspective, is that our minds have highly developed 'domain specific' mechanisms for dealing with our environment, the argument here is that literature, its production and consumption, are a special kind of human 'domain' (Carroll, 2004).

This theoretical stance provides a very different justification for ensuring that students have an experience of literary reading. It proposes that students should develop an understanding of how literature provides a very special set of resources for comprehending human motivation and behaviour. Literature is too often narrowly conceptualised and justified in the curriculum (as in England) as a form of nationalistic heritage (especially in secondary schools). In contrast, in Darwinian terms it is a means to help students understand that literature is a universalist project, however it is usually inflected, often dominated, by notions of national identity and survival. Literature therefore *should be studied* by all students, its teaching should lead to both understanding the tribal nature of nationalism but also the universality of literary knowledge

Darwin's impact on Biology, and to some extent other sciences, was almost immediate, not because his extraordinary theory was accepted, but because it threatened and challenged so much received wisdom, it had to be answered. It has taken about 150 years for it to begin to challenge received wisdoms in the arts, humanities and social sciences (Carroll, 2004). Expressed simply, what Darwin proposed was that we are intelligent animals, highly evolved and continuing to evolve, therefore we remain absolutely formed by the early stages of our species' evolution and the evidence of that formation is perpetually all around us.

One useful starting point in introducing the new school of Darwinian thinking is that it offers a united rejection of Post-modernism. What Post-modernists did (certainly unintentionally) for the new Darwinians was make them react to their claims that anything 'natural' has no meaning, all texts are exploitative lies, humans are, therefore, the victims of vicious ideologies and are naïve enough to think texts do have meanings and can be enjoyed at many levels. Post-modernism offered many valuable insights into human life and this is not in dispute with no space here for lengthy explanations but it was a profoundly reductive conceptualisation of what matters to real people, whereas life and literature matter to 'ordinary' people very much indeed (see Sayer, 2011). So, the question kept emerging, why waste time on reading literature if it offers so little of importance to human experience? To my knowledge, post-modernism had no effect on school teaching at all. Teachers of literature in school continued to believe texts were very important (Goodwyn, 2012, 2016) and helped young readers to value and enjoy them. As the post-modern vacuum needed to be filled, so a number of brave literary critics began a search for significance that led to Darwin and the conviction to put literature back at the heart of culture and help answer our desperate search for meaning in all of our lives. This new focus is a fundamental shift in the way literature can be understood, insisting it is part of the universal experience of being human, not merely the nation state.

A theory linked to post-modernism, critical literacy, certainly did affect schools in some countries, chiefly Australia where it has its origins. Its position was that students need to resist the seductions of texts because they were full of temptations like believing in romance, caring about 'good' and 'bad' characters, these texts were out to 'get you'. I have strong affinity with Critical Literacy because it wanted to make young readers savvy, critical and self-aware, because some texts *are designed to seduce you* and some are infused with racism, patriarchy, ideology, the list is endless. However, from a Darwinian perspective, this affective dimension is part of our species' intellectual property, and does not destroy our enjoyment of texts, indeed demonstrates we learn huge amounts about human behaviour from the literary representation of that behaviour. In the spirit of post-modernism, Critical Literacy argued, correctly, that texts are deceptive and dangerous, literary reading is a powerful and risky business, that, of course, is why it matters and is one reason why studying literature should be compulsory.

Summarising current Darwinian theory in relation to the Arts (including Literature)

This new paradigm, gathering momentum over the last 25 years in a number of disciplines, most recently the Arts, draws on Sociobiology, Evolutionary psychology, Philosophy, Political Science and others. The best account in my view is by Joseph Carroll in his 2004 *Literary Darwinism: Evolution, Human Nature and Literature*, and also 2011, *Reading Human Nature: Literary Darwinism in Theory and Practice.*

Of course our biology is very real, literature is not 'real', its value lies in its distance from and relationship to our lived experience which is grounded in 'reality', as much as we can comprehend it, which we do through our senses and apprehensions. Darwinian literary theory maintains that Literature is a huge achievement of our species and a fundamentally valuable means of understanding our bewildering human experience, indeed, it is in many ways 'as good as it gets', for understanding 'ourselves'. Science tries to explain how the world works and Art, and especially literature, examines how we work in that world.

In the popular imagination phrases like 'The evolution of the species through natural selection' and 'The survival of the fittest' are well known. More recent thinking has put more emphasis on the essential importance of Adaptation and especially the idea of the adaptive mind; that is that we are not just physically evolving but also psychologically, a simple example is self-regulation, the fact that we can recognise our instinctive impulses but then control them. Many people in the Arts in the past reacted against any suggestion about our genetic imprint because of concerns about biological determinism, arguing that artistic creativity is 'free', not programmed. However, it is very clear that we are principally determined by our genes—making us all similar and part of a shared humanity, but, because of the adaptive mind of each individual, reacting with the dynamic environment, each individual has 'uniqueness', including the artist. Indeed our evolutionary drives make us agents of our own individual development and creativity.

From this Darwinian perspective it can be stated 'All human knowledge derives from a process of interaction between man as a physical entity, an active perceiving subject, and the realities of an equally physical external world, the object of man's perception' (Lorenz, 1978 p. 1). However, this is not a return to simple positivism. As Popper stated, 'All science and all philosophy are enlightened common sense' (Popper, p. 34), I interpret this as arguing for humanity's fundamental ability to interpret the world, make sense of it whilst recognising that the act of making 'common sense' is a construct, not reality itself. So, this is not a view that only Science can produce truth, all human interpretive acts, such as art or literature, seek for truth.

However, Darwin was very clear that we are clever animals—not angels—our truth is grounded in our human capacity to make sense. There are genetic constraints on human behaviour and there are human universals i.e. similarities between all human beings and their dispositions and their biological and psychological needs. There are more *deep* structural commonalities than there are individual or group e.g. racial, differences, we have psychological dispositions performing regulatory functions. Some dispositions are 'hard wired' e.g. the regulation of vital bodily functions (you cannot stop your heart beating). Most psychological dispositions are 'open' i.e. subject to self-regulation e.g. we are designed as sexual, reproductive beings but may never have children—there may be 'psychic cost' in such regulation e.g. the practice of celibacy as part of a religious order.

It is important to recognise that both Darwin himself and modern interpreters did not see the 'survival of the fittest' as the key principle of evolution but as part of species development and what is clear about humans is that their mental model is one of inclusive fitness—that is the capacity to care for more than immediate kin and to sustain and develop relationships across social groups.

To return to art and literature, clearly art making and imaginative play are part of normative human development, as is the acquisition of language. Human beings may well have the longest period of infant caring, allowing for the development of the larger brain, this larger brain as we currently understand it seems to be a key evolutionary change in the development of human mental capacity.

Art and symbolic ornamentation seem to have been around for as long as humans have themselves been 'around'. The Art instinct (as it is increasingly called, see for example Dutton, 2011, Carroll, 2011) is comparatively well-established, probably emerging with sensual apprehension (sight, sound, touch, smell, taste). Also it can be suggested that in humans, sight and hearing are the most highly developed senses because, for us, environment is predominant.

It can therefore be argued that humans have developed ways of storing knowledge through the arts that are not ephemeral i.e. dependent on one living subject and The Arts are themselves an evolving system of interpretation of the world and storing and passing on 'knowledge' and human 'truth'. Literature is a late (in evolutionary terms) part of this evolving system, dependent in its contemporary form on writing systems themselves but ultimately deriving from human narrative and poetic instincts. One might locate the origins of literature in the development of human language and then stories linked to 'telling' and retelling, leading to the use of artistic language also involving rhythm and rhyme. The purpose of the present argument is to demonstrate that human nature and experience is the subject of literature, which in written form is a very new 'tool' in the cultural/symbolic tool box. Literature is a special body of knowledge in a figurative form, amongst many such forms therefore there also universals in all the arts, derived as they are from human senses. As a specialised form of knowledge ordinary parlance is not sufficient to describe literature's complexity, so it also has a specialist metalanguage and theories, students of literature find this language useful as they become more sophisticated.

Literature specifically

So Literature is a figurative structure that reveals our evolutionary schemata and drives (motives). Such Figurations can be seen as on a continuum with realism at one extreme and symbolism at the other. All humans who have normative development and capabilities appear able to handle complex symbolic systems and to use them e.g. reading and writing. There is no contradiction here between this fundamental human capacity and the need for specialist knowledge and terminology to access the complexity of literature. What we have is 'ordinary parlance'—the way 'untrained' readers talk about literature and human nature—so Romeo and Juliet can be talked about as 'real people' who live and then die tragically—whereas, depending on your literary theory, they can be described in much more exact terms, even as simple a word as character signals that Romeo and Juliet are constructs.

Culture then may be conceptualised as a principally psychological tool and through its artefacts provides evidence of the adaptive and adapting mind. Culture is highly concerned with both cognitive and affective orders, creating cultural artefacts, for example, novels, helps 'make sense' for the creator, using such artefacts—for example reading novels, helps the reader 'make sense' of life. Literature's figurations give us access to aspects of human experience and its themes tend to be dominated by biological imperatives, mating, family, kinship, shelter, death. Literature is especially concerned with describing the evolved psychological dispositions that regulate motives and behaviour. So, literature is extremely useful to our species and will continue to evolve. As our human experiences are both universal and very individual, so humans will always experience conflict when determining meaning in literature, an important factor for the classroom.

Literature's figurative systems vary enormously in complexity and ambition—this is part of the authorial intention but also partly determined by the reader's capability to comprehend e.g. level of practice (at reading) and level of experience as a human being; this is where teachers make such a difference by choosing the right texts. Reader Response Theory (Rosenblatt, 1938, 1978) was the breakthrough in recognising that texts change to the reader as the reader changes. Part of literature's unique value stems from the way it enables the individual access to articulated human experience and also the 'group' who can share reflection on both the figuration and their own reality as human beings. It provides representations of cognitive order—we seek to 'make sense' of our environment and the behaviours and motives of others.

There is profound relationship between human beings and literary representation, for example, character (organisms), setting [the environment] and plot [actions]. Subjective orientation is dominated by the desire for coherence or systemic integrity in a theoretical or figurative structure e.g. inner coherence and cognitive order (symbolism, introversion). Objective orientation concentrates on depicting the correspondence between the structure and reality e.g. depicting the experiences of other human beings (realism, extraversion). All symbolic representations of human nature and cultural order are necessarily interpretations from the perspective of an individual mind and a distinctive identity—consider, for example, Reader Response Theory.

Literature is part of our adaptedness, a sign of our capacity for infinite regulation (heroes) and failure to regulate (villains). Literature can be studied 'scientifically' but adolescence is unlikely to be the period to do so. However, literature as the study of human nature, how and why we behave well and badly—how long we have been 'behaving', reflecting on our human nature and trying to understand ourselves—so, old and new texts and their contexts will always be valuable and the nascent identity of the adolescent can have a dynamic relationship with these depictions of possible lives. The writer and context (environment) are always important. The author's intentions are important but are not 'the truth' of a text. The contemporary audience's reactions are important. Every response has importance, especially if it is 'generative'. So many current aspects of literature teaching already 'chime' with a Darwinian approach.

Some texts are much more complex than others. They can be sub-divided into genres and forms and also into a relativist hierarchy of value—some books are 'better' than others, as are some interpretations—our interpretations are subject to psychobiological influences but are not subjected by them. Literature is dominated by our biological imperatives food, shelter, environment, danger, reproduction, kinship, dominance, death. The individual and the complexities of identity are always central to literary meaning.

Literature is much focused on 'normative ideas' but literature explores all aspects of human nature—humans seem to inhabit an environment and form a group developing 'norms' as a form of collective regulation. Adolescents find literature helpful in describing and questioning such 'norms'. In terms of such questionings, we will need some new language to talk about literature e.g. 'mating', 'kinship' as well as 'love' and 'family'. Darwinian theory helps us understand the concept of kin and the expanded group—that conflict is a human universal as are psychological regulations. Nationalism and having a 'national literature' may be associated with a primal drive—nations may be conceptualised in terms of nationalism as more or less 'open'. As literature is produced by unique individuals it does not 'belong' to any one group. Nationalism can be conceptualised as a tribal, and therefore important concept, but one open to regulation.

Humans like (perhaps need) to work with complex symbolic systems. They like to work in groups and share knowledge (inclusive fitness). Almost all humans can work with and produce symbolic texts and that is something we ask of them in schools. Meanings made from texts are individual and connected to identity and conflict about meaning is 'natural' i.e. discussion is vital. Treating characters like 'real people' is fundamental and treating authors as real people is important. The environment in the text and the environment of the text are important. The production of individual meaning is more important than an agreed meaning. On a practical note for teachers, if texts become a threat, we will avoid them. A strong Darwinian argument for studying literature is that it helps us all in developing a theory of mind, it requires to enter into the mindsets of 'others' and it insists on the importance of recognising the emotions of others and the consequences if we do not.

Implications for literature teaching in schools

So, a Darwinian rationale for studying literature in schools makes it absolutely fundamental for adolescents. This does not belittle other subjects and indeed this theory also places much greater emphasis on the Arts generally. Literature is a fundamentally important resource for children and adolescents as they move towards adulthood and to taking full membership in the human species and indeed, begin reproducing it. Most literature study focuses on individuals, who exist within the family, then social groups, then a local community and finally much larger communities; like a series of Russian dolls, beginning with the neighbourhood, then place [town/village/city], the region, the nation, the continent, the planet—even 'the universe'. This is not a platitude as we return to the individual human's identity and the desire to 'belong' echoing our early tribal organisation. Inclusive fitness made it clear that the tribe was a more powerful place to live than just the family. Darwin made it a principle that we might overcome human division once we understood our nature more profoundly. After the horrors of the 20th century we may feel only that we can reduce it significantly but perhaps, with the horrors of the early 21st century, never remove it entirely.

At a practical level for teachers of English this approach to literature substantiates its importance to all students and reinforces its place as the key subject and demonstrates that literature does has a powerful relationship to human identity, which includes the 'nation', but, much more importantly, it reveals our universal human nature, what unites all of us as humans. So, for example, Shakespeare is not only not for an age but for all time and he is also for all humanity. He does not 'belong' to England, although we understand why tribes love their treasures, he belongs to our species.

Research over the last decade (Goodwyn, 2016) has investigated various issues about literature teaching in schools and in the professional lives of English teachers, and demonstrated that literature remains central to the work and values of English teachers and that a 'love of reading' was generally the strongest motivator for becoming an English teacher, the importance of literature remains central as an ongoing inspiration for teaching English; nothing new there. What the research investigated was whether this centrality of literature was still *as central* and also whether it had survived, in England, in an age of Ofsted, league tables and performance management. It also investigated the relationship between the assessment regime and the values that English teachers hold dear. The findings were clear that English teachers wanted far more autonomy over textual choice and much more emphasis on students' personal and creative response to literature. This research over two decades illustrates some real ambivalence for English teachers towards the notion of national cultural heritage and they have consistently resisted the idea of a single heritage whilst acknowledging the power of the English Literary canon.

These findings are important and they provide evidence that English teachers do not passively accept the increasingly narrow and nationalistic notions of literary heritage illustrated at the beginning of this chapter. Terry Eagleton, the famous Marxist literary critic, once remarked that all English students, and by implication English teachers, are Leavisites whether they know it or not (Eagleton, 1983, p. 31), I suggest that they may, more importantly, be nascent Darwinians, i.e. teachers principally concerned with literature as a store of human experience of deep significance to all humans, regardless of race, gender or nationalism. In this regard it does not matter whether they have tired of reading about post-modernism and critical literacy and enjoyed a 'Darwinian turn'. What matters is that English teachers can provide experiences of literature that explore the importance of literature to identity, including the complex and conflictual concept of national identity but ultimately to the fundamental place of literature in our human heritage.

References

Carroll. J. (2004) *Literary Darwinism: Evolution, Human Nature and Literature*, London: Routledge.

Carroll, J. (2011) *Reading Human Nature: Literary Darwinism in Theory and Practice*, Albany, State University of New York Press.

Cox, B. (1992) *The Great Betrayal: Memoirs of a Life in Education*, London: Chapman Publishers.

Darwin, C. (1981) [ed. Bonner. J.T. and May, R.M.] *The Descent of Man, and Selection in Relation to Sex*, Princeton, NJ: Princeton University Press.

DfE (2016) *The National Curriculum for English*, London, The Department for Education.

Dutton, D. (2011) *The Art Instinct: Beauty, Pleasure and Human Evolution*, Oxford: Oxford University Press.

Eagleton, T. (1983) *Literary Theory: An Introduction*, Oxford: Basil Blackwell.

Goodwyn, A. (2010) *The Expert Teacher of English*, London: Routledge Falmer.

Goodwyn, A. (2012) The status of Literature teaching in England. *English in Education*, Volume 46, Issue 3, pp. 212–227.

Goodwyn, A. (2016) Still growing after all these years? The resilience of the 'personal growth model of English' in England and also internationally. *English Teaching, Practice and Critique*, Volume 15, Issue 2, pp. 7–21.

Lorenz, K. (1978) *Behind the Mirror: a Search for a Natural History of Human Knowledge*, New York: Harcourt, Brace, Jovanovich.

Popper, K. (1979, rev. ed) *Objective Knowledge: An Evolutionary Approach*, Oxford: Oxford University Press.

Rosenblatt, L. (1938) *Literature as Exploration*, New York: Appleton-Century.

Rosenblatt, L. (1978) *The Reader, The Text, The Poem: The Transactional Theory of the Literary Work*, Carbondale, IL: Southern Illinois University Press.

Sayer, A. (2011) *Why Things Matter to People: Social Sciences, Values and Ethical Life*, Cambridge: Cambridge University Press.

INDEX